Iran at the Crossroads

Iran at the Crossroads

Edited by John L. Esposito and R. K. Ramazani

IRAN AT THE CROSSROADS
© John L. Esposito and R. K. Ramazani, 2001
Softcover reprint of the hardcover 1st edition 2001 978-0-312-23816-2

All rights reserved. No part of this book may be used or reproduced in any manner whatsoever without written permission except in the case of brief quotations embodied in critical articles or reviews.

First published 2001 by
PALGRAVE
175 Fifth Avenue, New York, N.Y. 10010 and
Houndmills, Basingstoke, Hampshire RG21 6XS.
Companies and representatives throughout the world

PALGRAVE is the new global publishing imprint of St. Martin's Press LLC Scholarly and Reference Division and Palgrave Publishers Ltd (formerly Macmillan Press Ltd).

ISBN 978-1-349-63165-0   ISBN 978-1-137-07175-0 (eBook)
DOI 10.1007/978-1-137-07175-0

Library of Congress Cataloging-in-Publication Data

Iran at the crossroads / edited by John L. Esposito, R.K. Ramazani.
    p. cm.
    Includes bibliographical references and index.

    1. Iran—Politics and government—1979-1997. 2. Iran—Politics and government—1997 3. Islam and politics—Iran. 4. Iran—Foreign relations—1979-1997. 5. Iran—Foreign relations—1997- I. Esposito, John L. II. Ramazani, Rouhollah K., 1928-
DS318.8 .I656 2000
320.955'09'049—dc21   00-062610

A catalogue record for this book is available from the British Library.

Design by Westchester Book Composition.

First edition: February 2001
10 9 8 7 6 5 4 3 2 1

Acknowledgments

This volume began as a conference, "The Iranian Revolution after Twenty Years: Retrospect and Prospects," held at the Edmund A. Walsh School of Foreign Service, Georgetown University. The conference was co-sponsored by the Center for Muslim-Christian Understanding: History and International Affairs and Washington's Middle East Institute in February 1999. Subsequently, a volume was developed, drawing on the best papers and adding several others to assure breadth as well as depth of coverage.

As with all such projects, many were involved in making it a successful effort. While we do not have room to thank all of them, several must be cited. Ambassador Roscoe Suddarth, President of MEI, and David Mack, Vice President, were supportive throughout the process. Andrew Patrasilitti (MEI) and Patricia Gordon (CMCU) were invaluable and tireless from start to finish. In putting together the volume, Thomas Dean Jordan, CMCU Administrative Assistant, whose oversight of the many details organizing this manuscript for publication, proved invaluable.

We are particularly grateful to our colleagues, who patiently revised their manuscripts several times in light of subsequent developments in Iran and international politics.

John L. Esposito   R.K. Ramazani

Introduction: From Khomeini to Khatami

John L. Esposito

For more than two decades, the Islamic Republic of Iran has been a dominant concern of policymakers in the Muslim world and the West. Iran's Islamic Revolution of 1978–79 was clearly one of the major turning points of twentieth century history. It shattered the myths of modernization and development theory, which presupposed the Westernization and secularization of society, and signaled the resurgence of Islam in Muslim politics and society. Much of the 1980s was dominated by the image of the Ayatollah Khomeini and the threat of Iran's export of its revolution. Indeed, Iran pursued twin goals: institutionalization of the revolution at home and its export abroad. Shortly after the revolution, the militant clergy moved quickly to consolidate their power. Early lay reformers and leaders such as President Abolhasan Bani Sadr and Prime Minister Mehdi Bazargan were forced from office as Iran emerged clearly as a clerically dominated state. The clergy assumed key positions in political, judicial, and educational institutions, and dominated the Islamic Republican Party and the media. Any and all significant opposition, clerical and lay, were silenced.

The influence and impact of the revolution could be felt across the Muslim world and in the West. Iran's export of revolution served as a catalyst in the emergence of Hizbullah and Islamic Jihad in Lebanon; support for radical organizations and movements across the Muslim world resulted in kidnappings and hostage taking and contributed to uprisings and protest demonstrations in Saudi Arabia and the Gulf. Although some warned of a domino effect in the Muslim world, Iran in fact proved more effective as a symbol and exemplar of revolution than an effective model.

Many were inspired by the spirit and example of Iran, not by a desire to replicate it. Iran became embroiled in a war with Iraq (1980–1988) that left the country devastated with massive loss of life and casualties that touched virtually every Iranian family, and with an economy in shambles. At the same time, the excesses of the revolution discredited or disenchanted many early enthusiasts. The death of the Ayatollah Khomeini in 1989 brought an end to the first phase of the postrevolutionary Iranian experiment.

The 1990s witnessed the second and third phases of the revolution. Ali Akbar Hashemi Rafsanjani attempted to focus Iran's energies on pragmatic political, economic, and ideological reforms. This included an attempt to reestablish Iran's place in the Islamic world and with the international community, with a special emphasis on economic development. The current phase of the Islamic Republic's history was signaled by Mohammad Khatami's sweep of presidential elections with a broad base of support for reform and his subsequent call for civilizational dialogue with the West.

At the dawn of the twenty-first century, we are witnessing a continuing attempt to redefine and reform the Islamic Republic, with a struggle at times between President Khatami's reformist agenda and more militant conservative forces led by Ayatollah Khamenei, Iran's Supreme Religious Guide. The Islamic Republic of Iran at 20 is a place of new promises and aspirations whose political, economic, and sociocultural struggles have significance not only for Iranians but also for Iran's relations with the international community. *Iran at the Crossroads* provides an intimate view of Iran, domestically and internationally, and the current struggle to reconstruct and, thus, to relegitimate the revolution.

From Khomeini to Khatami

Distinguishing myths from realities has long been a problem when dealing with the Islamic Republic of Iran. Twenty years of mutual satanization (in particular between Iran and the United States) produced a climate in which both the hyperbole of Iran's ideologues and the animosity of its adversaries have obscured facts on the ground. Few observers today, however, would dispute the fact that Iran—slowly, under Hashemi Rafsanjani, and more aggressively since the election of President Khatami—has been the scene of vibrant and heated public debate and discourse in the push for reform. Attempts by the ruling clergy to control personal and public space and suppress dissent in the name of Islam have been countered by the rise of a middle class that demands greater liberalization and reforms. Among the most fundamental of issues have been the nature of the Islamic Republic, the role of religion and the ulama in the state, democratization and civil society, pluralism, the rule of law, and the status of women. As Mehrzad Boroujerdi in "Paradoxes of Politics in Postrevolutionary Iran" (chapter 1) notes, "The balance sheet of the last 20 years is interestingly bewildering—unprecedented progress juxtaposed against regressive changes." The tendency to focus on the negative has often overshadowed the positive aspects of a more inclusive political climate and public discourse. Despite limitations, the Iranian Republic has institutionalized voting and elections—in particular, uninterrupted parliamentary elections, whose results have been relatively free of fraud and accepted by the ruling establishment. Electoral politics have witnessed the emergence of a more diverse and inclusive electorate and political elite whose voices and votes led to the turning point signaled by the election of Mohammad Khatami.

The catalyst for the current ideological and political struggle in Iran was the presidential elections of 1997. As Mohsen Milani in "Reform and Resistance in the Islamic Republic of Iran" (chapter 2) comments, what surprised and stunned many was the fact that the "favorite son" of the ruling elites lost in a landslide to the "Cinderella candidate," Seyyed Mohammad Khatami, who received 69 percent of the vote. He did so running on a liberal platform in a country where "liberal" was synonymous with "Western decadence."

Critical to understanding the politics of the Islamic Republic has been and continues to be its factions and shifts of power. Milani traces the history of factionalism and the loss of equilibrium and increasing polarization among the governing elites. Reeling from the impact of the revolution, the devastating losses in the Iran–Iraq War (1980–88), and the drastic decline in living standards as Iran's economy tumbled, the pragmatists gained an upper hand. Rafsanjani, responding to the deep political and economic changes, championed a policy of economic reform and moderation. Khatami built on this pragmatic orientation and espoused a progressive platform (in contrast to Nateq-Nuri's status quo platform) that resonated with the discontent of many, such as Iran's youth, women, workers, and intellectuals. Milani highlights the gains and losses and its future prospects as Khatami attempts to realize the mandate of his election, the establishment of governance based more on popular sovereignty in a system in which the balance of power remains with Iran's conservative forces.

Few observers of Iranian politics, whatever their political or ideological position, would not have been struck by the fundamental changes that have occurred in public space. Within Iran's clerical form of government, this has meant political discussion and debate over the nature of Iran's government and, with it, the challenge to the conceptualization of clerical guardianship during parliamentary and presidential elections in the late 1990s. That challenge has continued since Khatami's election. As Farideh Farhi in "On the Reconfiguration of the Public Sphere and the Changing Political Landscape of Postrevolutionary Iran" (chapter 3) notes, "It seems that for the first time in modern Iranian history a substantial part of the Iranian population is engaged in a political discussion about the rules of the games."

Open public discussion and debate of democratization, civil society, and the rule of law has been accompanied by factional disputes over the concept and future of the institution of the Faqih. The debate has included both a questioning of the historical and theological legitimacy of the concept of *velayat-i faqih* (clerical guardianship) as well as the limits that popular sovereignty and civil society and rule of law place on the institution. In addition, both the credentials and qualification of its current incumbent, Ayatollah Khamenei, have been challenged by prominent ayatollahs, other conservative as well as liberal clergy, and other voices in public for and in the press. Farhi discusses the implications of the current critical reassessment of the idea of clerical guardianship and "wavering hold on society."

When the clergy came to power, few thought that women and women's rights would be a major issue in the Islamic Republic. Initial attempts to exclude women from public life resulted in a politicization of Iranian women. After two decades of struggle, resistance, and organization, women play a significant role in politics and society. Farhi demonstrates how, ironically, "the symbolic use of women as instruments of state building has opened the way for women to make counterclaims on the state for further rights." The representation of women as culture bearers made them a primary symbol in the search for authenticity and cultural revival in the period of revolutionary state building. A state that was often charged as using women to foster its conservative or antiliberal agenda has, however, often yielded to, even at times taken credit for, the broadening of women's political, social, and economic participation.

In "The Politics of the 'Women's Question' in the Islamic Republic, 1979–1999" (chapter 4), Haleh Esfandiari traces the history of Iranian women's struggle for equality, noting that at its core has been "a new generation of women, the majority from their own "traditional" constituency, who would prove forceful, imaginative, and vociferous in demanding and pursuing education, jobs, legal reform, expanded rights, and participation in almost all areas of public life." Esfandiari shows how women from a broad social spectrum after the revolution have become a major force in their empowerment. Contrary to the expectation of many, among the most forceful voices for change have been women from less affluent, working-class and traditional families, as well as those from more Westernized backgrounds. They have resisted attempts at sex segregation in public life and the workforce, harsh imposition of an "Islamic" dress code, and suspension of the Family Protection Act and Family Courts initiated under the Shah's regime. At the same time, women have voted in large numbers in parliamentary and local elections, run for office, and established their own magazines and newspapers. Moreover, women voters across the political, social, and age spectrum were among the strongest supporters in Khatami's stunning victory in presidential elections. The gains of women have not been achieved without major resistance from conservative forces. Despite setbacks, however, women have achieved significant victories in the many battles that have been part of their struggle.

The ideologization and politicization of politics and society has also had a profound effect on economic development as well. Bijan Khajehpour in "Iran's Economy: Twenty Years after the Islamic Revolution" (chapter 5) analyzes the impact of the revolution and the effects of the Iran–Iraq War, U.S. sanctions, emigration of many of its experts, flight of capital, and nationalization of industries, as well as differing economic orientations of Iran's leading political factions (conservatives, moderates, or pragmatists and revolutionary leftists have proved major obstacles in Iran's economic performance). Khajehpour maintains that the Iran–Iraq War proved to be a catalyst for the "inset of a degree of pragmatism that had triumphed over revolutionary fundamentalism" under the leadership of Rafsanjani. Liberalization of the economy was not achieved through partial privatization and capital formation: "The growth between 1989 and 1994 was mainly financed through the accumulation of some $30 billion in foreign debt. In 1993, the ratio of Iran's foreign debt to the country's GDP was alarming." The intensification of U.S. sanctions in 1995, unfavorable oil markets, as well as domestic factors—in particular factional political/economic differences—added to the deteriorating economic conditions as witnessed by the poor performance of the government in achieving the economic goals of its Second Five Year Plan. Khajehpour analyzes the current economic trends, a continued poor economy due to such factors as low oil process, a stagnant market, economic recession, and factional infighting.

Central to the development of Iran's postrevolutionary Islamic government has been the concept and the institution of *velayat-i faqih,* guardianship or governance of the jurist. Enunciated and implemented by the Ayatollah Khomeini, it legitimated his considerable power in overseeing and guiding the development of the Islamic Republic. Under his designated successor, Ayatollah Khamenei, the office of spiritual leader (often popularly referred to as Supreme Leader), continues to carry with it substantial religious and political power. Since the election of Khatami, as has been noted, both the office and its current incumbent have been questioned and challenged by those who wish to see ultimate political power in the hands of elected officials. The issue is critical to contemporary Iranian politics and the political role and influence of the clergy.

Abdulaziz Sachedina, in "The Rule of the Religious Jurist in Iran" (chapter 6), reviews the development of the historical and political context in which the doctrine of governance of the jurist developed with its political and legal consequences. Sachedina reminds us that unlike Sunni Muslims, Shii Muslims have long looked to their religious leaders for guidance (but not governance) in religious affairs and also in political and social matters. Religious leaders served as *mujtahid* (jurist-consult, that is, interpreters) of Islam or guides in the absence of the Hidden Twelfth Imam. Shiis believe that he is a direct descendant of the Prophet Muhammad who designated the line of his family to serve as supreme religiopolitical leader. The Twelfth Imam, who disappeared in 874 C. E., is believed to be in seclusion or hiding and will return at the end of time. In the interim, Shiism developed the office of *marja-i taqlid* (supreme legal authority accepted for emulation), a *mujtahid* whose reputation for learning and moral probity qualified him to serve as a spiritual-moral guide.

Sachedina reviews the history of the development of the belief in, or doctrine of, the jurist as a source of emulation (*marja-i taqlid*) and supreme leader of the community and notes that it did not crystallize until the eighteenth century, but that, most importantly, it was always understood as a position of guardianship, *not* governance. Moreover, he maintains that there is nothing in Shii classical texts to support the notion that the *marja* (the most learned juridical authority in the Shii community) is the deputy of the Hidden Twelfth Imam, as supreme religiopolitical leader of Shiism. It was not until the Islamic Republic of Iran that this belief was ideologically and politically introduced to promulgate the position of "governing jurist" in the Islamic Republic's constitution. Thus, as Sachedina points out, it has been responsible for providing the necessary Islamic legitimacy to the Shii nation-state of Iran, responsible in large measure for providing cohesion "in maintaining the spiritual-moral and related socialpolitical identity of the Iranian Shiis." It is this nationalistic element that has led to resistance by many in the world Shii community, who do not wish to see selection of the most qualified source for spiritual-moral emulation tied to Iran's national politics and international agenda. This redefinition and transformation of the supreme religious leader's role as a spiritual-moral guide into a supreme religiopolitical guide, whose political power exceeds that of the president and parliament, is challenged in Iran and internationally today and has become a source of factionalism in Iranian politics. Indeed, at the heart of the controversy today in Iran is the scope of the jurist's political authority in a modern nation-state that invests its authority in the constitution.

Iran and International Politics

Iran has been a major player in international politics. Often, distinguishing between myth and reality is obscured, however, by the Islamic Republic's rhetoric and the rhetoric and accusations of its opposition in the West and in the Muslim world. Wishing to reclaim its role in regional and international politics as well as to pursue its self-proclaimed role as the custodian of the Muslim ummah (versus that of Saudi Arabia), the Islamic Republic in its first decade sought to export its revolution. Under the pragmatic turn of Rafsanjani and, most recently, President Khatami, Iran has sought to reestablish its ties with the international community and its leadership in the Islamic world. Mohiaddin Mesbahi demonstrates in "Iran's Foreign Policy Toward Russia, Central Asia, and the Caucasus" (chapter 7), that nowhere is the geostrategic pragmatism of Iranian foreign policy more evident than in its relations with Russia, Central Asia, and the Caucasus. Iran's relations with Russia, its agreement for nuclear and military cooperation, motivated by considerations of security and strategic balance, have been a source of grave concern for countries such as the United States, Israel, and some Arab states. Iranian-Russian relations have been strained by disagreements over Russian policy in Central Asia and the Caucasus as well as the Balkans. Thus, despite their mutual condemnation of NATO intervention, Iran provided aid to Bosnia, whereas Russia supported the Serbs. Differences over Russian policy in Nagorno-Karabakh and Tajikistan have been intensified by those regarding Russia's wars in

Chechnya and Dagestan. Iran's failure to speak out forcefully, Mesbahi warns, risks its being seen as siding with an "anti-Islamic Russia."

In Central Asia, as in the Middle East and elsewhere in the Muslim world, Iran's relations with the United States, Russia, and other states remains affected by concerns of an Islamic threat, often used by governments to delegitimate political opposition or justify repression of dissent. Mesbahi discusses the reasons for Iran's fundamentally pragmatic approach in its foreign policy. Despite Iran's profession in recent years of noninvolvement in revolutionary Islamic movements and export of its revolution, the militant rhetoric and actions of Iran's hardliners and the manipulation of Iran's "Islamic threat" by some Western governments and regimes in Russia, Central Asia, the Caucasus, and elsewhere will continue to affect its ability to strengthen state-to-state relations.

Despite a noticeable thaw since the election of Khatami, U.S.–Iranian hostilities continue to affect Iran's role internationally. The tensions of the past affect the present. Mesbahi provides an extended discussion and analysis of how "concern over the Islamic/Iranian threat has now become the conceptual and the policy bridge linking security discussions of Central Asia and the Caucasus with those of the Persian Gulf/Middle East."

It has often been commonplace to speak of Iran versus the West and, thus, to lump Europe with the United States. As Fred Halliday demonstrates, however, in "The Iranian Revolution and International Politics: Some European Perspectives" (chapter 8), Iran's relations with Europe have, in general, often differed from those with the United States. European governments sought to continue trade and some degree of diplomatic contact. Thus, Halliday concludes, although there have been significant difficulties in relations: "The Europeans maintained a dialogue with Iran, while Washington exerted strategic, military, and economic pressure."

Iran's post-revolutionary threat to export its revolution and its intrigues in the Gulf have left a negative track record that impacts on any attempts at normalization. Yet, at the same time, Halliday argues, it is important to distinguish between myths and realities in Gulf politics. In recent history, Saddam Hussein's Iraq, rather than Iran, has been a more persistent threat to the security and stability of the Middle East and, in particular, the Gulf. The realities of the 1990s have shown that in the Gulf, "The causes of opposition are not made in Iran but in the denial of democratic and legal guarantees to the populations of those countries."

Halliday, like Mesbahi, underscores the pragmatism and nonideological nature of Iranian foreign policy. From Afghanistan and Tajikistan to Central Asia, it has not formulated its policy on the basis of Islam or

Islamic ideology, nor has Iran necessarily aligned itself with Islamic movements. In the Arab-Israeli dispute, however, Iran has until recently taken a hardline ideological stance against the existence of the state of Israel, been a major supporter of Hizbullah, and supported Islamic movements in Palestine. Yet, Halliday maintains that the situation has shifted somewhat in recent years. Thus, the major obstacle to Arab-Israeli peace became the "provocative obstructionism" of the Israeli government of Benjamin Netanyahu. It fostered Palestinian rejectionism just as continued Israeli occupation of southern Lebanon was a major cause of Hizbullah's continued military activities in southern Lebanon while it integrated into mainstream Lebanese politics (parliament). Halliday addresses two particularly contentious issues: Iran's weapons of mass destruction and its support for terrorism. Although it is probable that Iran has a nuclear weapons program, its concerns, particularly regarding Iraq's nuclear capability, must be taken into account, as well as the need to create a regional security program. Although Iran has supported acts of terrorism, as in other areas, real support must be distinguished from blanket generalizations such as those made regarding Iran's involvement in the Oklahoma bombing and TWA 800 disaster, as well as the Khobar bombing in Saudi Arabia, attributed to Iran by the United States but denied by the Saudi government. As Halliday concludes, future relations between Islam and the West will require "strong nerves, and some patience and understanding" against a background in which talk of historical wrongs is two-sided.

As Gary Sick notes in "The Clouded Mirror: The United States and Iran, 1979–1999" (chapter 9), for the first two decades after the revolution both countries shunned each other. Both pursued a policy of mutual hostility rooted in history and domestic politics. Although historically and politically understandable, it has had real costs. Among the results that significantly affected U.S.–Iran relations was "a mythology . . . on either side that . . . [became] comfortably embedded in the national psyche" and the replacement of earlier officials who possessed knowledge and experience of the other with those whose knowledge is too often derived "from the prevalent demonology of detachment and indifference." Sick provides an insightful summary and analysis of key turning points (the humiliation of the hostage crisis, the U.S. tilt to Iraq in the Iran-Iraq War, Iran Contra, the Iran-Libya Sanctions Act) that have influenced U.S.–Iran relations, "fear of Islamic fundamentalism and a deep-seated paranoia about terrorism" that made Iran untouchable. He traces presidential policies down to the Clinton administration and its movement from its dual containment policy and its characterization of Iran as a rogue or terrorist state to the

Clinton/Albright response to President Khatami's call for a civilizational dialogue. As the Clinton administration and Iran's President Khatami seek more amicable relations, both countries have identified issues that they wish resolved. Sick discusses the agenda, from Iran's call for a lifting of sanctions and the settlement of its claims regarding its frozen assets, to U.S. concerns about Iran's opposition to Israel, its support of terrorism, and pursuit of weapons of mass destruction. Looking to the future, both Iran and the United States, despite shifts in policy, have not been willing to face the risk in their domestic politics that would be caused by moving their relationship to the next level. Awareness of the extent to which both Iran and the United States are mirror images of themselves provides an insight into the difficulties of the past and of a still uncertain future. As Sick observes, both tend to be moralistic and self-righteous, are inclined to be ideologically rigid, see themselves as indispensable states, and possess a sense of humiliation and grievances that often make the line between foreign and domestic policies indistinguishable.

The Islamic Republic of Iran, as the monarchical polities that preceded it, has struggled with defining its national interest. R. K. Ramazani, in "Reflections on Iran's Foreign Policy: Defining the 'National Interests'" (chapter 10), argues that it is a crucial challenge as Iran enters the third decade of its revolution. He identifies three different models that have emerged from the Islamic Republic's experience thus far: Khomeini's Ideological-Islamic Interest, Rafsanjani's Pragmatic-Islamic Interest, and the Democratic-Islamic Interest currently espoused by President Khatami.

During the Khomeini era, Iran's foreign policy was guided more by ideology, as embodied in his interpretation of Islamic governance (*velayat-i faqih*), than Iran's interest as a nation-state. Leery of nationalism, Khomeini privileged and pursued an Islamic world order or paradigm. This was reflected in the well-known slogan, "Neither East, nor West, but the Islamic Republic," which epitomized Iran's rejection of the superpowers' dominance of the international system and the position of an Islamic alternative and in the Islamic Republic's commitment to export its Islamic revolution. Yet, as Ramazani notes, as a nation-state, Iran had to live in the real world of the international system. Thus, Khomeini/the Islamic Republic also demonstrated a pragmatic side, as in Iran's secret purchase of arms from the United States and Israel. The Rafsanjani era ushered in a significant shift in the balance between ideology and national interest. The death of Khomeini and need for orderly political succession, the devastating economic impact from the Iran-Iraq War domestically, and realization of the need to focus on its political independence and territorial integrity and to restore its place in the international political and economic system produced a more pragmatic path. The presidential victory of Seyyed Mohammed Khatami on May 23, 1997, marked a further transitional stage. Khatami has projected a vision and model of Democratic-Islamic Interest to define Iran's national interest in guiding its domestic and foreign policy. Thus, emphasis on democratization, civil society, and the rule of law also have been complemented by a vision of a dialogue between Islamic and Western civilizations. Iran has improved relations with OIC states and Europe, reasserted its role as a player in regional politics both in the Middle East and Central Asia, and moved U.S.–Iran relations from decades of mutual satanization to dialogue. Yet, Khatami also has had to struggle with stiff and, at times, fierce resistance. In the end, only time will tell whether, as Ramazani notes, the Islamic Republic will become increasingly compatible with the realities of the modern world and Iran's century-long disrupted, but enduring, democratic movement.

Iran has for centuries been the home of empires, religions, and cultures. In the last half of the twentieth century, it emerged under Pahlavi rule as a major modernizing Muslim state and society. Hailed by many to be on the fast track to rapid modernization and development, its supporters and critics alike were stunned by the seemingly impossible, the overthrow of Pahlavi rule and the creation of the Islamic Republic of Iran. Both periods of modern Iranian history were symbolized by two men, Reza Shah and Ayatollah Khomeini. Both are gone now, as Iran struggles to define or, perhaps more accurately, redefine the nature of its government and its place in the new millennium. At the dawn of its third decade, the Islamic Republic of Iran, President Khatami, and his supporters are locked in a struggle to redefine Iran's political and economic future at home and abroad. Despite its accomplishments, major obstacles domestically and internationally remain. No better example of the factionalism and fragility of Iranian politics can be found than the parliamentary elections of February 2000 and their aftermath. An electoral turnout of more than 70 percent and the victory of pro-Khatami progressive candidates who gained a plurality of seats in parliament seemed a signal of Iran's movement toward a modern democracy. However, in the months that followed, conservative forces flexed their political muscle. The Council of Guardians quietly nullified eleven national constituencies and the judiciary closed down more than 30 reformist newspapers and journals. Thus, the significance and future impact of Khatami's quiet revolution, and the future of Iran, remain difficult to fully assess or predict.

1

The Paradoxes of Politics in Postrevolutionary Iran

Mehrzad Boroujerdi

> *The way of paradoxes is the way of truth. To test Reality we must see it on the tight-rope. When the Verities become acrobats we can judge them.*
> —Oscar Wilde, *The Picture of Dorian Gray*

Anachronistic, bewildering, enigmatic, incongruent, intricate, ironic, multidimensional, paradoxical, permutable, recondite, serendipitous, and unpredictable are among the oftmentioned descriptions of the intellectual and political landscape of Iran over the last two decades. Why has the Iranian intellectual milieu acquired such traits?

In answering the above question, this essay proposes the following points: (a) to understand the subtlety, specificity, and the seemingly contradictory intellectual heritage of contemporary Iran, one needs to develop an ear for the whisperings of irony and an eye for the nuances of paradox which have baptized Iran's revolution over the last two decades; (b) the profound cultural, economic, and social transformations of the postrevolutionary era have endowed Iranian politics with a degree of sophistication and multidimensionality previously unimaginable—consideration of this fact should remind us not to perpetuate the analytical error of the revolution's first decade by attributing the monumental political transformations that have taken place to any leader's words or deeds; and (c) since coming to power in 1979, the clerical establishment and Shii jurisprudence have been ambushed by politics and entrapped in the epistemological labyrinth of modernity.

The Benison of Irony

The paradoxical nature of political truth in contemporary Iran is clearly on display once we look at the following characteristics of the postrevolutionary polity:

- A constitution that simultaneously affirms religious and secular principles, democratic and antidemocratic tendencies, as well as populist and elitist predilections.
- A society in which many cultural, political, and social institutions are Western and modern in pedigree and configuration, yet native and traditional in iconography and nomenclature.
- A "hyperpoliticized" polity that does not benefit from the presence of recognized, legitimate, or effective political parties.
- A theocracy where religion is an axiom of political life and yet secular agents, aspirations, ideas, institutions, language, and motifs continue to survive and—more importantly—manifest their significance in the realms of private and public space.
- A society where the eclectic texture of its popular culture have made the practicality—let alone desirability—of religiously sanctioned statecraft very much doubtful. This reality has led to a gradual but consistent disillusionment with the belief that "Islam is the only [political] solution."
- A clerical leadership that has claimed to protect tradition but has amended and broken numerous age-old religious protocols for the sake of state expediency.
- A society whose Islamic intellectuals resort to the writings of Western thinkers to validate their own "Islamic" critique of the West.
- A citizenry that has come to enjoy an era of intellectual prosperity while living under a politically repressive state.
- A society where women's rights were trampled upon, yet women continued to make serious strides into the educational, cultural, and employment domains, thereby increasing awareness of women's rights and issues at the social level.[1]

There are other bewildering and contradictory trends and structures as well. For example, although many Muslim modernists denounce Western modernity and portray Islam as the solution to all their social ills, the Iranian Shii modernists—who have been the target of attacks by the ruling clerical establishment—are calling for a secular system of government to rescue religion from becoming even more mercantile and utilitarian. What makes this paradox even more interesting is that "secular Islamists"— another oxymoron—are advocating secularism at a time when many Western experts on Islam argue that Shiism is one of the religions least prone to secularization.[2]

One needs only to survey questions debated by scholarly and political elites to gauge Iran's intellectual barometer during the last two decades. Among the most pressing topics of debate and questioning are the following eight:

(1) *Democracy:* Is democracy merely a method of governing? Can one embrace democracy without adhering to humanism? Is epistemological pluralism the most central pillar of democratic practice? In the case of conflict between democratic rights and sacred law, which should prevail? Should the ballot box supercede religious interpretations in the Islamic Republic? Should leaders and managers be elected by the people or be appointed by religious authorities? Can a religious democracy be formed by simply embracing such Islamic concepts as consultation (*shura*), consensus (*ijma*), and allegiance (*bayat*)? Has there ever been a civil society in Iran? Is the "Islamic Republic" an oxymoron? What is the future of *velayat-i faqih* (rule of the juris-consult)?

(2) *Epistemology and Interpretation of Islam:* Should religion be relegated to the domain of individual consciousness? Should Islamic jurisprudence be subjected to epistemological analysis and hermenutical readings? Would such an exposure lead Muslims toward deism?

(3) *Islam and Ideology:* Is an ideological interpretation of religion possible, desirable, and/or inevitable? Is Islam a political religion by nature? Should professional/administrative competence take precedent over ideological commitment? Is Islam compatible with nationalism? Should the practices and rhetoric of revolutionary activism continue more than two decades after the revolution?

(4) *Islam and Modernity:* Can modernity be overcome? Can modernity be reconfigured? Are there non-Western varieties of modernity? Is it possible for criticisms of modernity to serve as a cultural-historical shortcut to the future for non-Western soci-

eties? Can Muslims borrow anything from the postmodernist criticism of modernity? Should Islam be interpreted in terms of the principles of modernity? If not, how should Islam be interpreted? How can Iranians become modern?

(5) *Islam and the West:* Are secularism and Westernization one and the same? What have been the repercussions of Muslims' and Christians' different and nonsynchronous encounters with modern civilization? Should criticisms of Eurocentric ideologies lead to incrimination of Enlightenment principles? Is selective philosophical borrowing from the West possible? What is Western thought? How do you thwart or create immunity toward Western "cultural invasion?"

(6) *Pluralism:* Is pluralism compatible with religiosity? How can one reconcile the belief in one religion leading to salvation with the diversity of religions? Does Islam allow for pluralism or only coexistence and tolerance? Can there be different ways of reaching the truth? Should religious pluralism be distinguished from sociopolitical pluralism? Does religious pluralism pave the way for secularism? Is religious pluralism an appropriate topic of discussion for the masses or just the intellectual elite? Are clerics the sole trustees of the community?

(7) *Religion and Science/Technology:* Is science a disinterested entity? Does science need philosophy—especially a spiritually endowed Eastern or Oriental one? Is technology merely a tool at the disposal of humans, or is it the embodiment of a new and subjugating metaphysics of being? Is there a future for religion in a world dominated by scientific thought?

(8) *Rights and Freedoms:* Can the social rights of atheists be accepted in a religious society? Should religious minorities benefit from the same rights and freedoms as Muslims? Do freedom and justice oppose one another? Is freedom an Islamic concept? Is there a human rights discourse in Islam? Should the Universal Declaration of Human Rights be accepted? Are there first- and second-class citizens in an Islamic republic? Should heretics and nonbelievers enjoy freedom of expression? Is society's interest and security more threatened by limiting freedom or enlarging it?

These questions illustrate the zest and complexity of the Iranian intellectual community. The disagreements concerning the nature of science, religion, and secularism in the modern world testify to the existing gap between text and practice, ought to be and is, politics and jurisprudence, and local and global. One venue for comprehending these gaps is to examine the relationship between religion and politics.

Cajoling a Muscular State

In addition to the institutions it had inherited from the ancien régime—state ministries, public universities, schools, courts, parliament, and so on—the Islamic Republic felt compelled to manufacture a plethora of assemblies, committees, councils, courts, foundations, and organs to exert its ideological control. The appropriation of the inherited institutions and the invented new organs modified the contours of Iranian statecraft by making the state even more "muscular."[3]

The advantages of having a muscular state became evident in the volatile political ambiance of the early 1980s, as the clerical regime moved swiftly to subdue its opponents. The state could now afford to regard public opposition of any kind as seditious and to restrict or repress any political activity outside its purview. Many of the above organs, usually run by zealous believers, showed no restraints in their power to ingress upon individual and civil rights or to devour civic initiatives and institutions. Overtime, however, as they became arenas for factional infighting, overlapping responsibilities, and conflicting policies, the government decided to consolidate them into more established and bureaucratic agencies. As the system moved from populist agitation toward state consolidation, its statesmen came to rely upon codified laws and bureaucratic procedures. Hence, another paradox was born. Even when the advocates of the interventionist state managed to strip from the constitution many of its democratic and legalistic elements in the name of political expediency, they, nevertheless, came to realize that codified law, bureaucratic rules, and standard operating procedures can be binding. If not already, the clergy may realize in due time that the takeover of the institutions of the modern state has forced them to submit to its implacable logic, bow to its imperious demands, and embrace the alienation that goes with all power.

A more challenging endeavor facing the ruling clerics was how to purify Iranian culture from its non-Islamic traits and make the citizenry's lives compatible with "Islamic" teachings. Most indicators so far point to the fact that the clergy have failed in their social engineering. While the "vice police" roamed the streets of Iranian cities, they failed to fundamentally alter the dynamics of private life and discourse in a country where charm, compassion, dignity, grace, and subtlety are considered as given rules of social etiquette. Domestic and familial life may never have been fully secularized in Iran, but it was not about to fall prey to religious extremism or revolutionary hysteria either. People came up with ingenious forms of camouflage and double talk to safeguard their privacy. Moreover, they managed to undermine or at least dilute the severity of the clergy's edicts by resorting to adroit humor, conspiracy theories, cynicism, dissimulation, irreverence, nostalgic rehabilitation of the old regime, perversion of the laws, secrecy, symbolic discourse, and outright dissent.

Resistance to clerical rule by fiat has been most evident among Iran's stoic, and predominantly secular, middle class. As the middle class's economic capital has drastically shrunk in the turbulent postrevolutionary Iran—resulting from the gap between the cost of living and annual wages—they hang on more than ever to their most precious badge of honor—their "habitus."[4] Moreover, this class has used its "cultural capital"—the general cultural background, knowledge, disposition, and skills that are passed from one generation to the next[5]—to subvert the present theocracy. The oppositional behavior of the middle class is a form of resistance to an ideological state that has not been able to deliver on its promises. Meanwhile, due to increasing rates of urbanization, literacy, and bureaucratization of state power, the middle class has been able to perpetuate itself. Apparently, an increasing number in Iran's ruling circle are reaching the conclusion that they need to stop, if not reverse, the process of devaluing and depreciating the cultural capital of Iran's influential middle class. They seem to have realized that the state can no longer afford to ignore the candid calls of a critical mass of secular-minded technocrats, professionals, and industrialists, all of whom are demanding the liberalization of the educational system, relaxation of artistic and cultural restraints, abandonment of cultural xenophobia toward the West, and legal moderation. Moreover, considering the changing demography of the country, they also need to be concerned about the revolution of rising expectations among Iran's increasingly urban, literate, and young population.[6]

Another bone of contention between the clerically dominated state and its secular interlocutors is the issues of nationalism and pre-Islamic Iranian identity. The Islamic regime initially had a troublesome relationship with ancient Persian lineage, customs, traditions, artifacts, and festivals. In their attempt to properly "Islamicize" the cultural reference point of many Iranians, they felt that they had to fight Western cultural influences, while deprogramming Iranians from any attachment to their notions of pre-Islamic values and ideas. They soon realized that diluting the richness of Persian culture was not an easy task and, therefore, they somewhat relented their cultural offensive against Iran's pre-Islamic traditions and icons. The new leaders reluctantly learned that they had no choice but to coexist with pre-Islamic Iranian culture, symbols, practices, and identity, as Iranians were in no hurry to abandon their collective memory of a glorious past that is still sufficiently attractive.[7] They also had to digest a speedy ideological rapprochement with Iranian nationalism as the war with Iraq broke out in 1980. Those who had lamented nationalism as an insidious ideology for Muslims now had to wrap themselves in its mantle, embrace its iconography, and partake in its passionate discourse. Whereas the war with Iraq enabled the clergy to consolidate their power and subdue their opponents, the hostilities also bolstered Iranians' sense of self-confidence and "national" pride.

The Janus face of the Islamic Republic is most abundantly clear in the cultural realm. The 1979 revolution yielded a flourishing press. By the middle of 1979, more than 260 government-owned as well as independent papers were published in Iran, with a majority devoted to political and social themes.[8] The "spring of freedom," however, did not last more than a few months. The new regime could not tolerate the rampant debates in the pages of the print media about the form, nature, and legitimacy of the new republic and its revolutionary institutions.[9] By 1982, only 66 legally approved papers were in operation.[10] To compensate for the lack of political parties in a society marked by intellectual ferment and an agile generation demanding greater freedoms, however, the clerics had to loosen, at least slightly, restrictions on the press. This is not to suggest that there was a smooth transition to cultural opening. In 1987, Esmail Fassih, one of postrevolutionary Iran's most popular novelists, inaugurated his article on the status of the writer in contemporary Iran with the following witty remark: "In the Bejeweled Land of (traditionally *Shahanshahi*) Persia, a good writer is a dead writer."[11] Furthermore, in his resignation letter of July 1992 as Minister of Culture and Islamic Guidance, Hojjatolislam Mohammad Khatami sharply wrote:

> Unfortunately for a while now we are witnessing that in the field of cultural affairs all legal, religious, ethical, and secular norms are being violated. We have gotten way beyond the realm of critique and evaluation (even unfair ones). Nowadays every means is justified in the name of certain ends and

as such the order of things is about to lose its logical and legal relevance. As such, an unhealthy and turbulent atmosphere is about to be created. The most immediate effect of this ambiance is the discouragement and insecurity of fine and distinguished thinkers and artists, even those who are firm believers in the revolution and Islam.[12]

Nonetheless, in due time, Iranian society came to experience an explosion of publications—presently estimated to be around 1,300; a booming translation industry; and a thriving cinema industry.[13] The track record of the press corps demonstrates that they have played a crucial role in shaping Iranian public opinion, producing ideas different from that of the state, making the citizenry conscious of their rights, and enabling people to express their views within the established boundaries.[14] Thanks to the presence of a critical mass of independent papers and literati, Iranians have come to enjoy serious journalism and a lively press. Considering its catalytic powers, the press has the potential to exert further pressure on the state to embark upon political liberalization.[15]

In short, Iran's political barometer indicates that despite its propaganda and bravado, the Islamic Republic has failed to inundate its secular opponents. As champions of a modernist subculture and a secularist discourse, both the nationalist and the leftist forces constitute a formidable alternative to a clerical leadership beset by epistemological and political hazards. The theoretical self-criticism and growing intellectual maturation of these forces, which is reflected in their adoption of indigenous and ingenious new political positions, will most certainly enhance their public fortune and should beget them an ample pool of disciples in a more open political ambiance.[16] We should also bear in mind that, whereas many former Islamists are now defecting to the secularist camp, there have been no consequential defections in the other direction. As such, the fallacious temptation to dismiss the legitimacy of the secular forces and the viability of their discourse should be avoided. Present projections about the withering away of secular thought in Iran may prove as shortsighted as prophecies about the demise of Islam rampant in the 1970s.

Politics Invades the "Republic of Virtue"

The 1979 revolution was the culmination of an invasion of politics by religious forces determined to set up a "republic of virtue." Ironically, however, the materialization of Ayatollah Khomeini's theory of divine rule of jurists (*velayat-i faqih*) entrapped the clerical establishment as well as Shii jurisprudence in a political quagmire. The new revolutionary elites faced economic and political problems not reducible to or analyzable by means of religious givens. The antiquity and the private character of *shariah* law made it rather ill equipped to deal with the legal and public needs of a modern, stratified, and revolutionary polity. Consequently, the ruling clerics had to invoke the "exigency of the state" argument.[17] The periodic and public invocation of this argument, in turn, further diluted the legitimacy of the theory of *velayat-i faqih*. Not only this central theoretical principle of the Islamic Republic remained a minority position among the highest ranking Shii theologians—a great majority of whom remained apolitical—but it was also repudiated by members of the new politically active class of religious intellectuals. Abdolkarim Sorush (b. 1945), the leading contemporary theoretician of this class, discarded the theory of *velayat-i faqih* in the following fashion:

> The language of religion (and Islam in particular) as reflected in the Qur'an and the hadiths is more a language of obligation rather than right. The tone of the scriptures is one of an all powerful and mighty Lord who commands and prohibits the humans and reminds the believers of their duties.... In my view, one of the reasons which has made the comprehension of *velayat-e faqih* and Islamic government difficult for both supporters and followers is this very issue. A government of *velayat-e faqih* is one that is based on duties [obligation or onus] while the mind of the modern man and most of new political philosophies bases government on rights and consent of the citizenry. It is a dangerous and destructive eclecticism when the ruler and the ruled fluctuate from speaking and behaving in accordance with principles of rights and speaking and behaving in accordance with the duty of obligation.[18]

Sorush maintained that modern man is one who has reserved for himself the "right" to obligation (not the "duty" to be obligated) to God. Moreover, he does not recognize anyone's right to claim divineness in politics and government. One of Sorush's colleagues went a step further and argued that the theory of *velayat-i faqih* was the last and most important attempt at (or catalyst for) secularization of Shii jurisprudence.[19] According to him, when a religious system moves toward the formation of a state, it becomes incumbent upon it to modify its religious laws in accordance with the new conditions at hand. A prerequisite for doing so is to prepare a strong digestive system to swallow an entity referred to as the "state."[20] Secularization is the catalyst that enables religion to absorb the state and, in turn, precipitates the absorption of religion within the machinery of the state. As the state is the guardian of the national interest and as the protection of national interest requires the acceptance of "prudence or expediency" as a principle of statecraft, the theory of *velayat-i faqih* opens the gate for all types of willful and whimsical interpretations of *shariah* or the constitution.[21]

These modernist intellectuals maintain that such a trend has a deleterious impact on religion, because as soon as religion becomes tied up with the material interest and political considerations of a particular group (and, thus, becomes an ideology), its opportunity to develop and progress is diminished. They warn their religious brethren that considering the homegrown and spontaneous nature of the above developments in the Islamic Republic, the process of secularization will be more permanent and irreversible in Iran than in countries where it was induced by the irreligious.[22] As such, they maintain that a secular state is a better alternative to a theocratic system in which religion becomes tainted with the impurities and utilitarian compromises of politics and clerics become mere civil servants.

In the conclusion of his book, *The Constitution of Iran,* Asghar Schirazi echoes some of the same sentiments—albeit from a secular perspective:

> While members of the clergy have held on to their turbans and robes ever more tenaciously, they have at the same time increasingly taken over the offices of state and thus neglected their religious duties. Indeed, they have been transformed into state functionaries. It is not they, the bearers of religious authority, who have conquered the state and subordinated it to the rule of religion. Instead the reverse has happened: the state has conquered the clergy and along with them religion.[23]

Toward a Pensive Politics

The balance sheet of the last 20 years is interestingly bewildering—unprecedented progress juxtaposed against regressive changes. Whereas much of the current scholarship on postrevolutionary Iran has been concerned with the negative traits of this era (human rights abuses, fundamentalism, economic hardships, political violence, etc.), the more positive developments (deep-rooted socioeconomic changes, emergence of a self-defining, vibrant, and critical public discourse) have been more or less ignored or downplayed. I believe an accurate and holistic assessment of the balance sheet of postrevolutionary Iranian politics also requires an acknowledgement of how the tangled realities of social production have had somewhat of a cathartic effect on sociopolitical thought. By way of concluding this essay, I shall present a few examples of these hitherto disregarded positive trends.

One of the most noticeable developments during the last two decades has been the emergence of certain formal processes, institutions, and norms that are real and/or legitimate. For example, voting and elections have become institutionalized as candidates representing narrow but real rival groups compete with one another. Iran's ruling establishment seems to have more or less accepted the results of the electoral process as evidenced by the relatively low instance of voter fraud. While the parliament (*Majles*) operates within very defined parameters, it can no longer be considered as a rubber-stamp institution. Instead, it has become an effective debating chamber and a springboard for airing grievances by parliamentarians who engage in incessant politicking and do not shy away from using procedural rules such as vote of confidence and impeachment to accomplish their agendas. Furthermore, a new generation of political elites—many of whom hail from the provinces and have impeccable revolutionary credentials—has emerged, which is trying to increase its elbowroom in Iran's contentious political world. The incorporation of these and other political constituencies is making Iranian political life increasingly more inclusive. Today, one can argue that political factions in Iran are for real and their disagreements, particularly about cultural issues, are genuine and deeply held. These factions use such legally endowed institutions as the parliament or the press to wage their political/ideological fights or to jockey for power in a system distinguished by its overlapping power centers.

An even more positive omen of political maturity in postrevolutionary Iran is an increasing preference, across the political spectrum, for reformist rather than revolutionary change. This is an extremely important development, considering the historical proclivity of political movements in Iran to have called for the revolutionary overthrow of any governments of which they disapproved. After experiencing two revolutions and numerous other political upheavals in one century, it may now be finally possible to embrace a political culture that advocates the prudence and efficacy of reformist change.

Finally, one can argue that the excesses of the last two decades, which have been exorbitant and tragic in monetary and human cost, also have inadvertently contributed to positive changes in Iran's intellectual milieu.

Today, keen observers of Iranian politics cannot help but notice the changes in the intellectual orientation of some of the most doctrinaire organizations. Leftists as well as Islamic thinkers are questioning the credulity and corrupting influence of ideological thinking. Having freed themselves from the cordon of previously luminous ideologies, many of Iran's intellectuals are now busy articulating serious and sophisticated criticisms of autochthonous and quotidian features of Iranian political life such as authoritarianism, censorship, clientalism, cult of personality, *etatism*, fanaticism, influence peddling, partisanship, and violence. I believe that their earnest demands for accountability, civil rights, democracy, human rights, liberty, a limited state, political heterogeneity, social justice, tolerance, and transparency bodes well for Iran's future.

Notes

1. The following set of educational, employment, cultural, and social facts testify to this claim: (a) By the mid-1990s, females' literacy rate (aged six and over) climbed over 74 percent; girls and women constituted 46 percent of K-12 students; 50 percent of high school graduates; 40 percent of university students; 31 percent of graduates of higher education centers; 38 percent of all students getting MS, Ph.D., or postdoctorate degrees in medical sciences; 18 percent of university faculty; (b) while 65 percent of Iranian women are still housewives, their rate of participation in the economy has steadily increased. This participation rate has been most visible in the service sector, which accounts for over 45 percent of all female employment; (c) women now comprise a notable constituency of avid book readers, buyers, translators, editors, and authors, as well as poets, painters, photographers, art and film critics, actors, screen writers, makeup artists, directors, and cinematographers; and (d) the emergence of an increasingly potent women's movement is subjecting Islamic legal doctrines, patriarchal social practices, and sexist cultural norms to a rigorous feminist critique.
2. The advocates of this approach often mention such features of Shiism as its ideological grievances toward temporal authority, its tendency toward oppositionalism along with its communal, paternalistic, and highly emotional qualities to support their argument. For a criticism of this view, see Mehrzad Boroujerdi, "Can Islam be Secularized?" in M. R. Ghanoonparvar and Faridoun Farrokh , eds., *In Transition: Essays on Culture and Identity in the Middle Eastern Society*, (Laredo, TX: Texas A&M International University, 1994), pp. 55–64.

The Paradoxes of Politics in Postrevolutionary Iran 25

3. I have borrowed this concept from Fred Halliday. See his essay entitled "Portrait: Mohammad Khatami," *Prospect*, January 1998, p. 43.
4. Pierre Bourdieu has defined "habitus" as "a system of lasting, transposable dispositions which, integrating past experiences, functions at every moment as a matrix of perceptions, appreciations and actions." He maintains that habitus "could be considered as a subjective but not individual system of internalized structures, schemes of perception, conception, and action common to all members of the same group or class and constituting the precondition for all objectification and apperception." See Pierre Bourdieu, *Outline of a Theory of Practice* (Cambridge: Cambridge University Press, 1977), pp. 82–83, 86.
5. For Bourdieu's discussion of cultural capital, see Pierre Bourdieu, "Cultural Reproduction and Social Reproduction," in Jerome Karabel and A. H. Halsey, eds., *Power and Ideology in Education* (New York: Oxford University Press, 1977).
6. In this regard, some of the more salient facts to keep in mind are the following: an urban population rate of 61.3 percent; a private sector that employs over 65 percent of the labor force; a population median age of 19.4 years (1996); and a literacy rate of 79.3 percent. In regard to the last fact, it is particularly noteworthy to remember that almost one-third of Iran's population (20 million) are students and that it has over five million people with postsecondary education.
7. Nor were the clerics, it seems, able to keep Western cultural influences at bay. In their "home territory," many members of Iran's middle and upper classes treated the specter of Western (and particularly American) popular culture—with its dynamic, modern, and youthful qualities—as an invisible guest. In other words, Western cultural traditions and icons may have been driven underground, but its presence could still be felt.
8. *Ayandah*, vol. 5, nos. 10–12 (Winter 1979), pp. 916–21. This was almost twice the number of newspapers and periodicals that were published in 1974.
9. In a famous speech in November 1980, Ayatollah Khomeini denounced the press and rhetorically asked the officials, "Why do you not stop these newspapers? Why do you not shut their mouths? Why do you not stop their pens?" See Shaul Bakhash, *The Reign of the Ayatollahs: Iran and the Islamic Revolution* (New York: Basic Books, 1984), p. 148.
10. The clampdown on the press was preceded by a few months with attacks on the universities, which began in earnest in June of 1980 with the launching of the Cultural Revolution campaign. The government's eagerness to silence opponents became apparent, as armed gangs of hooligans loyal to

the hardline clergy assaulted campuses with the proclaimed goal of evicting the offices of politically affiliated groups. In 1984, the Minister of Higher Education gave the world a glimpse of the devastating consequences of the cultural revolution by revealing that "3,500 university teachers had been fired or had resigned during the period after the closing of the institutions of higher education." Cited in Asghar Schirazi, *The Constitution of Iran: Politics and the State in the Islamic Republic*, trans. John O'Kane (London: I.B. Tauris, 1997), p. 139.

11. Esmail Fassih, "The Status: A Day in the Life of a Contemporary Iranian Writer," *Third World Quarterly*, vol. 9, no. 3 (July 1987), p. 825.
12. "Saranjam Doktor Khatami Raft" [Dr. Khatami Finally Left], *Adineh*, no. 72 (Mordad 1371 [August 1992]), p. 5.
13. For further elaboration of these cultural developments, see Mehrzad Boroujerdi, "Iran's Intellectual Panorama," *Bulletin of the Center for Iranian Research and Analysis*, vol. 11, no. 3 (Spring 1996), pp. 22–24.
14. Particularly noteworthy in this regard are the facts that the circulation rate of the country's press is now approaching almost three million copies per day, and that the number of *provincial* journals is on the rise.
15. The fact that during the first 20 months of President Khatami's reign, 52 publications were banned temporarily or closed outright and that over 250 lawsuits were filed against various press personalities demonstrates that the ghost of censorship continues to haunt the Iranian press. However, the use of such draconian measures along with the beating and assassination of press personalities also reveals the effectiveness of the press in exposing power brokers and shaping public opinion.
16. For example, a good section of the Iranian leftist movement has engaged in a serious critique of the legacy of Marxism-Leninism, the Soviet Union, armed struggle, and the necessity of a "revolutionary" transformation. They have substituted many of their previously orthodox positions with neoleftist and social democratic positions. Similarly, Iran's monarchists and republicanists have engaged in animated discussions concerning factionalism, pluralism, republicanism, reformism, and the legacy of the Pahlavi dynasty.
17. In this regard, it is worth remembering the following words of the Polish journalist, Ryszard Kapuscinski, who writes: "Although a system may cease to exist in the legal sense or as a structure of power, its values (or anti-values), its philosophy, its teachings remain in us. They rule our thinking, our conduct, our attitude to others. The situation is a demonic paradox: we have toppled the system but we still carry its genes." Ryszard Kapuscinski, *Independent* [London] (September 1, 1991).

18. Abdolkarim Sorush, "Mana va Mabnay-e Sekularism" [The Meaning and Basis of Secularism], *Kiyan* 26 (August-September 1995), pp. 9–10.
19. Jahangir Salehpour, "Farayand-e Urfi Shodan-e Feqh-e Shi'a" [The Secularization Process of Shii Jurisprudence], *Kiyan* 24 (April-May 1995), pp. 20–21.
20. Salehpour maintains that just as it happened in the West at the dawn of the formation of the nation-state, in Iran, as well, political thought has tilted toward an "absolutist state." Although in a peripheral country such as Iran, the Shii anxiety for establishing a powerful state also can be attributed to the unconscious attempt to deal with the problem of underdevelopment (the same way German idealism contributed to the formation of the powerful Prussian state). Ibid., pp. 22–23.
21. As proof of this trend, we can offer the following examples: Ayatollah Khomeini's famous edict that the interests of the state take precedence over even the most important tenants of faith (i.e., prayer, fasting, and hajj); Ayatollah Khomeini's dismissal of Ayatollah Montazeri as his designate heir apparent without first securing the consent of the Council of Experts; creation of *Shoray-e Tashkis-e Maslahat-e Nezam* (Council for Discernment of Governmental Expediency); distinguishing between the position of *Marja-i Taqlid* (source of emulation) and the leader; the appointment of little known Ayatollah Araki as the marja after Ayatollah Khomeini's death and declaring Hojjatolislam Khamenei as the new supreme leader; overnight upgrading of religious titles; and granting the Council of Guardians the power of approbation (*Nezarat-e Estesvabi*).
22. Salehpour 1995, p. 23.
23. Schirazi, *The Constitution of Iran*, p. 303.

2

Reform and Resistance in the Islamic Republic of Iran

Mohsen M. Milani

> *I have made a covenant with the nation to move with it towards justice.* . . .
> *They try to say religion and freedom do not mix.* . . . *They are striving to say that security and freedom do not mix and that in order to have security, freedom must be crushed. But the nation will not be fooled.*
> —President Mohammad Khatami in Hamadan, Iran, July 27, 1999

Infused with infinite idealism and righteousness, young revolutionary regimes are obdurately resistant to internal reforms. When such regimes fuse politics with religion, when their ultimate legitimacy emanates from God, and when the aim of reform is to empower the people, then the obstacles to reform become that much more insurmountable. This explains the formidable opposition to Iran's new reform movement, which has polarized that country's politics and society to an unprecedented and potentially dangerous level. The catalyst for the emergence of this new movement was the 1997 presidential election.

It was not the "favorite son" of the governing elites, Hojjatolislam Ali Akbar Nateq-Nuri, but the "Cinderella candidate," the relatively obscure Seyyed Mohammad Khatami, who stunned the establishment and won the election by a landslide, receiving more than 20 million votes, or 69 percent of the total. In a book he had written before declaring his candidacy, Khatami argued that liberal democracy, despite all its shortcomings, is one of the West's greatest achievements and that its basic tenets must be warmly embraced by all modern societies. As a presidential candidate, Khatami, a committed cleric with impeccable loyalty to the Islamic

Republic, defended a liberal doctrine in a country where the word "liberal" was synonymous with "Western decadence," and was practically purged from the tolerated language of political discourse. His mantra was political development—strengthening civil society, respecting the rule of law, cherishing freedom, and institutionalizing tolerance—all of which, in the convoluted vernacular of revolutionary Iran, meant democracy. Perhaps to Khatami's own surprise, his soul-soothing message was precisely the formula that energized millions of voters. As president, Khatami has come to personify a reform movement whose objectives are to empower the people or establish popular sovereignty as one of the bases of governance and to make the Islamic Republic gentler, kinder, and more tolerant and transparent.

The structural configuration of the Islamic Republic consists of both Islamic and republican components, with the former purposefully designed to dominate the latter. During the presidential race, Hojjatolislam Nateq-Nuri supported efforts to continue and strengthen this imbalance of power, while Khatami advocated the fundamental right of the citizenry to exercise popular sovereignty. Make no mistake: The debate between those clerics was not for or against Islam, for or against the *velayat-i faqih* (the ideological basis of the Islamic Republic), for or against secularism. Rather, it was a debate of Islam against Islam. In one Islam, popular sovereignty and the *velayat-i faqih* must become compatible and complimentary, and in the other, the *faqih* speaks the last word and limited popular sovereignty can be exercised only within the boundaries he defines. One Islam attempts to embrace modern ideas; the other is confident that its divine regulations transcend time and space. The roots of both perspectives can be traced to the Constitutional Movement of 1906: One was represented by the sagacious Mirza Mohammad Hossein Gharavi Naini, the most eloquent defender of constitutionalism, and the other by Sheikh Fazollah Nuri, the most articulate opponent of constitutionalism.

Because of the dynamic political climate Khatami has helped create, the genie of democratization appears to be temporarily out of the bottle in the land with 2,500 years of autocratic tradition. To what extent has Khatami succeeded in reforming the Islamic Republic, and what are some of the main obstacles he faces? I will answer these questions by discussing the impact of the 1997 election on the factional balance of power, Khatami's campaign platform and strategy, Khatami's major achievements, and the obstacles to reform in the Islamic Republic.

Factions and the Power Shift before the 1997 Election

From its inception, the Islamic Republic has been dominated by rival factions. Powerful factions, with differences in their paradigms, have emerged in revolutionary Iran as a result of the polycephalic nature of Shiism and the ulama-dominated political milieu of the Islamic Republic. In Shii Islam, the highest religious authorities, the ayatollahs, enjoy the discretion to offer different and sometimes contradictory interpretations of Islamic and political issues. Even at the zenith of Ayatollah Ruhollah Musavi Khomeini's popularity and power in the early 1980s, for example, there were other ayatollahs who not only had their own considerable mass following but also expressed views different from Khomeini's. In revolutionary Iran, factional rivalry has provided some room for the factions to articulate their views, mobilize support, build institutions, and nominate candidates for political and religious offices.

In the beginning, two factions, the Conservatives and the Islamic Leftists, competed within the confines of the Islamic Republican Party, Iran's largest party of the time. The Conservatives had the support of many senior clerics and controlled most of the seminaries and the Guardian Council, the institution designed by the Islamic Constitution to protect the Islamic nature of the Islamic Republic. The Conservatives interpreted Islamic jurisprudence with little flexibility, championed free enterprise, and favored restricted implementation of Islamic laws and enforcement of what they called Islamic morality. The other faction, the Islamic Leftists, consisted of younger clerics with strong populist proclivities. They believed in a dynamic Islamic jurisprudence, one that can be rendered compatible with the needs of the modern world. Known in the West at the time as the "hardliners," the Islamic Left supported nationalization of the major industries and a Soviet-style economic planning of sorts, minus Marxism. The Islamic Leftists were quite powerful within both the government and the newly created revolutionary institutions, such as the Revolutionary Courts. Ayatollah Khomeini saw in them a powerful force against the Conservatives, whose rigidity in interpreting Islam he disliked intensely. The Islamic Left's indirect involvement in the Tehran hostage crisis also increased its power. Hojjatolislam Mohammad Khoeiniha, a darling of the Islamic Left, for example, was the spiritual leader of the students who occupied the American Embassy for 444 days of the hostage crisis. If we apply Crane Brinton's model of the "phases of revolutions" to Iran, which he developed in *Anatomy of Revolution,* we must conclude that the Islamic Leftists were certainly the main force behind the extremist phase of the Islamic Revolution, when all opponents of the Islamic Republic were eliminated and Islamization of all aspects of life was the government's top political agenda. Oscillating between the Conservatives and Islamic Leftists were the Pragmatists under the leadership of Hojjatolislam Ali Akbar Hashemi Rafsanjani, the Zhou Enlai of the Iranian Revolution. Eclectic in orientation, and few in number, the Pragmatists gradually gained power as effective power brokers between the Islamic Left and the Conservatives.[1]

Standing above those factions was the charismatic Ayatollah Khomeini, whose decisive leadership no faction dared to challenge. He kept the factions competitive, never allowing one to dominate or eliminate the others. This balancing act was essential to maintain the equilibrium of the Islamic coalition he had so successfully forged to defeat his opponents. The differences between the Conservatives and the Leftists were so irreconcilable, however, that Khomeini had no choice but to dissolve the Islamic Republican Party in 1987. This led quickly to a major split within the Ja'maye Ruhaniyat-e Mobarez-e Tehran (The Society of the Combatant Clerics of Tehran), the ulama's most powerful organization, controlled by the Conservatives. Subsequently, the Majma-ye Rouhaniyoun-e Mobarez-e Tehran (The Association of the Combatant Clergy of Tehran) was formed. Sheikholislams Seyyed Mohammad Khatami, Mehdi Karubi, and Mohammad Khoeiniha were among the founders of the new organization, which has remained the mouthpiece for the Islamic Leftists.[2]

Even before Ayatollah Khomeini was buried in 1988, the governing coalition began to become polarized. This process began in June 1989, when Seyyed Ali Khamenei was elected the new *Faqih* by the Assembly of Experts for the Leadership, with 60 votes cast in his favor and 14 against. Two months later, the pragmatic Hashemi Rafsanjani was elected president, receiving more than 15 million votes (Table 1). Hojjatolislam Karubi replaced Rafsanjani as Speaker of the Majles, placing the Islamic Leftists in control of that institution. Ayatollah Khamenei quickly formed an alliance with President Rafsanjani that has lasted until today. Old comrades whose friendship dates back to their anti-Shah activities in the 1960s, they exercised power in distinct domains and refrained from conspiring against each other. Rafsanjani focused on the economy, while the *Faqih* concentrated on building his network both inside and outside of the government and increasing his religious legitimacy within the clerical establishment, which the Conservatives controlled. After all, the *Faqih* was in need of recognition and acceptance, having been elevated from the rank of a hojjatolislam to the higher rank of an ayatollah. In a few years, however, his representatives and appointees were visible in all government agencies and in revolutionary institutions and he became the country's most powerful figure.

The ascendance of the Pragmatists in 1989 reflected deep changes in the country's social and political landscapes.[3] At the time, the population was angry, frustrated, and thirsty for reform: In the previous decade, Iranians had experienced one revolution, eight years of war with Iraq with devastating consequences, and a drastic decline in their living standard. Rafsanjani correctly read this prevalent mood. He promised "economic reconstruction" and the reversal of the economic policies of the Islamic Leftists who, under premier Mir Hussein Mussavi for most of the 1980s, had pursued a statist, if not socialist, economic policy. It was under President Rafsanjani that Iran began its drive toward social and economic reform and a conciliatory foreign policy.[4]

The Islamic Leftists misread the country's mood and continued to express extremist views that had little popular support. Although Rafsanjani tried to coopt some of them by allowing, for example, Khatami to stay in the cabinet, the Islamic Leftists continued to oppose his reforms. They condemned Rafsanjani's "liberal economic policies" as benefiting the rich and hurting the poor. They opposed Rafsanjani's moderate approach to the West, arguing that such a policy would allow the West to dominate Iran again. They unabashedly portrayed their Islam as authentic, while denouncing their rivals' as "the American Islam."[5] They were no less hostile to the new *Faqih*. Morteza Alviri, a Tehran Majles Deputy, claimed in 1991 that some one hundred Majles deputies were followers of Ayatollah Hossein Ali Montazeri, a direct challenge to the *Faqih*. There were suggestions here and there that the *Faqih* must be elected by a national plebiscite and that the Guardian Council be abolished altogether.[6]

In short, the Islamic Left's vehement opposition to Rafsanjani's moderation and reforms and its questioning of Khamenei's new role as the *Faqih* further marginalized it, solidified the alliance between Rafsanjani and Khamenei, and pushed the Pragmatists to form a brief alliance with the Conservatives. The Left's fall from power accelerated during the elections for the Fourth Majles in 1992. Before the elections, the Leftists introduced several futile pieces of legislation to change the existing electoral laws.[7] Moreover, the Guardian Council, in collaboration with the Interior Ministry, disqualified several Leftist candidates, openly declaring that only those who would support and obey Khamenei were fit to hold office. Speaker Karubi denounced the Guardian Council for eliminating hundreds of candidates, which, he said, was tantamount to dictatorship.[8] Some eight hundred candidates out of the total of 3,733 were disqualified, many of them from the Left, some of them former Majles deputies. Most famous among the disqualified candidates were Hadi Ghaffari, a cleric well known for his adventurism, Mrs. Atefeh Sadighi Rejaii, the wife of a former president, and Ayatollah Saddeq Khalkhalli, famous in the West as the "hanging judge." Even those Leftists who were not disqualified did not do that well. Consequently, the Islamic Left lost the control of the Majles and the Conservatives gained the upper hand. Hojjatolislam Nateq-Nuri received some 203 votes out of 240 and became the Majles Speaker, placing the Conservatives in the Majles's leadership positions.

In control of the Majles and supported by Ayatollah Khamenei, the Conservatives became more aggressive in pursuing their economic and political agenda. Hojjatolislam Mohtashemi summarized the collective feeling of the Islamic Left: "The Right [Conservatives] has made flagrant efforts to remove the Left from all positions of participation and legislation."[9] Out of power, the Islamic Leftists went through an ideological transformation, became more democratically oriented, and moved closer to all the disgruntled elements within the Islamic Republic. In campaigning for the Fifth Majles, for example, many Leftist candidates emphasized new issues, such as freedom, personal liberties, and pluralism of thought.

In 1996, as Iran approached the Majles elections, Rafsanjani ended his alliance of convenience with the Conservatives. Alarmed that Nateq-Nuri's victory in the upcoming presidential race would significantly tilt the balance of power toward the Conservatives and push the country irreversibly toward "absolute rule by the *Faqih*," Rafsanjani began to institutionalize his support in order to become a major player in both the Majles and presidential races. At his urging, Rafsanjani supporters created the Servants of Construction, a small group of moderate, high-level technocrats dedicated to economic reconstruction of Iran. The small group became a major power broker in both the Majles and presidential races.

As before, the Guardian Council disqualified a substantial number of candidates for the Fifth Majles: some 40 percent of the 5,121 applicants, many of them from the Left. No one faction won the absolute majority; the Conservatives won 110 seats, the Left and the Servants of Construction 60 seats each, and the Independents 15. Speaker Nateq-Nuri received the lowest vote of any Majles speaker since 1979, which symbolized the end of the alliance between the Conservatives and the Pragmatists.[10] In the upcoming presidential election, the Islamic Left and the Pragmatists became strange new bedfellows.

Khatami's Campaign Strategy and Platform

Electoral competition, with all its trappings, strategies, and manipulations, has become an integral component of Iran's factionalized politics. Once candidates jump the difficult hurdle of being approved by the Guardian Council, they engage in fierce electoral competition. To reach the pinnacle of power, Khatami prudently exploited the factionalized system of the Islamic Republic.[11]

The open campaign for the presidency began in mid-1996, when President Rafsanjani publicly announced his intention to step down at the end of his second four-year term, thus ending all speculations and rumors about a possible revision of the Constitution that would allow him to run for an unprecedented third term. Internal bickering prevented the Servants of Construction from nominating any candidates. The Islamic Left's favorite candidate, Mr. Mir Hossein Mussavi, tested the political waters and decided not to enter the race. The Conservatives, however, were organized and united, with Nateq-Nuri as their anointed candidate. The election was theirs to lose. Nateq-Nuri was supported by many influential ayatollahs, Majles deputies, and organizations, including the Society of the Combatant Clerics of Tehran, Qom's Theological Lecturers, which consists of a group of senior clerics, and the Jameyate Motalefeye Islami, which is a small but highly organized and disciplined organization that was established in the early 1950s. The public perception was that Nateq-Nuri was Ayatollah Khamenei's favorite candidate, although he never publicly endorsed Nateq-Nuri. The radio and television networks, controlled by the Conservatives, certainly supported his candidacy, too.

Ironically, the euphoric optimism that Nateq-Nuri was sure to win became a major liability. The fear that his victory would institutionalize the absolute rule by an appointed *Faqih* and give the Conservatives monopolistic power over all the major institutions of the Islamic Republic became the glue that cemented the electoral alliance between the Pragmatists and the Islamic Left. But it was up to Khatami to expand the popular base of that alliance.

Khatami announced his candidacy in November 1996. The most important organizations that endorsed Khatami were the Majma-ye Rouhaniyoun-e Mobarez-e Tehran, the Organization of Iran's Islamic Revolution, and, belatedly, the Servants of Construction. It was generally believed that Khatami would inject much enthusiasm and vibrancy into the race and, therefore, increase voter participation. No one, not even those in Khatami's inner circles, believed that Khatami could actually win the presidency.[12] Had he so desired, Ayatollah Khamenei, who was quite familiar with Khatami's views, could have readily gotten Khatami disqualified; much to his credit, he did not.[13]

The backgrounds of the frontrunners, Nateq-Nuri and Khatami, and the public perception of what they symbolized were distinctly different. Unlike Nateq-Nuri, who, as a revolutionary, had been jailed several times by SAVAK, Khatami was not active and had never been jailed and was in fact director of the Islamic Center in Hamburg, Germany, in 1978. Nateq-Nuri's intellectual interests were largely confined to Islamic studies, while Khatami was recognized as an avid reader, a philosophy enthusiast with great interests in the arts, and an author of two books.[14] And, finally, Nateq-Nuri's body language, mannerisms, and oratorical style were generally regarded as typical of a traditional clergyman, while Khatami, always immaculately dressed with a contagious smile on his face and a graceful manner, was seen to represent the aristocracy of the ulama establishment. His blunt and self-deprecating style contrasted sharply with his opponent's. In the war of symbolism, Khatami represented "modernity" and Nateq-Nuri "traditionalism." Their campaign platforms reflected this distinction.[15]

Khatami's progressive platform accurately reflected the ideological transformation he experienced in the early nineties. Khatami's political career in the Islamic Republic began when Ayatollah Khomeini appointed him editor of *Kayhan*, a leading newspaper, in 1979. He left a legacy of professionalism, high ethical standards, and even-handedness. After resigning, he was elected to the First Majles in 1979. The turning point was his appointment as the Minister of Culture and Islamic Guidance in 1983, a cabinet post he held for nine years under two administrations controlled by the Islamic Left and the Pragmatists—testimony to his flexibility and political savvy.

When extremism was mainstream, when the Islamic Revolution was in its most radical phase, and when Ayatollah Khomeini's cultural revolution was pushing to completely Islamicize all aspects of life, Khatami pursued an enlightened and tolerant policy toward intellectuals and artists. During his tenure, the Iranian film industry flourished as he provided generous subsidies to filmmakers, and the number of foreign films imported into Iran was increased. By easing censorship, an impressive number of new books, journals, and newspapers were published. These policies and Khatami's strategy of building a bridge to the intellectual community were always harshly criticized by the Conservatives, who reluctantly tolerated him as long as Ayatollah Khomeini supported him.[16] After Khomeini's death and the Conservatives' parliamentary victory in 1992, the pressure became so unbearable that Khatami was forced to resign.

Khatami was then appointed as Director of the National Library, a politically innocuous job that kept him away from the corridors of power. In the solitude of the new job, he went into an ideological hibernation, with two books and a major ideological transformation as its auspicious products. Mostly a collection of his lectures while he was a cabinet minister, the first book, *Fear of the Waves,* published in 1993, is an implicit but scathing criticism of the Conservatives.[17] It calls upon Muslims to abandon dogmatism and fanaticism, embrace rational thinking and reasoning, and interpret Islamic jurisprudence more flexibly, reflecting the realities of time and place. Much of the book is devoted to discussing the thoughts of Khatami's greatest heroes, Ayatollahs Khomeini and Mottahari. Khatami praises Ayatollah Khomeini as an Islamic revolutionary and one of the greatest religious innovators of Islam. The book is the labor of a man still mesmerized by the Islamic Revolution who feels at home with the Islamic Left's overall perspective.

If in the first book Khatami represents the mainstream of the modernist Shii political thought whose most eloquent defender was Ayatollah Naini, he moves to the fringes of that tradition in *From the World of the City to the City of the World,* or perhaps altogether transcends it. In it, Khatami seems to have grasped the nature of the challenge Islam is facing in the modern world. He does not hide his utter contempt for the conspicuous absence of a well-articulated Islamic political philosophy. He subtly, and, by implication, questions the principle of the *velayat-i faqih* as elaborated in the Islamic Constitution. For him, Abu Nasr Farabi (ca. 870–950), the great Persian thinker, gave birth to Islamic political philosophy by being the first philosopher who sought to harmonize classical political philosophy with Islam. But when he died, the decline of that discipline began. Whereas Muslim thinkers contributed immensely to a variety of disciplines, he writes, Islamic political philosophy remained infertile, costing Islamic societies their intellectual vitality and ability to think. Exactly when the Islamic world was suffering from this debilitating intellectual vacuum, the West made gigantic progress in all fields of knowledge, including political philosophy.

The importance of Khatami's second book, which is mostly based on secondary sources, is not its discussions of the great Western political thinkers, from Plato and Aristotle to Rousseau and Locke. Its significance lies in its remarkable conclusions with their shattering implications. In Khatami's own words:

> In the new age of political thought, what has received the approval of modern men is the idea that there is no "superior will" beyond the rational subjectivity and the will of humans, and that the only source of civil society is the existence of agreements, or the perception of the existence of such agreements, for the creation of certain kinds of relations, a sense of obligation for relations, and finally the creation of institutions and social organizations that can help sustain these relations and ensure their efficient operation. In other words, *consensus and a social contract are the real source for the "superior will" and civil society* (my emphasis).[18]

Khatami then acknowledges that "liberal democracy," founded on a contractual basis of relationship between the ruled and the rulers, is one of the greatest achievements of the past few centuries. Although he does criticize liberal democracy for failing to address the spiritual needs of the people, he nevertheless insists that all modern societies must embrace its essentials.[19] One can easily discern Khatami's eloquent subtlety in reconciling Islam and liberal democracy. Khatami believes that an Islamic government based on popular sovereignty can meet the material as well as spiritual needs of the people.

With such ideas, Khatami knew that his campaign for the presidency would become a minefield which he must somehow manage to cross safely. He, therefore, had to sugarcoat his message. Khatami developed a well-defined platform and an effective electoral strategy based on his analysis of the country's mood and its changed demographics. He focused on the nation's political needs.

After the end of the Iran–Iraq War in 1988, Rafsanjani's economic reconstruction began to change the social fabric of Iranian society and the demands of its population. In 1997, the population, one of the youngest in the world, saw a huge increase in the number of students, especially at the institutions of higher education. Moreover, Rafsanjani's economic policies had increased the size and power of the private sector while he had brought to power a young and pragmatic group of Iranians. Thus, the youth and the modern middle class had emerged as potentially powerful constituencies, Iran's silent majority.[20] Moreover, social tension was visible everywhere: Inflation was rampant, unemployment high, the standard of living lower than before the Revolution, and many people were frustrated by the moral restrictions the government imposed upon them. In short, there was widespread discontent—and only Khatami addressed that discontent.[21] Khatami's winning strategy was to attract not only the constituencies that had previously participated in elections but also the passive, apathetic, and disgruntled segments of the population with little prior interest in voting.

Khatami promised to establish an Islamic government whose legitimacy emanates from a free people and whose *raison d'être* is to serve the people.[22] His themes of a more open, transparent, and representative government, and of more freedom and liberty were attractive to youth, women, and the modern middle class. Khatami understood that young people are rarely interested in history and yearn instead to hear something new about their future. Khatami's emphasis on freedom and his occasional but explicit flirting with Persian nationalism tantalized the young and the modern middle class. His insistence on judging people on merit and not gender and his endorsement of a woman minister in his cabinet were exactly what many Iranian women were anxious to hear. Khatami recognized that many people were disenchanted with the constant and obtrusive interventions of the moral police and would enthusiastically welcome promises of personal freedom and limited government. His emphasis on rational thinking rather than dogmatism, peaceful coexistence rather than violence and aggression, and dialogue rather than confrontation, as the basis of the political system felt like a fresh breeze, giving hope to millions of disenchanted voters. To present himself as the people's candidate, he refused to ride in a bulletproof automobile. To spread his message, he organized various trips to many parts of the country with his White Bus, mingling with the people face to face. Altogether, some five thousand persons worked voluntarily for Khatami's nationwide organization.[23]

Contrary to Khatami, whose platform was national in scope and offered new ideas, Nateq-Nuri's status quo platform was attractive to the hardcore Islamists and addressed the nation's economic needs. Just when Nateq-Nuri was speaking about "melting into the *velayat*" (*zoub dar velayat*), which meant complete and unconditional obedience to the *Faqih*, Khatami was declaring that the citizens of the Islamic Republic did not necessarily have to believe in the doctrine of the *velayat-i faqih;* their practical acceptance of the Constitution was sufficient. Khatami insisted that different people are entitled to different interpretations of the *velayat-i faqih* and the Islamic Revolution. Just when Nateq-Nuri was warning the population about "tahajom-e farhangi," or Western cultural imperialism, Khatami was insisting that Iran and Islam can indeed learn a great deal from the West. Just when Nateq-Nuri was stressing economic liberalization and reconstruction, Khatami maintained that without political development Iran could have neither liberty nor economic prosperity. In the heat of campaigning what mattered was not the feasibility of the candidates' proposals but their ability to win the imagination of the electorate. And Khatami succeeded in doing so.

The presidential race entered into a new phase around the Persian New Year in March 1997, when the Conservatives recognized that Khatami's popularity was growing exponentially, precipitating a series of negative campaign attacks against him. Newspapers supporting Nateq-Nuri argued that in Iran's factionalized politics, Khatami lacked the temperament, perseverance and resilience to be president, and reminded voters of his two prior resignations. A few pro-Khatami rallies were interrupted by small groups of the Ansar-e Hezbollah, which chanted anti-Khatami slogans such as "Death to liberals" and "Death to the anti-*velayat-i faqih*."[24] Ayatollah Mahdavi Kani feared Iran would repeat the Constitutional Movement, in which the ulama first became divided and then were pushed into oblivion.[25] Some senior clerics introduced the notion of "selecting the most pious (*entekhab-e aslah*)": electing the candidate with the best religious credentials. In that vein, Ayatollah Zhazali publicly confirmed that within the Guardian Council, Khatami had received fewer votes than Nateq-Nuri, implying Khatami's inferior qualifications.[26] It was rumored that while the majority, if not all, of the revolutionaries backed Nateq-Nuri, the forces of *kufr*, or infidelity, were supporting Khatami. The Motlalefe-ye Islami urged people to vote for the candidate for whom they thought the *Faqih* was voting, which it implied was Nateq-Nuri. A short film was distributed all over the country, showing young men and women carrying Khatami's picture and jubilantly singing and dancing in the streets of a prosperous Tehran neighborhood.[27] The demonstration had supposedly taken place on 'Ashura, the day when faithful Shiis mourn the violent death of Imam Hussein, the symbol of martyrdom. Khatami quickly disassociated himself from the film, which was designed to portray his supporters as antireligious. Finally, rumors were spread that the Conservatives would disrupt the election or tamper with the ballots, all to discourage Khatami's supporters from going to the polling stations. Those rumors ended when Ayatollah Khamenei declared that the candidate with the most votes would be the next president and Rafsanjani warned sternly in a Friday sermon that "changing the ballots, or disrupting the election's positive trend is an unforgivable treason."[28]

Khatami supporters had their own negative campaign strategy. They helped popularize the idea that should Nateq-Nuri become president, he would establish a religious dictatorship and impose the same draconian rules that the Afghan Taliban had imposed in Afghanistan; at best, he would transform Iran into a Shii version of Saudi Arabia.[29] They succeeded in turning the election into a referendum for or against freedom. But Khatami benefited most from the miscalculations of the Nateq-Nuri campaign, where hubris became more visible by the day. As if his victory were assured, he sent Mohammad Javad Larijani, a Majles deputy and Nateq-Nuri's foreign policy advisor, to London to meet with British authorities and to emphasize how Nateq-Nuri was determined to normalize relations with the European Community. When the news of the private meeting between Nick Brown, who later became British ambassador to Iran, and Larijani was publicized, the Nateq-Nuri camp suffered a serious blow.[30] In April 1997, Nateq-Nuri went to Russia and met with President Yeltsin. Treated as a head of state, he acted like a president. The reception in his honor was repeatedly shown on national television. Forgotten in all of this was the historical propensity of Iranians to support the underdog and to move in the direction opposite to that recommended by the elites. Thus, the more Nateq-Nuri was presented as the candidate of the establishment and the more he acted like a sure winner, the more popular Khatami became.

Finally, with 200,000 security forces protecting the 33,400 polling stations, some 29 million Iranians cast their votes, 13 million more than in the 1994 presidential elections (Table 1). The voter turnout was the highest Iran had ever seen—higher than in some mature democracies.

Khatami's election further legitimized election as the most efficacious method of resolving disputes. Even the typically cynical Iranians are beginning to accept that their votes do count. This acceptance is the seed from which democracy may grow: While electoralism is not tantamount to democracy, without competitive elections democratization cannot begin. Saeed Hajareyan saw the previous elections as a "*beyat*," reenacting an Islamic tradition in which the masses declare allegiance to their leaders.[31] In 1997, the voters made a clear choice. But is the Islamic Republic ready to accept that choice?

Achievements of Khatami's Presidency

Khatami's landslide victory was a political shock to the Islamic Republic. On the one hand, the Conservatives were so disoriented from their humiliating defeat that they were forced into a defensive mode. This is why the

Majles gave a vote of confidence to every member of Khatami's cabinet. On the other hand, Khatami's winning coalition, the Second Khordad alliance, which consisted of the Pragmatists and the Islamic Left, boasted about the solid popular mandate it had received and proclaimed itself as champion of reform and its opponents as antireform. To change the public perception of its prior association with extremism, the Islamic Left enthusiastically wore the new robe of reformism. But soon the Conservatives recovered from their initial shock and the Second Khordad alliance awoke to the reality that it is easy to make campaign pledges and much more complicated to turn them into policy.

Recognizing that his rivals have more power, as he only controls the executive branch, Khatami has pursued a three-pronged strategy to push the Islamic Republic toward democracy: increase the people's political consciousness and change the nature of the tolerated political discourse, encourage and expedite the formation of political parties, and involve the people in the political process. In the early 1950s, Premier Mohammad Mossadeq often took his case directly to the people in order to pressure Mohammad Reza Shah Pahlavi and the Majles to endorse his policies; similarly, Khatami appears convinced that educating and politicizing the population is the only practical way to tilt the balance of power in his favor.

Khatami's greatest achievement and his legacy thus far has been popularizing the elementary alphabets of democracy, while making the Islamic Republic somewhat more transparent and open. Not since the beginning of the Islamic Revolution has the content of the political discourse been so rich and provocative as it has been during the past few years. There are heated discussions in the thriving media and within intellectual circles about civil society, tolerance, the rule of law, the undesirability of applying brute force to achieve political goals, and different interpretations of the *velayat-i faqih*. Of course, secular and religious intellectuals, most notably the philosopher Sorush, were debating these issues before Khatami came to power.[32] Sorush and others, however, have only reached a very small and highly educated constituency, whereas Khatami's message has reached a larger national audience. Khatami, skilled in speaking the common vernacular, as the ulama are specially trained to do, has changed the lexicon and the content of the popular political discourse, all with the intention of introducing the alphabets of democracy in a land long accustomed to autocracy. Consider the public discussion about Islam. Most of the past two decades witnessed much debate about "American Islam" versus "authentic Islam of Prophet

Muhammad." Only a cleric with impeccable religious credentials like Khatami could have changed the direction of that discussion. Now, people are distinguishing between a "compassionate and peaceful Islam" that relies on logic and persuasion to spread its gospel and a "violent or regressive Islam" that depends on brute force. Only someone with a mind and soul like Khatami's could have popularized the notion that Islam and tolerance are two sides of the same coin and that Iran must nurture the "culture of tolerance," allowing people to express their opinions without fear of retribution.[33]

The public discussion about the wave of assassinations in 1998 may be the most interesting and revealing aspect of both the new political transparency and the unprecedented polarization of the political elite, which has left its mark on Iran's intelligence community. The media, backed by the Khatami Administration, strongly condemned and raised serious questions about the mysterious killings of Daryoush Fourohar, a well-known and outspoken critic of the Islamic Republic and a fierce Persian nationalist, and four other less-known writers in 1998. Khatami pledged not to rest until the perpetrators of those crimes were identified and prosecuted, recognizing that he was entering into a dangerous zone. Eventually, under intense pressure, the Ministry of Intelligence acknowledged that some of its "rogue" elements had masterminded and executed the atrocious crimes. Rarely do the intelligence agencies of any country publicly accept responsibility and apologize for their illegal acts, especially assassinations. But exactly that occurred in Iran. In the end, the Minister of Intelligence was forced to resign, a new minister was appointed, and a few officials of the Ministry of Intelligence were arrested and are now awaiting prosecution. According to the Ministry, the alleged mastermind of the operation, Saeed Islami, committed suicide in his solitary prison cell. The media continues to pressure the government to reveal more about the entire unfortunate episode.

The public discussions about the assassinations would not have taken place without the relative freedom the media enjoys today. Although the radio and television networks, whose powerful director is appointed by the *Faqih*, play a disproportionate role in disseminating information and news, the private and semigovernment print media have become more vocal and popular in the past few years. Not since 1979 has Iran witnessed the proliferation of so many new newspapers and magazines. Never before has the media been so polarized and so partisan: some dailies, such as *Khordad, Neshat,* and *Asre-Ma,* openly support reforms, while others, such as *Kayhan, Joumhuri-e Islame,* and *Resalat,* blatantly challenge the wisdom of Khatami's programs. In the absence of disciplined and organized political parties, the press has taken advantage of its relative freedom and has been playing an increasing role in educating and informing the population and sometimes determining the day's political agenda. And this explains why the Reformists and the Conservatives, as I will discuss in the next section, have been engaged in a fierce battle over the control of the media. Although a sizable portion of the press is owned and operated by one of the three competing factions, the government's impact on the news media remains substantial: it provides them lucrative subsidies. The task ahead is to allow the nonfactional newspapers to benefit equally from government subsidies.

Khatami has a rather weak record in expediting the formation of political parties and professional associations in the past two years; only a few have formed. The most consequential are the Servants of Construction, a pro-Rafsanjani group that became a party in 1998, and the Jabhe-ye Moshrekhat-e Iran-e Islami (The Participation Front of Islamic Iran), Iran's largest pro-reform and pro-Khatami party. Ironically, the Conservatives have yet to form their own parties; its most powerful organized force is the Heyatha-ye Motalefe-e Islami, which is more of a disciplined group than a cohesive political party. The existing parties and professional associations are controlled by the rival factions. Not a single opposition political party has been allowed to form. Not even Iran's Liberation Movement, a small group of reformist Islamic intellectuals, which the late Mehdi Bazargan created in the early 1960s, can operate freely. The foundation of civil society is the existence of free, competitive political parties and free professional associations. The challenge is to allow all parties that accept the Islamic Constitution to operate freely.

If Khatami has not been able to expedite the formation of political parties, he has made a significant initiative to engage the people in the decision making process. The elections for the local and municipal councils in 1999 represent Iran's closest encounter so far with grassroots democracy. Although the Islamic Constitution contains one chapter and eight articles about the necessity of such elections, they had never before been held. In his campaign, Khatami pledged to hold such elections, and he kept his promise. Having been soundly defeated in the presidential race, the Conservatives were not enthusiastic about elections. They argued that the voter turnout would be embarrassingly low because of the two national plebiscites in the previous year, one for the presidency and the other for the Assembly of Experts for Leadership. The Reformists stressed that local and municipal elections are the real foundation of republicanism and a pillar of the civil society that Khatami had promised to build and sustain. They believed that the local and municipal councils could behave like little parliaments, decentralize power, allow the people to participate directly in the decision-making process, and diminish the power of the nongovernmental groups that the Conservatives controlled.[34]

Two remarkable aspects of the local councils elections were the number and diversity of the candidates and the conspicuously large number of women and independents. The platforms of the two factions were identical to the 1997 presidential race: The Conservatives stressed loyalty to the Revolution and the *Faqih*, while the Reformists pledged to make the government responsible and responsive and to create a civil society.[35] Eventually, some 334,141 candidates competed for 20,000 seats on local councils. More than 23.6 million, or 64.5 percent of the eligible voters, cast their ballots.[36] Although this was five million fewer voters than in the 1997 presidential race, the turnout was still remarkably high. This was an impressive victory for the Islamic Republic as the citizens of all major cities and thousands of remote villages throughout the country participated in selecting their representatives.

The elections results were another decisive victory for Khatami and his supporters and a reliable indicator of the relative strength of the main organized groups. In the largest cities, the Reformists won 71 percent of the seats, the Conservatives 14.6 percent, and the Independents 14.4 percent. In Tehran, of the 15 candidates from the Second Khordad Coalition, 13 were elected and two others became alternates. In nearly every major city, at least one woman won a seat.[37] Only one member from the Motalef-ye Islami won a seat in on the Tehran council—which speaks volumes about the popularity of that organization.

The local councils are still relatively powerless: They merely prepare bylaws and protocols for dealing with the central and local governments. Still, their impact has already been felt. In Tehran, for example, the city council elected a new mayor in 1999. More work, however, must be done to empower the local councils and make them an integral component of the decision-making process.

Obstacles to Reform

Khatami began his presidency with high hopes for creating a democratic Islamic Republic. But he has faced many obstacles in implementing reforms. His Second Khordad alliance, the basis of his cabinet, is inherently fragile, consisting of factions with irreconcilable interests and a questionable commitment to democratic ideas. Moreover, the Iranian economy, as Khatami has said repeatedly, is "sick" and structurally weak. Khatami's popular base of support is destined to decline if the economy continues to deteriorate. What has helped Khatami, however, is the public perception that the country's economic difficulties result mostly from declining oil prices on the international market—beyond Khatami's control. But these obstacles, important as they are, seem pale when compared to the hurdles that the Islamic Constitution and the Conservatives have placed in the path of reform.

In his terse inauguration speech in 1997, Khatami used the word "people" more than 30 times and made not a single reference to the *velayat-i faqih*.[38] He mentioned Ayatollah Khamenei's name only once as the leader of the Islamic Revolution and the Islamic Republic. This calculated symbolism did not go unnoticed: Ayatollah Janati admonished Khatami that his obligation was to God, the Prophet, the Twelve Imams, the *Faqih*, and the people, in that order.[39] Ayatollah Mohammad Yazdi, the Chief of the Judiciary, warned that at a time when we have a qualified *Faqih* as the leader of the Islamic community, the rest of the people have no right to interfere in the delicate business of running the state.[40] Mr. Assadollah Badamchian, a senior member of the Heyatha-ye Motalef-e Islami, expressed a somewhat similar view: "The 20 million votes cast for president Khatami in 1997 did not belong to him. It was only when this was ordered and encouraged by the Supreme Leader [Khamenei] that this event took place."[41] In all three cases, the implication was unambiguous: The *Faqih*, and not the president with 20 million votes, is the ultimate source of authority in the Islamic Republic. The spirit and the letter of the Islamic Constitution support the Conservatives' view.

Establishing popular sovereignty was certainly one of goals of the 1979 Revolution. The architects of the Islamic Constitution, however, deliberately designed a bifurcated system in which the Islamic component, symbolized in the institutions of the *velayat-i faqih* and the Guardian Council, is superior to the republican component, reflected in the presidency and the Majles. Moreover, the framers designed an elaborate constitutional mechanism to prevent any president from challenging the *Faqih*, the system's most powerful authority and the commander of its armed forces. Originally, the presidency was designed to be weak, with real power in the hands of a prime minister who was to be approved by the Majles. The Guardian Council, whose 12 members are not popularly elected, was also empowered to examine the compatibility of Majles legislation with Islam and the Constitution and approve the credentials of all the candidates for the Majles and the presidency. The elitist justification for a feeble presidency was predicated on the belief that ordinary people lack the perspicacity to distinguish good from evil and desperately need guidance from a powerful *Faqih* to protect themselves from their own temptations. The framers referred repeatedly to the gullibility of the masses who could be deceived by a "demagogic president" who then could impose "presidential dictatorship" and challenge the *Faqih*.[42]

The 16 month tenure of Mr. Abolhassan Bani Sadr as Iran's first president revealed the remarkable effectiveness of the constitutional mechanism to control the president. When Bani Sadr tried to create an imperial presidency and challenge Ayatollah Khomeini, he was ousted quickly and escaped to Paris. After Bani Sadr, neither President Mohammad Ali Rejaii, killed in a bomb explosion, nor President Seyyed Ali Khamenei (1981–1989), challenged the *Faqih*. The system worked as designed.

At the urging of Ayatollah Khomeini, the Constitution was revised in 1988. The president became more powerful, taking on the powers of the prime minister, whose office was eliminated. At the same time, the *Faqih*'s powers were increased and his constitutional control over the executive branch was kept intact. (Rafsanjani's proposals to make the president commander of the armed forces and to impose a ten-year limit on the *Faqih*'s tenure were rejected.) The constitutional tentacles of the *Faqih*'s power reach the judiciary, the Guardian Council, the armed forces, the security forces, and the national radio and television networks (the last two powers were added in 1988); meanwhile his extraconstitutional prerogatives include the control of all major private foundations and the selection of the Friday prayer *imams*, among others. The legitimacy of the Islamic Republic emanates from the *Faqih* and not the people. It is the *Faqih* who must give his blessing to the president-elect before he can legitimately assume office. And it is the *Faqih* who determines the country's general direction. The framers declared unambiguously that while the people enjoy the discretion to freely vote for their representatives, no one can violate the divine boundaries of Islam, which are to be determined by the *Faqih*—accountable only to Allah. In short, without the *Faqih*'s blessing, no reform or policy may be implemented.

Although the powers of the *Faqih* were substantially increased, the necessary qualifications of the occupant of the most powerful institution in the Islamic Republic were lowered. The *Faqih* is no longer required to be a *marja*, a popularly acclaimed source of emulation, nor is he to be recognized and accepted by the majority of the people, the two main qualifications of the 1979 Constitution. These revisions narrowed the popular base of support for the *Faqih*, rendered him more vulnerable to challenges by the country's leading ayatollahs, increased the possibility for the people not to emulate the ruling *Faqih*, and sowed the seeds of discontent within the clerical establishment. There were many ulama who opposed the revisions. Ayatollah Montazeri, the most outspoken of these ulama, declared that the new revisions could move Iran closer to a religious dictatorship. That discontent became the unspoken force behind much of the support Khatami received from the Islamic Left and others in the presidential election.

The Conservatives, who support these revisions, have used their enormous power to stop the spread of ideas they deem harmful to the unity and cohesion of the Islamic Republic. Clearly, they are most sensitive about the doctrine of the *velayat-i faqih*, which explains why Hojjatolislam Mohsen Kadivar was found guilty and imprisoned in 1999. A young cleric who, like Khatami, has both traditional Islamic and modern education, Kadivar has written prolifically about the *velayat-i faqih* doctrine. His work is significant for his well-documented conclusion that there are competing interpretations of the *velayat-i faqih* and that there is a distinguished and rich tradition in Shii jurisprudence that advocates an elected *Faqih* with a supervisory, and not executive, role as the leader of the Islamic community; this is the exact opposite of the doctrine the Islamic Constitution espouses. Kadivar believes that the *velayat-i faqih* can become compatible with popular sovereignty, a position Khatami seems to support implicitly.[43]

Ultimately, Ayatollah Khamenei will play a decisive role in determining the outcome of the struggle between the Reformists and the Conservatives. To understand his role, we must understand his situation: As the *Faqih*, he must maintain a factional equilibrium among the governing elites, must remain accountable to the clerical establishment, traditionally controlled by the Conservatives, and must be concerned about his own popularity and legacy. It is dangerously simplistic to portray him as siding completely with the Conservatives against the Reformists. An objective analysis of Khamenei's public positions during his presidency and his declarations after assuming leadership, for example, clearly shows that his temperament and ideological orientation are more harmonious with the Pragmatists than with either the Islamic Left or the Conservatives. Ayatollah Khamenei certainly does not want to be portrayed as a force against reform, desired by two-thirds of the electorate. As the protector of the whole system, he recognizes that as long as factions compete peacefully and as long as the original coalition formed by Ayatollah Khomeini remains intact, the Islamic Republic will remain stable. However, he is seriously concerned, as are the Conservatives and some Pragmatists, that quick reforms will generate forces in the Islamic Republic that no one will be able to contain. He, therefore, is cautiously supporting those aspects of Khatami's reforms that he deems not to destabilize the system. The case of the Conservatives, however, is different.

Since Khatami took over the presidency, the balance of power has disproportionately favored the Conservatives. They still control the Fifth Majles, the judiciary, the Revolutionary Courts and the special court for the clerics, the Guardian Council, the Assembly of Experts for the Leadership, the Sound and Vision of the Islamic Republic of Iran, most of the Friday prayer *imams*, the leadership of the security and armed forces, the enormously rich private foundations that continue to be exclusively accountable to the *Faqih*, and most of the paramilitary, vigilante groups, such as the Hizbullah and the Ansar-e Hizbullah, which serve almost as private armies. Khatami controls the executive branch, although the *Faqih's* representatives are also visible in that branch, and enjoys the good will of 20 million voters.

Every step of the way, the Conservatives have challenged or stalled Khatami's reforms. The 1998 public trial of Tehran's former mayor, Mr. Gholamhossein Karbaschi, who published one of the most popular dailies and played a critical role in Khatami's victory, was the first signal that the Conservatives are not about to capitulate to the Reformists. He was tried on six charges, including embezzlement and illegally contributing 250 million Rials ($80,000) to two candidates for the Fifth Majles in 1996.[44] He was found guilty of most charges and now is in prison. It was generally believed that he was prosecuted for the critical support he and his office provided Khatami during the presidential race.

The Reformists and the Conservatives have been engaged in a cat-and-mouse game over the freedom of the press. Ataollah Mohajerani, the Minister of Culture and Islamic Guidance and a staunch supporter of the freedom of the press, not only has been questioned by the Majles for his "soft" policy of granting publication permits to unfriendly elements, but was also physically attacked and injured by zealous vigilantes in 1998. Often when the courts shut down an unfriendly newspaper or journal, the Ministry of Culture and Islamic Guidance comes to the rescue: With a new name, the banned publication receives a new permit and resumes its activities. This is why the Conservatives proposed a repressive *bill* to curb the freedom of the press in May 1999. When the daily *Salam*, Khatami's most loyal supporter, published an allegedly classified document relevant to the proposed bill, it was shut down by an order from the court that deals exclusively with the ulama. When a few hundred students staged a peaceful demonstration to protest the closure of *Salam,* the vigilante groups, helped by some elements of the security forces, stormed the students' dormitories, ransacked the building, and physically attacked and injured scores of students. For reasons not entirely clear at this time, the peaceful protest movement became violent, as agent provocateurs chanted anti-Khamenei slogans and created chaos. Only after Khatami sternly warned the rioters did the disturbances end. But the psychological and political implications of the bloody crackdown are still reverberating in Iran.

Future Prospects: Whither Iran?

The transition to democracy has been slow and often bloody everywhere. Democracy cannot be built overnight. It is a painful process. Consider England: It took some 683 years before Parliament became sovereign, from 1215, when King John signed the Magna Carta and thus recognized the limited power of the higher nobility, to 1689, when Queen Mary II accepted supremacy of the Parliament. During that turbulent period, England experienced a religious split, a civil war, a royal beheading, and a military dictatorship by Oliver Cromwell. Once Parliament became "sovereign," it took another 296 years to extend voting rights to all segments of the population who were 18 years of age and older. Only in 1960 could all men and women over 18 years vote.

In Iran, too, the transition to democracy has been, and will continue to be, painfully slow and violent. It started at the dawn of the twentieth century with the constitutional movement. Although Iran is still far away from becoming democratic, some improvements were made in the twentieth century. Iranian democrats must be patient and must welcome every step, no matter how small, toward democracy. Clearly, Khatami's election was an important step in the transition to democratic rule.

The exuberance after Khatami's unexpected electoral triumph was reminiscent of the popular enthusiasm for the Islamic Revolution in 1979. In a way, Iran experienced its first electoral revolution in 1997. Candidate Khatami promised much but President Khatami has thus far been unable to deliver all that he promised. Not a single major legislation or policy has been introduced to address the needs of youth, women, and the middle class, the three core constituencies that made Khatami's victory possible. The greatest challenge is to gradually open the political system to all forces that accept the Islamic Constitution. Still, Khatami has left a positive impact on people's lives and continues to enjoy immense popularity, because people believe in the sincerity of his convictions and understand his predicament.

Khatami's victory was a mandate to establish popular sovereignty as the basis of governance. Significant strides have been made to open the political process and make the Islamic Republic more transparent: A few political parties—all loyal to the Islamic Republic—have been formed, censorship of the press has been relaxed somewhat, and the unprecedented elections for the local and municipal councils were held successfully and peacefully in 1999—Iran's closest encounter so far with grassroots democracy. But Khatami's greatest legacy is popularizing the alphabet of democracy in a land long accustomed to autocracy. A sophisticated political discourse is developing around issues such as the urgent need to make the state the servant, rather than the master, of the people, the compatibility of Islam and democracy, the necessity of nurturing a culture of tolerance, and denunciation of violence. Auspicious as these developments are, Iran, I must emphasize, has a long way to go before establishing popular sovereignty as the basis of governance.

But Khatami has to operate within the confines of a system that was deliberately designed to prevent any president from challenging the *Faqih* or initiating quick or radical change. Khatami's reforms have created a constitutional crisis by accentuating the constitutional friction between the executive branch and the institution of the *velayat-i faqih*. This, in turn, has created mistrust and polarized the elites. Questions have been raised about the role and powers of the *Faqih* and the Council of Guardians.

Khatami is now pressured from two opposing sides. On the one hand, his powerful rivals maintain that Khatami has gone too far too fast and that continuing his policies would generate a political avalanche that neither he nor anyone else could contain; therefore, they say, he could inadvertently cause the demise of the Islamic Republic. They insist that the single greatest challenge is to rebuild Iran's shattered economy and not to open up the political process. On the other hand, some of Khatami's staunchest supporters are frustrated by the glacial pace of reform and urge him to push for more and quicker reforms. Both groups offer recipes with far-reaching consequences. The first group has yet to comprehend that Khatami's electoral victory was a referendum in favor of reform. To reject reform is to oppose the aspirations of two-thirds of the electorate. Without peaceful reforms now, the long-term alternatives are hardly attractive: violence, radical change, further loss of legitimacy, or dictatorial rule based on brute force. The second group appears too idealistic and naive, incapable of either planning strategically or understanding that the balance of power disproportionately favors the Conservatives. Clearly, they are influenced by forces so disenchanted with the Islamic Republic that they would prefer the uncertainty and instability that quick reforms usually generate to the pain and frustration of slow and thoughtful reforms. The impatient reformers should not take lightly the possibility of the suppression or reversal of the current reform movement by their powerful rivals.

It is not difficult to understand the current calculus of power: Khatami enjoys a remarkable degree of soft power, which emanates from his electoral victory and popularity, but is devoid of much hard power, confined to his control of the executive branch. His opponents possess considerable hard power: They control most of the republic's strategic institutions. Khatami needs to translate his immense soft power into the much-needed hard power. Having still not institutionalized his own popular base of support, and having no control over the security forces, Khatami would now be well advised not to accelerate reform, which can bring to the surface forces that no one in the republic can control. Instead, Khatami must institutionalize what he has already achieved, empower the local and municipal councils, and prepare for the parliamentary elections of the Sixth Majles, scheduled for February 2000. Only with the backing of a reform-oriented Majles can Khatami begin to translate his soft power into hard power.

But most critically, Khatami must develop a prudent modus operandi with Ayatollah Khamenei, without whose support the credentials of candidate Khatami would not have been approved by the Guardian Council and without whose support President Khatami's reforms are unlikely to succeed. It is a dangerous mistake to assume that Ayatollah Khamenei belongs to the Conservative camp. He is trying to stand above the factions. The Islamic Republic functions only when there is collaboration between its Islamic and republican components, between the *Faqih* and the chief executive. The student protest in June 1999, which evolved into mindless violence, appears to have pushed the *Faqih* and the president closer, convincing them that united they will continue to rule over a stable Iran, but divided they will jeopardize the very existence of the Islamic Republic. Khatami seems to have grasped the reality that sponsoring quick reforms without thoughtful contingency plans is the prelude to instability, chaos, and then despotism.

Thus, Khatami confronts a dilemma: how to reform the system without destabilizing it. This, of course, is hard—but so is being a statesman. Today, the Islamic Republic is at one of the most dangerous crossroads in its two decades of existence. Only that precious art of statecraft—knowing when to compromise, what reforms to champion, and when to push for reforms—can steer Iran toward brighter days and prevent unnecessary bloodshed and chaos. And only history will judge if President Khatami is indeed blessed with that art.

Table 1. Presidential Elections in the Islamic Republic of Iran, 1979–97

Names	Candidate's Votes	Total Votes Cast	Percentage of total
Abolhassan Bani-Sadr	10,750,000	14,140,000	76.0
Mohammad Ali Rejaee	13,000,000	14,760,000	88.0
Seyyed Ali Khamenei	16,790,000	17,000,000	98.7
Seyyed Ali Khamenei	12,200,000	14,225,000	85.7
Ali Akbar Hashemi Rafsanjani	15,537,000	16,440,000	94.5
Ali Akbar Hashemi Rafsanjani	10,555,000	16,700,000	63.2
Seyyed Mohammd Khatami	20,100,000	29,100,000	69.0

Sources: Various Iranian dailies. All figures are rounded.

Notes

1. For the most comprehensive discussion of the positions of the Islamic Left, the Conservatives, and the Pragmatists, see *Iran Javan*, no. 99 (July 8, 1999), no. 100 (July 15, 1999), and no. 101 (July 22, 1998).
2. For the declaration of the founders of the organization, see Ettela'at, April 6, 1988.
3. See Mohsen M. Milani, "The Evolution of the Iranian Presidency: From Bani-Sadr to Rafsanjani," *British Journal of Middle Eastern Studies*, vol. 20, no. 1(1993), pp. 82–97.
4. See R. K. Ramazani, "Iran's Foreign Policy: Both North and South," *Middle East Journal*, vol. 393, Summer 1992, pp. 393–412, and Mohsen M. Milani, *The Making of Iran's Islamic Revolution* (Boulder, CO: Westview Press, 1994).
5. See, for example, *Bayan*, nos. 5 and 6, 1990. In the same issue of the paper, published by Hojjatolislam Mohtashemi, Rafsanjani was accused of giving key positions to liberals and members of the Hojatiy-e Society, a group of fanatic zealots known for their anti-Baha'ism.

6. *Resalat,* November 18, 1991, as quoted in Farzin Sarabi, "The Post-Khomeini Era in Iran: The Elections of the Fourth Islamic Majles," *Middle East Journal,* vol. 48, no. 1 (Winter 1994), Pp.80–107. Questions about the *Faqih* were also raised in *Salam,* April 25, 1992.
7. For more details, see Bahman Baktiari, *Parliamentary Politics in Revolutionary Iran* (Gainesville, FL: University Press of Florida, 1996).
8. *Resalat,* March 10, 1992.
9. As quoted in Sarabi (1994).
10. For the complete results of the elections, see *Asr-e Ma,* no. 46, 1996.
11. For more details, see my "Political Participation in Revolutionary Iran," in John Esposito, ed., *Political Islam: Revolution, Radicalism, or Reform?* (Boulder, CO: Lynne Rienner Publishers, 1997), pp. 77–94.
12. See Babak Dad, *Sad Rooz Ba Khatami* [One Hundred Days with Khatami] (Tehran: Ministry of Education and Islamic Guidance, 1998), p. 20. This journalistic book offers the most detailed and interesting description of Khatami's inner circle and campaign.
13. Only four out of 230 declared presidential candidates were determined qualified by the Guardian Council: Nateq-Nuri, Khatami, Reza Zavarei, deputy head of the judiciary, and Mohammad Mohammadi Rayshahri, former Interior minister.
14. For their very short but accurate background information, see *A'sh'naee ba Majles-e Shora-ye Islami* [Introduction to the Islamic Consultative Assembly] (Tehran: The Islamic Majles Press, 1982), pp. 139 and 184.
15. For three different analysis of Khatami's presidency, see Shaul Bakhash, "Iran's Remarkable Election," *Journal of Democracy,* vol. 9, no. 1(1998), pp. 80–94; Eric Hooglund, "Khatami's Iran," *Current History,* (February 1999), pp.59–64; and Farhang Rajee, "A Thermidor of Islamic Yuppies?" *Middle East Journal,* vol. 53, no. 2 (Spring 1999), pp. 217–231.
16. See Sussan Siavoshi, "Cultural Policies in the Islamic Republic: Cinema and Book Publications," *International Journal of Middle East Studies,* vol. 29 (1997), pp. 509–530.
17. Seyyed Mohammad Khatami, *Beam-e Mouj [The Fear of Waves]* (Tehran 1993).
18. Sayyed Mohammad Khatami, *Az Doniya-ya Shahr Ta Shahr-e Doniya* [From the World of the City to the City of the World] (Tehran: Nay Press, 1994), pp. 35.
19. Ibid., p. 28.
20. For a good analysis of how these changes influenced the outcome of the presidential race, see Abbas Abdi, "The Invisible Nucleolus of the Recent

Election," in *Entekhab-e Nou* [A New Choice] (Tehran, Tarh-e Nou, 1999), pp. 93–105.
21. See Jahanger Amuzegar, *Iran's Economy Under the Islamic Republic* (London: I.B. Tauris, 1993).
22. For Khatami's platform, see *Salam* (Supplement), Spring 1997.
23. Dad (1998), p. 89.
24. *Iran Times*, April 25, 1997.
25. *Salam*, April, 1997.
26. Dad (1998), p. 209.
27. Ibid., pp.138–143. He claims some 40 thousand videos of the event were distributed throughout the country and were shown in many mosques.
28. *Iran Times*, May 23, 1997.
29. Personal interview about the presidential race with Mr. Mohammad Esmail Haydar Ali, Editor of the weekly *Khozaresh*, Tehran, December 19, 1998. Mr. Haydar Ali thought that this was one of the most effective propaganda campaigns against Nateq-Nuri.
30. *Iran Times*, July 11, 1997. Pro-Khatami students accused Larijani of "treason."
31. Saeed Hajareyan, in *Entegha-be Nou* (1998), p. 56.
32. For a good summary of his thought, see Valla Vakili, *Debating Religion and Politics in Iran: The Political Thought of Abdilkarim Soroush* (New York: Council on Foreign Relations, 1997).
33. See, for example, *Khordad*, March 6, 1999.
34. Personal interview with Dr. Mohsen Mirfakhraie, member of the editorial board of *Salam*, Tehran, March 19, 1999.
35. See, for example, *Resalat*, February 20, 1999. The headline of the paper is: "Vote for those loyal to the Revolution, the Imam, and the Leadership." See also *Shoma* [You], the publication of the Motalefe-ye Islami, February 25, 1999. For the pro-Khatami candidates, see *Asr-e ma*, February 26, 1999.
36. *Hamsharhi*, March 15, 1999.
37. *Mosharekat* (publication of the Front for Participation in Islamic Iran), March 8, 1999.
38. President Seyyed Mohammad Khatami's Inaugural Speech to the Islamic Consultative Assembly (Tehran: n.p., 1997).
39. *Iran Times*, June 6, 1997.
40. Ibid., July 25, 1997.
41. As quoted in *IranFile*, vol. 2, no. 2, June/July 1999, p. 4.
42. See Mohsen M. Milani, "The Transformation of the *velayat-i faqih* Institution: From Khomeini to Khamenei," *Moslem World*, vol. 82, nos. 3–4 (July/October 1992), Pp. 175–190.

43. See Mohsen Kadivar, *Nazari-yehaye Doulat dar feqh-e Shi'i* [Views on the State in Shi'i Jurisprudence] (Tehran: Ney Press, 1998); and *Houkomat-e Valla-e* (Tehran: Ney Press, 1998). The first book is the most comprehensive discussion of the *velyat-i faqih* published in the recent years in the Persian language.
44. See *Mohakeme va Defa* [Trial and Defense] (Tehran: Farhanq va Andish, 1998). The book is the complete version of Karbaschi's trail. There is very little about Karbaschi's campaign contributions. See pages 5, 173, and 174.

3

On the Reconfiguration of the Public Sphere and the Changing Political Landscape of Postrevolutionary Iran

Farideh Farhi

In a poignant moment in Mohsen Makhmalbaf's movie opus about Iranian identity, culture, and self-representation, *Salaam Cinema,* an aspiring actress, abused and taunted by the director in her attempt to perform, turns around to abuse and belittle others once she is given a position of power. Makhmalbaf's commentary about Iran's political culture is clear enough, reflecting a position held by many Iranians: It is the Iranian political culture, fed by centuries of arbitrary rule, that builds, destroys, and rebuilds authoritarian rule. A similar argument is made on a purely political plane, positing modern Iranian history as a vacillation between dictatorship and chaos. Placed in this context, the Iranian revolution rather than being a rupture or beginning is seen as yet another recurring cog in Iranian history's wheel. The chaotic and rapidly unfolding events in contemporary Iran entailing total discrediting of the clergy and established religion, it is said or feared, are simply preludes to expected closures to come. This is of course a weighty, if not thoroughly researched, argument. It is also a position that is very difficult to debunk, especially if it is held by many. Positions, after all, have a way of becoming self-fulfilling prophecies if widely held.

At the other end of spectrum, there is an opposite argument that is equally unexamined. Increasingly, particularly after the May 1997 election, a case is being made that the political changes Iran is experiencing are the logical outcome of underlying socioeconomic transformations that have come about at the "bottom" of the Iranian society, on the whole empowering the strata previously excluded from decision-making processes. From this perspective, vigorously espoused by many of the Iranian reformers intent on making a case for the need for nonviolent political change, the May 1997 vote was an announcement, exposing new identities and sources of social power that have been suppressed or ignored by those in power and their propaganda apparatus.[1] A more responsive and transparent politics, rather than being an act of choice, is presented as the inevitable outcome of socioeconomic change. In this fight between modernity and tradition, "political development" is presumed to be both what is needed and the eventual winner. If in the former conceptualization Iran's political future is held prisoner to its cultural history, in this latter line of argument it is thoroughly indebted to the underlying forces of social change irrespective of the political innovations and ruptures.

In this paper, I do not intend to take sides in the battle between culture and socioeconomic change. Plainly stated, in the business of assessing the impact or outcome of revolutions, 20 years is simply not sufficient time. After all, it took almost a good two hundred years for the historians of the French revolution to declare that event over.[2] Instead, unlike both of the positions stated above, I would like to take the question of political innovation seriously, focusing on the dynamics of revolutionary action rather than effects (or noneffects) of the revolution. Instead of discussing the possibility or impossibility of a new political landscape as the automatic effect of something else, be it a new Islamic ideology or a set of narrowly defined political activities or uninterrupted socioeconomic change, I would like to focus on the efforts to reconstruct the political landscape along new lines.

To do this I will mainly give attention to what appear to be fundamental changes in the boundaries as well as content of the public sphere in Iran. By public sphere, I mean a theater in modern societies in which political participation is enacted through the medium of talk. It is a space in which citizens deliberate and debate about their common affairs.[3] It is also an arena in which individuals and groups articulate the competing claims they make upon one another and upon the whole. Whether or not the changes that are occurring in the manner of deliberating and debating are in keeping with new socioeconomic realities, is a question I leave to others. What I do claim is that the ways public speech and sphere are being reformulated are quite unprecedented and the understanding of this reconfiguration will tell us much about the changing nature of politics as well as the way previously closed borders are turning into uncharted territories. Accordingly, rather than focusing on the contest of the moment to see which side is "winning," the idea is to explore how political and ideological contests are recreating and transforming Iran's political landscape. Rather than focusing on the actors, I would like to examine the conversation.[4] The underlying socioeconomic changes that have occurred and are occurring, of course, should and can not be ignored but neither should the political choices and arguments made at these critical times in Iran's history.

Before beginning the discussion, however, one important caveat needs to be mentioned. More than any other revolution, perhaps with the exception of the French case, the Iranian revolution altered and obscured the line between public allegiances and private life. Private choices became loaded with public political meaning and each individual's legitimacy became dependent on his or her private morality. This invasion of "public" or "publicity" into what had formerly been considered "private," as many have noted has been the bearer of much turmoil and anxiety over gender roles, the relationship between men and women, and the relationship among generations in Iran. In this paper, I do not intend to get into the impact of the invasion of public into private on the Iranian political culture and the distortions that this process has borne, although the topic is certainly worthy and in need of much more research. In what follows I would like merely to offer a preliminary analysis of the boundaries of public "talk" set by the revolutionary drama and then move on to an analysis of the shifting sands under those boundaries as well as some of their more intractable characteristics.

Revolution, Nation, and Public Speech

No matter which side of the debate on the Iranian revolution as a historical break or politics as usual one stands, there can be no denying that the revolution did at least one thing. For yet another time in the twentieth century, it made public questions related to the terms of Iran's global integration and means and forms of local autonomy and interconnectedness. By loudly making these questions a public issue, the revolutionaries, along with other things, were attempting to constitute the new confines of public speech. And for a variety of reasons that have still not been fully laid bare, these confines were set in an extremely austere and severe manner. This meant that the terms of local autonomy and connectedness could initially only survive as a negation of a cultural—read national—loss and not as affirmation of a process through which people generate narratives of individual and social meaning and purpose. Of course, let us not forget that all this was immediately followed by a war—a rather solemn and grim war, but also a war that moved to the realm of "unreal" or "unwar" in globalized cultural space as the world literally looked the other way; even when all the powers that be knew that with the aid of their technology and intelligence information, the Iranian landscape and population were being devastated. Hence, solemnity and severity at least had a very good public defense.

During this era, the terms of reference for the so-called West were defined, codified, and officially stamped in very clear terms, mostly drawn from notions prevalent during the age of high imperialism of the late nineteenth century. In other words, in the era of globalization,[5] the contours of Iran's understanding of the self and global engagement were set, some would say in stone, in terms of conflict, confrontation, war, invasion, and the required discipline, martyrdom, and presumed selflessness that society had to reproduce in order to defend and recreate itself concurrently.

Having been defined in these terms, the end of the war simply afforded a rather easy shift from the focus on physical invasion and physical survival to the "real" and more "authentic" battle against cultural invasion. The Iranian revolution, it was said, was not about bread and butter issues or mere political reform but a battle for the souls of men and women who had been led adrift in this rather soulless and immoral world. Of course, this conceptualization only made sense if a unified national identity of the supposedly "invaded" culture was assumed. Culture was defined as the repository of national—read Islamic—habits, customs, and ultimately souls, while the Iranian people, unified and determined, were represented as upholders of structures that were deemed generally fixed, but nevertheless in desperate need of stern guardianship.[6] As such, there was a tendency to elide cultural and national identity as "the nation," in this case the Islamic nation, appeared to be a more concrete and identifiable entity than "culture."

The thought of constructing a nation on the basis of ideas, rather than an aggregation of existing cultural plurality, was obviously intended, along with other things, to prevent the entry of individual speech into the public arena unless it echoed the official rendition. Indeed, the mere act of speaking as an individual and not as representative of a nation has generally been enough to make citizens "suspect" in terms of their allegiance to the Islamic republic and create a whole category of people that Changuiz

Pahlavan has so aptly called "second class citizens."[7] These citizens have been somewhat allowed to lead their own particular way of life, albeit under constant threat of attack, but have not been permitted to make a public defense of their way of life. Accordingly, in a resistive format similar to "un-Islamic" gatherings that are held behind closed doors, public speech was once again forced to retreat into the already familiar realm of political gossip.

The closure of public space in the name of the nation is of course nothing new in Iran or elsewhere. It happened during the Shah's time and, as Vaclav Havel keeps reminding us, remains the most compelling mark of closed societies. In a discussion about the reshaping of the public space, however, it is the understanding of the particularity of each case that becomes important. In Iran, I would also like to argue, the revolutionary closure of the public space has been based on three fundamental pillars: clerical guardianship, representations of female modesty, and the cult of martyrdom. I also would like to argue that it was against the backdrop of these confines that a quintessentially "liberal" public discussion has taken shape. At the center of this discussion is a call for the overhaul of the political process or rules of the game based on liberal principles of accessibility, transparency, rationality, and the suspension of status hierarchies in conjunction with an almost total neglect of concerns for socioeconomic cleavages and change. As mentioned above, the changed socioeconomic context is taken as a given and begging for political reform/development. The conversation is about the need to agree about a process that will allow the Iranian political system to adjust to the changes that have already occurred. The dynamics, of course, is that while the confines are being questioned, they also set the terms of the debate as well as serving as the backdrops whose questioning unsettles the boundaries of the Islamic Republic itself. Let us now turn to the terms of the debate.

Clerical Guardianship

When all the ideological or religious defenses of notions such as *velayat-i faqih* or institutional inventions such as the Guardian Council are stripped to their essence, the most important political innovation of the Islamic republic rested on the clerics' claim to direct rule. This, of course, did not mean that no one else could become part of the leadership and the decision-making processes. It also did not mean that no diversity is allowed in opinions or actions. It simply meant that, using a variety of rhetorical as well as institutional instruments, the "clerics" were posited as the final decision as well as "king" makers. This assured that, like the previous monarchist system, governance continued to be primarily based on acquiescence to superior force rather than on consent supplemented with some measure of repression.

The term "clerics" should of course be used delicately here. The idea of clerical guardianship was not intended to connote that all clerics should be politically involved or that it is through their unanimity that clerical rule was made possible. Rather, it simply suggested that first of all there was a will to rule, no matter at what cost, and, second, there existed certain interpersonal and nontransparent dynamics among the revolutionary clerics that would allow them to negotiate their way out of political crisis. In short, the notion of clerical guardianship portrayed the revolutionary clerics as deliberate, determined, and flexible in their claim to power and this has been an important source of political legitimacy in a society in search of stability.

Ayatollah Khomeini was, of course, the most important figure in the construction of the idea of clerical guardianship. He not only resurrected the idea as a purely political formulation, but also, as others have said it better than me, epitomized the idea in flesh. He was deliberate, determined, and flexible. He was a political man who also could rise above it all and be the final arbiter among political men. Yet, Ayatollah Khomeini's dominant presence should not overshadow the ideological dimension of clerical rule. Even without Ayatollah Khomeini, the Iranian revolutionary leadership has always striven to derive legitimacy by relying on the existence of de jure or de facto authorities, be it individuals, institutions, or behind-the-scene negotiation processes, that could rise above the everyday scenes of partisan politics and define the parameters of accepted public speech and actions.

Here it is important to note again that, given the diversity as well as the sheer number of centers of power, the idea of clerical guardianship in Iran has never taken the form of complete control over the public sphere. Indeed, even in the midst of the war, there were serious disagreements over a number of substantive issues that related to the running of a modern political economy. Clerical guardianship was also never intent on undermining the multiple centers of power. The idea, as said before, was that a nontransparent, nontangible tacit agreement among the clerics would always prevent policy disagreements and, more important, power struggles from getting out of control.

The first public display of cracks in this conceptualization of clerical guardianship came during the fifth parliamentary elections in 1995.[8] As is well known, during these elections, a new political faction *(Kargozaran-e Sazandegi,* or Servants of Construction) splintered from the dominant political faction of the moment *(Rohaniyat-e Mobarez,* or Society of Combatant Clergy). This emboldened an alienated faction *(Rohaniyoon-e Mobarez,* or Militant Clerics Society) to reenter the election process as well. The first round of elections suggested important gains for the upcoming factions. However, intervention on the part of the *vali-e faqih* and warnings against the "creeping" influence of the "liberal" or "secular" forces closed the competitive window that was opened and led to the reversal of some of the perceived gains in the first round. But the reversal in the election results could not hide the damage done to the idea of clerical guardianship as the final arbiter among competing factions.

The damage done in the fifth parliamentary elections became clearly manifest and also further extended during the presidential election. By the time it became possible to think of Khatami's candidacy as a real one, it was clear that the idea of clerical guardianship was being taken prisoner of partisan politics rather than acting as a mechanism to rise above it. This became quite apparent when attempts to extend the notion of clerical guardianship as a means to control the outcome of the election failed miserably. The argument that reputable clerics (and, by implication, *vali-e faqih*) should render judgement on who is the rightful *(aslah)* candidate and the subsequent public positioning of many clerics in favor of Ali Akbar Nateq-Nuri, created a public spectacle not easy to control.

The notion of clerical guardianship was actually undermined in two ways during the presidential election. On the one hand, by openly coming out in favor of one candidate and then justifying it in religious terms, the clerical guardians opened themselves to the charge of using religion in an instrumental fashion.[9] On the other hand, by not being able to influence the outcome of the election, they revealed their inability to control events in Iran. This latter point is particularly important in light of the fact that the Iranian electorate fully expected tampering with the election outcome. Satirical journal *Gol Agha*'s now all-too-famous pun, "Protect the Persian language, write Khatami, read Nateq-Nouri," deftly reflected this popular understanding as well as the expectation that how people vote at the election booth will not be properly reflected once the vote is read. At the same time, the mere fact that the possibility of cheating was publicly discussed was itself a major blow to the notion of clerical guardianship as the glue that holds the system together. No wonder that the presidential election brought the first direct personal attack on Ayatollah Khamenei, the current *vali-e faqih,* who fully embodies the idea of clerical guardianship as well as its wavering hold over society. And no wonder that the election also articulated the need to give attention to the rules of the political game and brought calls on the president-elect to shy away from behind-the-scene deal making among clerical guardians. Hidden negotiation and exchange in the "black market" of politics, it was argued, would bear no results but bankruptcy for the new administration.[10] The new president, after all, owed his election to an open political game and was not the price setter or most powerful in behind-the-scene negotiations. As such, an open political process was seen as not merely a popular aspiration but also a practical necessity for enhancing the power of reformers.

If the presidential election revealed a failure in the black market of Iranian politics, the arrest of Tehran's mayor disclosed a further reality about a political system willing to ravage itself from within. Internal conflicts no longer could remain fully hidden and this partial transparency has brought a degree of indeterminacy to public space.

One particular moment in Mayor Karbaschi's trial is a telling example of what this indeterminacy may have in store for the future of Iran's politics. As is now well known, a large part of the evidence against Tehran's mayor was gathered through interrogations of mayors of various municipalities in the city of Tehran. Throughout the trial, Karbaschi and his lawyers argued that the evidence gathered through interrogation should be considered inadmissible because of the suspicious circumstances that surrounded the gathering of this evidence. On this issue, the judge's opinion and reasoning wavered, at times claiming that no such evidence will be relied upon and at other times relying precisely on that evidence. The judge's confusion reached its height when he asked the city's chief financial officer to come forward and reconfirm the details of financial misuse he had recounted in his written prison confession. But when the financial officer skirted the direct question and instead insisted on talking about the kind of pressures imposed upon him in prison, the judge was forced literally to order his removal from the courtroom as a means to cut short his public speech about the existence of torture in Iranian prisons.[11] This extraordinary scene, replayed on national television—presumably a fully controlled medium of public display, gives us some clues about the extent to which Iran's public arena has moved away from being fully orchestrated and staged. After all, it was not too long ago that the same medium was being used as a Stalinesque stage for confessions, tales of betrayal, and spiritual self-flagellation. With hindsight, we now know that this very public gesture on the part of the Tehran's chief financial officer was a harbinger of future public tales of improprieties by security and intelligence forces becoming public.[12] With hindsight, we also know that the general admittance that torture does indeed occur in Iranian prisons or that information ministry officers are responsible for the murder of opposition figures is still a far cry from identifying and punishing the actual individuals responsible for the transgressions. Full transparency is obviously not in grasp yet, but is nevertheless a significant component of the contest being waged over the nature of the political process.

Representations of Female Modesty

If the wavering hold of clerical guardianship gives us clues about a political deadlock and the resultant unpredictability of public dialogues and questioning of rule by a nontransparent decision-making process, the way discussion of women's issues has evolved hints at the direction in which public speech is headed. Much has, of course, been written about the symbolic use made of women by the revolutionaries.[13] For our purposes, it is sufficient to say that women all over the world have been represented as the most reliable bearers of the cultures in which they are embedded. Indeed, the slip from women to culture and back is usually done with such ease that the event is not even marked. But embedded in this complete identification with culture are two discursive moves that have proven troublesome for most women. The first involves a rather drastic homogenization of the category of women, which is itself made possible but also feeds into the second move of equating local culture with nationhood. In normal times, the interconnection between women and culture usually goes unnoticed; women and the cultural values they embody normally recede to the background, becoming part of the unseen web of what can be considered an imagined national identity.

But in abnormal times the situation completely changes. Women have traditionally been very important instruments in the envisioning of change in the shape of power on the basis of new language and symbols. As the embodiment of "correct" values, they also become guardians of those values, be it liberty as in the French case or Islamic modesty as in the Iranian case.[14] This kind of conceptualization, of course, has a flip side, which is that women as bearers and guardians can also very easily turn into very dangerous points of entry for cultural "invaders" or "infiltrators." Hence, they themselves must always be guarded with watchful eyes, lest they switch sides.

Both these dynamics played important roles in Iran's revolutionary drama. During this period of power struggle and revolutionary state building, the representation of domesticated woman came to symbolize the search for authenticity and cultural revival. Accordingly, as is well known, women's behavior, appearance, and range of activities, as well as public speech about women, came to be defined and regulated by the political and cultural objectives of various political movements, the state, and the leadership.

This story of austere revolutionaries and obliging women in the early stages of revolution should not, however, be taken at face value. By now, serious research has "unveiled" the innovative ways Iranian women have been able to inhabit the stereotypes imposed upon them by exploding these stereotypes from within. In the public arena this has meant that, while in no way speaking in unison, women's voices have been able to appropriate, mutilate, and reassemble the narratives produced by the official voices. For instance, veiling has been used as a license to enter into public space as well as a means to strike down barriers to entry into public space. Furthermore, questions regarding the absolute guardianship of the paternal side, blood money, and even inheritance have been put on the table, begging more egalitarian interpretation of Shii jurisprudence and tradition, and even direct Quranic verses.

Indeed, one could say in an almost ironic fashion that the symbolic use of women as instruments of state building has opened the way for women to make counterclaims on the state for further rights. This essentially "liberal" struggle for the rewriting of unequal laws, for more economic opportunities, and for more political representation and power sharing have all been directed at a state that explicitly used women to make an antiliberal claim. Now it has to respond to these liberal claims and quite often even take pride in its positive response to those claims. To be sure, women's struggle to claim further rights by focusing on their problems as sets of issues that need to be dealt with by the state has not been a story of uninterrupted success. Real changes in family laws and inheritance laws as well as criminal laws are yet to occur, and women are yet to be permitted to run for the Council of Experts or presidency. There is no doubt, however, that fundamental changes have occurred in the contest over the representation of women and women's issues.

Two recent parliamentary bills clearly show this shifting terrain. Ironically both of these bills can be considered the first "antiwomen" attempts since the immediate rollbacks that occurred in the early part of the revolution regarding women's rights. Both bills were introduced immediately after Khatami's election and in the midst of a turbulent political period when the Islamic republic is yet again in need of defining or redefining its identity as well as its sources of legitimacy. One of the bills called for the effective segregation of medical staff. The other bill pushed for an amendment to press laws, specifically demanding limits on the basis of *shariah* on the visual representation of women in the print media as well as on public discussions of women's rights that may inflame gender conflicts. The Khatami administration opposed both bills.

Both bills, introduced by women legislators, were apparently instigated by immediate events, that is, improprieties reported in the handling of dead female bodies at hospitals and morgues and the increased practice of publishing colorful full-size pictures of women, albeit fully covered, on magazine covers and newspapers. But this time around, the symbolic use of women as a means to close the public space did not go unnoticed. In fact, in the debate that followed the introduction of both bills, this symbolic use was immediately noted, criticized, and even ridiculed.[15] This outright criticism then allowed a direct public discussion about the merits of the proposed bills with less concern over the possibility of being branded counterrevolutionary, immodest, liberal, secular, and so on. More important, unlike the early revolutionary period when women were left on their own to defend themselves against the onslaught of legislation against them, this time around public discussion revealed the formation of alliances that went beyond gender divisions.

Outspoken women spelled out their opposition in their regular forums, but professionals also spoke. Women spoke about how the proposed law on the segregation of medical staff would put women's lives in danger, but doctors also pointed to the impossibility of implementing the law. They pointed to the dangers and costs of making yet another male-female interaction illegal and underground, but they also made the broader philosophical argument about how this law puts them in conflict with their professional oath to save lives. As to the limitations on press laws, women focused on the limits put on discussions related to women's issues and a very interesting slippage in the bill referring to women as objects. Journalists, by contrast, pointed to the legal fuzziness that was entailed in the proposed law and the possibility of this law being used as yet another vehicle for censorship. Finally, several legislators as well as political commentators pointed to the general pattern of legislating vague laws and the responsibility the parliament has in legislating laws that have a good chance of being properly implemented.

To be sure, opposition to these bills did not prove all that successful in the parliament. In fact, the bill segregating the medical staff passed the parliament although the Guardian Council later rejected it because it failed to provide funding for its implementation. At the same time, public discussion robbed these bills of any public legitimacy. It suggested that, unlike the early revolutionary period, "antiwomen" legislation can no longer remain taboo topics and be forcefully imposed purely on the basis of fuzzy notions of Islamic modesty. They must circulate and compete in a relatively open political market in which such vague notions of Islamic modesty are more easily interrogated and women themselves have a very important say in shaping the way their bodies and issues are discussed in public dialogues. As such, rather than being a mechanism for forcefully imposing a national identity, the "woman question" has become an entangled web whose "untangling" can be considered a key to overcoming the current legitimacy crisis faced by the regime.

Cult of Martyrdom

If an open discussion of the "woman question" is clearly coming out of the taboo category, there is still one boundary that has been more difficult to approach or poke holes into. Indeed, of all the rhetorical arguments used to bring closure to public debate, none has been utilized more effectively and conclusively than the call to respect the "blood of martyrs." It is an effective rhetorical argument, because it draws energy from an important divide that exists in the Iranian socioeconomic landscape between those who sent their "sons" to war and those who did not. Unfortunately, no serious study has been done regarding the socioeconomic background of those who went to war, the number of families who are living with the immediate effects of the war, and the political positioning of these families. There is, however, no doubt that the call to silence in the name of martyrs has been an effective tool and will continue to be so for awhile to come.

At the same time, even in this very sensitive area, walls are turning into possibilities. In order to shed light on the subtleties involved, it is important to note that up until very recently the call to respect the "blood of martyrs" never had a definitional content. It simply was a powerful assertion. Once it was asserted that an act or a speech did not honor the "blood of martyrs," no matter what the act or speech was, the assertion itself was intended and mostly sufficient to silence. In the past year, however, subtle efforts are being made to define the meaning of honoring the "blood of martyrs" as well as question the propriety of appropriating the voice of martyrs in political discussions. One particular public incident brings out some of the important dimensions of this issue.

Interestingly, the public incident involved a not-so-public speech made by the head of the Revolutionary Guards, Rahim Safavi. In a gathering of the Revolutionary Guard's naval commanders in Qom, Safavi complained about the democratic direction the country was taking, discussing the possibility of using a "sword" to "cut the heads and tongues" of those not honoring the legacy of martyrs.[16] The Safavi controversy brought several issues regarding public speech into the open.

His first line of defense suggested that the speech given was actually not for public consumption and was an "internal Sepah matter, which was unfortunately distorted by the press."[17] The critics immediately pointed out the impropriety of denoting a gathering of Revolutionary Guard commanders as a private space. They also pointed that as a public official he is responsible for his words and the contradictions they pose for his presumably apolitical military position. "Could he maintain his position as a commander if his public speech is in direct contrast to the internal directives of the institution he commands?" was an often-asked question. Of course, Safavi did not answer any of the questions asked but the mere fact that these questions were posed was a novelty, implying a call for transparency and responsibility of a public official not voiced before in such a direct and nonabstract manner.

But the more interesting reaction to Safavi's comments came from another corner. In a stunning piece in *Jameeh,* Hamid Reza Jalaiepour, the license holder for that newspaper, brother of men killed in the war and early revolutionary struggles, and a war veteran himself, flatly declared to his former commander that time has passed for inserting the war martyrs into the political battles of the moment.[18] Dragging his family's impeccable revolutionary history into the public domain, Jalaiepour announced and others later concurred that the vision Safavi was embracing for Iran's future was not the one for which the martyrs had died. More important he identified Safavi's comments as yet another instance of instrumental use of the idea of martyrdom. To Jalaiepour, this kind of rhetorical move was no longer acceptable in a polity attempting to build legitimacy based on something beyond the division between the "true believers" who gave their sons for the country and the rest. This is especially the case if the ideology of "true believers" has become a transparent justification for a political system governed by a division between those who run the government and everybody else.

True Believers, Public Speech, and Liberal Politics

The division between the true believers/insiders and the rest/outsiders is indeed the teetering border against which public speech tests itself at this moment in Iran. The actual existence of this border has never been in doubt and of course, given the state of political organizing in contemporary society, the substantive vanishing of it is also quite far. We all know that the Islamic regime in Iran has relied on an elaborate and overlapping set of institutional innovations to create a political system that allows for a degree of competition and openness but is still closed to non-"believers" or nonpretenders. I have tried to argue that in order to remain closed, the Islamic regime has relied on a series of rhetorical tools delineated above. All these tools, however, are being increasingly rendered unavailing in the realm of public talk.

In a political conversation that began as a result of disagreement over the list of candidates for the fifth parliamentary election, every aspect of clerical claim to power has been questioned and the tools used to legitimize this rule also have been unearthed. More simply put, in the partisan struggle to gain control over the existing political institutions, public speech has begun to run "wild" and bring into question the very speech that has provided the ideological foundations for the closed system. In this regard, public speech has jumped far ahead of political institutions, be it political parties or civil society institutions. There are still no viable political parties that could legitimately be considered a party with a popular base. The cherished civil society is still in need of institutions that could mediate between public demands and the state. But the political language has become one of questioning the divisions made in the name of an undivided but diverse citizenry and one of confidence about the inevitability of political changes to come.

If there was any doubt about the rise of this new political language, it was washed away during the sixth parliamentary election of 2000. Suddenly and without much public display of uncertainty, the pithy and yet all-encompassing slogan of "Iran for all Iranians" became the mantra of the reformist political front that had become quite aware of its popular appeal.[19] The reformist candidates, insisting on their identity as both "national" and "religious" and using their pens and newspapers they now controlled, became the voice and conscience of a "nation in search of inclusion and respect." Theirs was a struggle to end "humiliation" for all and once again the message was well received. The electorate, of course, responded with no uncertainty in overwhelmingly voting for the reformist slots. This was despite the fact that the promoters of the "Iran for all Iranians" slogan did not offer much thought about exactly how and through which institutions they would endeavor to make the slogan into a reality. Of course, it wasn't that people were not aware of the dissonance between public speech and existing political institutions. But for now the act of making a political statement in public was deemed sufficient in maintaining the momentum of change that had been unleashed since the fifth parliamentary election.

Meanwhile, this dissonance between public speech and the existing political institutions continues to create a very interesting situation for the Iranian political landscape. Lacking a combination of political institutions to govern as well as any alternative institutions to begin the process of discussing how to reform the institutions that lack legitimacy—or how to come to grips with a dysfunctioning economy for that matter—the Iranian political discourse has turned to elementary concepts about rules of the political game. In the name of "citizens," claims are made for political openness and heterogeneous civil society. And in this claim to citizenship, "women" and "youth," "recent immigrants from the rural areas," and the "educated," placating the historical missions of "workers," "peasants," "the downtrodden," have become the best metaphors for a population in search of inclusion.

Yet, the decisive question remains whether Islamic nationalism can thrive with a nation open to competing conceptualizations, diverse identities, and a rich public discourse about controversial issues. Clearly, the claims to a tolerant and multicultural nation and open state are not enough. Even multinational, multicultural states require more than simply tolerance among diverse peoples. They require public discourse about diverse issues. Citizens, irrespective of status hierarchies and cultural differences, need to be able and willing to engage each other in discourse about the social arrangements which hold them together and order their lives.

It seems that for the first time in modern Iranian history a substantial part of the Iranian population is engaged in a political discussion about the rules of the games. These discussions are as much about who can enter the public debates now (i.e., who can speak and as what) as they are about what the Iranian political system will look like in the future. I guess it can be considered a credit to the Islamic republic that such a discussion has come about in a mere 20 years, before any political institutions could be consolidated enough to prevent such a discussion or merely make it a predetermined public show. And I also guess that this indeterminacy is the reason why public conversation is so closely watched by those engaged in it not only as a sign of future closure or openness (as is the case for Iran observers) but as a requisite for continuing the conversation.

Notes

1. This view is most clearly made in the introduction of a book edited by Abdol-ali Rezaee and Abbas Abdi on the May election, entitled *New Choice: A Sociological Analysis of the May 23 Phenomena*. This introduction has been translated by Alidad Mafinezam and was posted in one of the Gulf 2000 threads. The argument is rather simple here: A more educated, urbanized, and diversified (including women and youth) electorate needs and demands a more responsive and transparent political system.
2. See the seminal essay by François Furet, "The Revolution is Over," in *Interpreting the French Revolution* (Cambridge: Cambridge University Press, 1981), 1–79.
3. This understanding is obviously, although admittedly superficially, influenced by Habermas' account of the structural transformation of the public sphere. According to Habermas, the idea of a public sphere is that of a body of private persons assembled to discuss matters of public concern or common interest. In Europe, according to Habermas, it developed as a counterweight to absolutist states. Mediating between society and the state, the public sphere first aimed at requiring the information about state functioning be made accessible and subject to scrutiny and the force of public opinion. Later, it aimed at transmitting the general interest of the society via forms of legally guaranteed free speech, free press, and free assembly, and eventually through the parliamentary institution of representative government. See Jurgen Habermas, *The Structural Transformation of the Public Sphere: An Inquiry into a Category of Bourgeois Society*, trans. Thomas Burger with Frederick Lawrence (Cambridge, MA: MIT Press, 1989).
4. It should be noted that this conversation is extremely rich and multifaceted. In this paper, I make no claim to covering the whole or even the depth of the conversation. My attempt is to venture into what I consider to be some key points of the public conversation in Iran.
5. Unlike the era of high imperialism, globalization is an era of presumably far less coherent and culturally directed processes, less intended to spread a social system from one center of power across the globe but nevertheless involved in creating interconnection, interdependency, and homogeneity of all global areas. The Iranian postrevolutionary rhetoric, at least for a long time, did not seem to acknowledge this change.

6. As such, Iran's Islamic revival, despite all the initial use of extranational rhetoric, seemed to follow the pattern of all nationalisms in power quite closely. Here it is important to make a distinction between nationalism in power and nationalism in opposition. Nationalism in power often demands strict adherence to the authority of the official embodiment of national tradition while nationalism in opposition is generally a strong stimulus to cultural productivity. In Iran, both nationalisms seem to be present, making the country quite enigmatic and a place for all sorts of contradictory trends; for example, religious revival in the midst of theological dogma, increased openness in the midst of closures, etc.
7. Changuiz Pahlavan, "Dovome Khordad 1376 va Bohran-e Gozar" [Second Khordad 1376 and the Transition Crisis), Rah-e Vol 1, no. 5 (2 Khordad 1377/23 May 1998).
8. It could be argued that the first public display of the crack came in the 1991 election for the Council of Experts when the Guardian Council openly began to vet the candidates on the basis of factional allegiances. Still, the fifth parliamentary election remains a watershed for the attention it received and the way it energized the political process.
9. This is a charge that was bound to be repeated in every election, with the Guardian Council or other bodies acting in a very partisan fashion as instruments for sifting candidates and rejecting the candidacy of candidates deemed not worthy.
10. Different versions of this argument were laid out in the short life of the theoretically prolific monthly *Rah-e No* edited by Akbar Ganji.
11. That torture occurs in Iran is, of course, not a big revelation. Political gossip is full of its detail and the external human rights reports are all fairly well known. The novelty here is an open discussion within the country. The same can be said about the later stunning public statement about the involvement of the information ministry in the murder of opposition figures and writers.
12. Since the initial presentation of this paper in February 1999, much has happened to push Iranian politics in the direction of openness. Stunning developments have publicly revealed the involvement of the Information Ministry in the murder of dissidents and the trial of the former interior minister Abdullah Nouri in late 1999 set the stage for progressively breaking the taboo of discussing literally any topic in public. As such, there seems to be a hastening of the dynamics laid out in this paper. The nature of the dynamic, however, remains the same.
13. For an elaboration of this point, see my "Sexuality and the Politics of Revolution in Iran" in Mary Ann Tetreault, ed., *Women and Revolution in*

Africa, Asia and the New World (University of South Carolina Press, 1994).

14. Here I am not taking up an argument about the actual role of women in the revolutionary process. I think it is a fairly common theme in the literature on revolutions that at least at the early stages of all revolutions women's movements are suppressed. This is seen as caused by male revolutionaries' desire to legitimize their own quest for power by excluding women from the revolutionary process and because women's actions tend to threaten the stability of gender roles in both the public and the private sphere.

15. Ibrahim Nabavi, the satirist who was later arrested for his other transgressions in his Fifth and Fourth Columns in *Jameeh* and *Tous*, went so far as to suggest that after the passing of these bills the division of Iran into two segregated Islamic republics is the logical step. Gol Agha, drawing a caricature of a figure in chador wearing a moustache and attending to a female patient, touched on the dilemma of yet another male-female interaction going underground. For a discussion of these bills and more serious opposition to them, see *Zanan*, no. 43 (Khordad 1377/May 1998).

16. The story on Rahim Safavi's verbal indiscretion was first discreetly reported in *Jameeh* at the end of April 1998 in a very small column and then broke as a major public controversy the next day in stories in both *Salaam* and *Jameeh*. *Salaam* pursued the story in a more subtle but consistent manner. After publishing several harsh critiques, *Jameeh* was literally bullied into dropping the story. Later on, the Safavi protest became part of a multi-case suit brought against the newspaper in the press court that led to a ruling to close the paper.

17. *Salaam*, 13 Ordibehesht 1377/3 May 1998.

18. *Jame'eh*, 12 Ordibehesht 1377/2 May 1998.

19. It is my understanding that the slogan of "Iran for all Iranians" is not something that just happened in the heat of election. It was adopted after serious and heated discussion within the Islamic Iran's Participation Front. This newly formed political entity has as its members many of the leading reformists inside the government and in the press. Clearly, the heated debate came about because the IIPF members understood the implications of this far-reaching slogan for the still closed circle of revolutionary elite in Iran.

4

The Politics of the "Women's Question" in the Islamic Republic, 1979–1999

Haleh Esfandiari

The clerics who came to power and established the Islamic Republic in 1979 planned a traditional role for women under the new order. They imagined women primarily as housewives and mothers, modest of dress and in demeanor, pious, dutiful, committed to raising children and ministering to the needs and heeding the wise guidance of husbands, fathers and brothers. Little did they imagine that the "women's question" and women's rights would become a central public policy issue in the Islamic Republic. Nor did they foresee that they would be confronted with a new generation of women, the majority from their own "traditional" constituency, who would prove forceful, imaginative, and vociferous in demanding and pursuing education, jobs, legal reform, expanded rights, and participation in almost all areas of public life. The regime initiated the Islamic era intending largely to exclude women from the public sphere. Under immense pressure from women, they are today resigned to allow women a significant role in society.

This dramatic turnaround came about for a number of reasons. The revolution politicized the mass of Iranian women. Ironically, the clerics themselves played a role in this politicization. During the last year of the monarchy, when they helped mobilize society against the old order, the clergy urged women to come out into the streets and to march, demonstrate, and take part in strikes alongside the men. After the revolution, the clerical leaders continued to rely on mass rallies and marches, of both men and women, in order to demonstrate that their policies and their campaigns against their political rivals enjoyed public support. For example, women joined men in applauding the takeover of the American Embassy in Tehran, in condemning political factions opposed to the ruling clerics, and in supporting the war effort during the Iran–Iraq War (1980-1988). During the war, women were expected to offer up sons and husbands as "martyrs" for the war effort. Women left their homes to stand in lines for ration cards and rations. Difficult economic conditions forced many women into the workforce; the two-income family became quite common.

Once women came out into the streets, it proved difficult to send them back to their homes. Under the monarchy, girls and women had already joined the student population and entered the workforce in large numbers. Legal reform before the revolution strengthened women's rights in marriage, divorce, and child custody. Both before and after the revolution, clerical rhetoric regarding what the clergy described as the honored status women enjoyed under Islamic law sharpened an expectation among women of expanded rights. The regime also inadvertently reinforced these expectations by some of its policies. For example, as a gesture of appreciation toward war veterans and the war dead, the government extended certain privileges to their families, particularly wives and daughters. Ayatollah Khomeini himself intervened to allow war widows to gain custody of their children, no matter what Islamic law said on this matter.[1]

In addition, it turned out that girls and women from less affluent and religious families, no less than their much criticized middle and upper-class counterparts, aspired to education, access to jobs and civil service careers, and participation in public and social affairs. It was middle- and upper-class women who came out in the streets to demonstrate when the government first attempted to impose Islamic dress on women in the weeks immediately following the revolution. But it was largely women from working-class and traditional backgrounds who protested the suspension of the Family Protection Law and the Family Courts established under the old regime.

Moreover, "regime women," the wives and daughters of powerful clerics, very soon proved to be as ambitious as their counterparts under the monarchy. They, too, aspired to office, senior bureaucratic posts, well-paying jobs, and power. It was the wives and daughters of clerics and powerful officials who became the first women deputies in the Majles, or parliament, and ran government-sponsored charity organizations and hospitals. For example, Aazam Taleqani, the daughter of Ayatollah Taleqani, and Atefeh Rejaii, the wife of slain Prime Minister Mohammad Ali Rejaii, were elected to parliament in 1980. Fatemeh Karubi, the wife of Ayatollah

Mehdi Karubi, headed a chain of government hospitals when her husband was Speaker of the Majlis. Faezeh Hashemi, the daughter of former President Hashemi Rafsanjani, helped establish, then headed, a women's sports organization. Fatemeh Hashemi, the older daughter of Hashemi Rafsanjani, served in the foreign ministry. Zahra Mostafavi, the daughter of Ayatollah Khomeini, became president of an Islamic women's organization. Zahra Rahnavard, the wife of former Prime Minister Mir Hussein Mussavi, became the first postrevolutionary editor of the woman's magazine, *Ettelaat-e Banovan*.

Women from all classes resisted segregation in university classrooms, job and education discrimination, the harsh enforcement of the dress code, and regulations against the intermixing of young men and women, and barriers against female participation in certain sports. By voting in large numbers in the 1997 presidential elections and backing the candidate they believed supportive of issues important to women, women proved they have electoral clout and cannot be ignored by clerical leaders and politicians.

This article is in three parts. First, I will briefly discuss the status of women on the eve of the revolution.[2] Second, I will examine the legal, political, and social status of women in the 1979–97 period, that is, from the first revolutionary government to the election of President Mohammad Khatami.[3] Finally, I will examine the impact on women of policies adopted during the first two years of Khatami's presidency, a man for whom women voted in large numbers.

The Pahlavi Era

On the eve of the Islamic revolution in Iran, after five decades of Pahlavi rule, women in Iran were working in large numbers in both the private and public sectors. They worked as lawyers and judges, and taught in schools and universities. In the government, the number of women in decision-making positions was gradually expanding. There were women cabinet ministers, undersecretaries, directors-general, heads of departments, mayors, and diplomats. Women voted in elections and were elected to the two houses of parliament and to local councils. Young women fulfilled their military service requirements by living and working in rural areas and small provincial towns as members of the Literacy and Health Corps. Women served as traffic police officers and trained as pilots. The number of girls in schools and universities and adult literacy classes was expanding rapidly.

Under the monarchy, important changes also occurred in the status of women in the legal sphere. The Family Protection Laws of 1967 and 1975 for the first time gave women the right to petition the courts for divorce and gain child custody. Family Protection Courts were set up to settle family disputes. A husband could no longer unilaterally divorce his wife or automatically gain custody of the children. A husband could not stop his wife from working without good cause. Either party had the right to go to court and make a case against the other spouse's occupation. Women judges served on Family Courts, and women lawyers represented both male and female clients. The marriage age was raised from 13 to 15 and then to 18 for girls. Polygamy was made very difficult, and the court had the ultimate say as to whether a man could take a second wife. Temporary marriage was still legal but, socially, was increasingly frowned upon and was not widely practiced.

The veil had been abolished in 1936, but after the abdication of Reza Shah in 1941 a great number of Iranian women had gone back to wearing some sort of a headcovering. In the mid-1970s, the government for a brief period toyed with the idea of barring Islamic headdress from the universities but gave up the project. On the eve of the Islamic revolution in 1979, on the streets of Iranian cities, one saw both veiled and unveiled women. Women were free to observe the kind of attire they desired.

Abortion was legalized by removing a clause in the law that had criminalized performing and having an abortion. Family planning centers were set up; and, to slow rapid population growth, women were encouraged to take precautionary birth control measures.

Despite these advances, activist women were not fully satisfied. The inheritance law, based on Islamic law, was not touched. The passport law, which gave the husband the right to stop his wife from traveling abroad, was not changed. I remember occasions when senior women civil servants, about to leave the country to attend a conference abroad, were stopped at the airport because they did not have their husband's permission to travel. The right to choose a conjugal domicile was still the prerogative of the husband.

The government did not change Article 179 of the criminal code. The article prescribed no punishment for a husband who discovered his wife in a compromising position with another man and killed her and prescribed only 11 to 60 days in prison for a man who found his daughter or sister with a man who was not her husband and killed the couple. Such killings, committed in defense of family honor, were thus deemed justifiable under the law.

In the political arena, women secured the right to vote and to be elected to parliament in 1963. In 1978, on the eve of the revolution, women sat in parliament, representing Tehran and the provinces. Women served on local councils, and were appointed as mayors. Two women sat in the cabinet, and a number of women served as undersecretaries and directors general in government ministries. The first woman was appointed to the cabinet in 1968, when Farrokhru Parsa, an educator, was named Minister of Education. She was executed by the revolutionary government in December of 1979, after a revolutionary court found her guilty of "corrupting" young girls during her tenure at the ministry. A second woman also sat in the cabinet under the monarchy, as Minister of State for Women's Affairs. The post was abolished a few months before the revolution as a gesture to the growing Islamic sentiment in the country.

The changes in the status of women that took place under the monarchy were not limited to large cities and major provincial centers. Women across the country benefited from these changes through education, radio programs, and activities of the Women's Organization of Iran and its branches. Women had begun to vote in elections. Thus, when the antigovernment protests began in the late 1970s, women from all classes took an active part in demonstrations, strikes, and sit-ins. The revolutionary fever affected urban areas more than rural areas, and women's participation was greatest in Tehran and other major urban centers.

But the women participants included the educated and the less-educated, the religious and the secular, the affluent and the poor, political conservatives, moderates, and radicals. These women may have had different goals, but they all called for the overthrow of the monarchy and they all aspired to a new regime based on social and economic justice and political freedom. They fought to gain equality under the law. They did not expect to become second-class citizens.

Under the Islamic Republic

Within a very short time, women discovered that, when it came to gender issues, the Islamic Republic had a different agenda. This agenda was not in keeping with the expectations and promises made to women during the political protests that brought down the monarchy.

Women were suddenly confronted with a regime out of step with the concept of women's rights and with the gains women had made in the five decades preceding the revolution. They were faced with a state that believed in a traditional role for women within an Islamic context. Without consulting women, the state started dictating to women the role they could assume in public and even in the privacy of their homes, the jobs they could hold, the education they could receive, the dress they must wear in public, and the manner in which they may interact with men. The state promoted a traditional role of mother, spouse, and homemaker for women, discouraged family planning, and told women to bear more children. It emphasized the role of the man as provider, decisionmaker, and master of the household. The situation was fraught with ironies. Women were expected to be docile and subservient. On the one hand, the state repeatedly stressed that the "sanctity" of women must be respected. On the other hand, young gun-toting vigilantes routinely assaulted women for not observing the *hejab* or not being in the company of close male relatives.

The changes that occurred in the status of women were swift and affected women's lives in three areas: legal, political, and social.

One of the first acts of the revolutionary government was the suspension of the Family Protection Law and the Family Courts. Once again, a man was free to divorce his wife by declaration and gain exclusive custody of the children. A woman could not file for divorce unless such a right was stipulated in her marriage contract. A woman could not petition for custody of her children; according to Islamic law, a mother loses custody of her son at the age of two and her daughter at the age of seven. Restrictions on polygamy were removed. A woman was faced with the choice of putting up with a second wife or, if she insisted on divorce, being abandoned with no alimony. This threatened the economic well-being of all women, regardless of social class. The age of marriage was reduced to puberty for girls—nine under Islamic law. Although marriage at age nine is rare, it remains the law of the land.

The authorities began to speak approvingly of temporary marriage. During the Iran–Iraq War (1980–88), men were encouraged to take temporary wives from among war widows. Abortion once again was declared illegal and had to be practiced in back alleys. The government preferred women to be examined by female doctors, especially in the case of gynecologists. In 1981, parliament approved the Islamic Law of Retribution, imposing punishment by flogging, stoning, and payment of blood money for a series of crimes, including violation of the Islamic headdress, and adultery. Women were barred from becoming judges, in keeping with Islamic law and the Constitution of the Islamic Republic.

Women did not feel safe in the workplace for a variety of reasons. Women in decision-making positions were either dismissed, given early retirement, or demoted. Some government offices introduced segregation in the place of work, but abandoned the practice given its impracticality. Government-run daycare centers were closed, making it difficult for women to go to work. To encourage women to quit the civil service, some seemingly enlightened policies were introduced. For example, female government employees were permitted to work part-time and to retire after 15 years of government service. Women were slowly pushed into traditional female fields such as teaching and nursing.

Limited facilities prevented the segregation of women and men at the universities. But women were barred from a number of "unsuitable" fields, including agriculture, veterinary science, and some branches of engineering. Girls also were gradually excluded from technical and business concentrations in high schools and found it more difficult to major in the sciences. The large majority of science teachers were men, and male teachers were not permitted to teach young girls.

In the political sphere, women held on to the right to vote and to be elected to parliament, but in other areas did not fare as well. There were no women in the Revolutionary Council (1979–80), nor in the first cabinet formed by Mehdi Bazargan in February of 1979. Among the 72 members of the Assembly that drafted the Constitution of the Islamic Republic, there was only one woman, Monireh Gorgi. She did not act as a spokesperson for women's issues, but her presence in the assembly set a precedent for future participation of women in elected bodies.

The constitution of the Islamic Republic, ratified in 1979, defined women principally in the context of the family, in their role as wives, mothers, and homemakers, and what were deemed to be Islamic ideals. But the constitution also specified that all Iranians are equal under the law, and this provided the opening that allowed women in later years to contest unequal treatment.

Despite the opposition of the more conservative clerics, four women were elected to the first parliament of the Islamic Republic in 1980. It took over a decade for a prime minister to name the first woman deputy minister, and 17 years for a woman vice president to be appointed. The vice president, appointed in 1997, sits in on cabinet meetings.

The government's initial social policy toward women was harsh. No explanation was given for this policy. It was as if the ruling clerics felt threatened by the progress women had made under the previous regime and decided to remove women from the public sphere. They used Islam to justify their policies, not knowing that religion could be a two-edged sword and that women, too, would use the teachings of Islam to force their way back into the public sphere. The *hejab,* or Islamic dress, was imposed forcibly. It first became mandatory in government offices in 1979 and was then rapidly applied in all spheres of public life and regulated by heavy punishments. Showing a bit of hair became punishable by 70 lashes. In the last few years, lashings have become less common—although they still take place—and have been replaced by heavy monetary fines.

When the imposition of the *hejab* was first announced in March 1979, middle class and professional women came out into the streets for two consecutive days and protested. The demonstrators were attacked by club-wielding men and chador-dressed women, who called the demonstrators "prostitutes." Men and women going out together had to carry their identity cards to prove to revolutionary guards manning checkpoints that they were husband and wife or immediate blood relatives.

The attempt to segregate men and women in public places produced some strange sights. Buses were segregated, but taxis, which are shared in most Iranian cities, were not. Restaurants set aside some of their space for women, some for men, and some for families of men and women eating together. Men and women were not supposed to intermingle in public, yet they intermixed in stores and chatted while waiting in line for scarce goods or to get their ration cards from mosques. The government never seriously attempted to separate men and women in movie houses and theaters. Today, cinemas are a meeting place for young people, protected in the dark theater from the eyes of the morals police. Sport facilities were segregated, but women fought to participate in all kind of sports, including swimming, skiing, soccer, volleyball, and cycling. In skiing areas until 1999, men and women skied on different slopes, but sat together as "families" over lunch. Government offices and some universities have separate entrances and separate elevators for men and women, but the two intermingle once inside the office.

Government efforts to change the lifestyle of women and reverse the advances women had made in the previous decades did not quite succeed. Women fought back and managed to keep the question of women's rights at the forefront of the government's business. Even today, hardly a week goes by without a statement by a leading cleric or government official or a regime woman on the status of women. The regime women have acted as agents for change and have helped convince the government to present a progressive image of the status of women in what the regime considers a model Islamic society. The regime has, thus, remained steadfast on some issues; but it has compromised on many others.

Women have fared comparatively better in the political than in the legal or social sphere. The Constitution bars women from the position of spiritual leader—the highest post in the country. But it is silent on the sex of the president, prime minister, and cabinet members. This has allowed women in recent years to press claims to these positions. Women have served as deputies since the first parliament. In the parliamentary elections of 1996, two hundred women ran for seats and 13 women were elected to the Majlis. Faezeh Hashemi secured the second highest number of votes in the capital, after parliamentary speaker Ali Akbar Nateq-Nuri. Several women sought to stand as candidates for the presidency during the 1997 presidential elections. Aazam Taleqani was the most prominent among them. She was rejected by the Guardianship Council—but, significantly, because of an alleged lack of credentials rather than her sex.

During President Rafsanjani's tenure (1989–97), women's political participation expanded. An office for women's issues was set up under the president, and Shahla Habibi was appointed as advisor to the president for women's affairs. In 1995, the government announced the appointment of a woman as deputy minister of health. All ministries and provincial governments were instructed to set up offices for women's affairs. The government-sponsored Cultural and Social Council for Women fought to end discrimination against women in university level education. Today, men and women have equal access to all disciplines in higher education. In recent years, the number of women's Nongovernment Organizations (NGOs) also has grown. Although most of these NGOs are affiliated with the government, their activities range from domestic to international, from charity to education, environment, literacy, and vocational training. The government sent women representatives to most important international conferences on women and encouraged other official government delegations to include women among their members.

Women also have scored some victories in the legal field. Because of women's criticism and pressure, the government was forced to reintroduce some parts of the suspended Family Protection Law, but in a modified version. The government was faced with an avalanche of protests by women after it suspended the Family Protection Courts. Having first referred family disputes to regular civil courts, it then transferred such cases to special courts. Finally, the government was forced to reinstate the old Family Protection Courts but called them Special Family Courts. Clerics preside over these courts. Over the years, the number of complaints regarding the tendency of these courts to rule in favor of men led the government to assign women lawyers as special advisors to the presiding judges.

Under the modified version of the Family Law, a husband can petition to divorce his wife, but he has to abide by the court's ruling. Child custody is decided by the presiding judge, although unless the husband proves to be totally unfit he still gains the custody of the children. As a big concession to women in family matters, the government made available a marriage contract for about-to-be married couples. It gives a divorced wife the right to secure half the property obtained during a marriage, and the right to secure a power of attorney from her husband to divorce herself on 12 different grounds. In 1994, parliament enacted a law giving a divorced wife the right to monetary compensation in instances where the husband initiates the divorce proceedings and the wife is not at fault. Compensation is based on the length of the marriage. Polygamy and temporary marriage are still permitted, but the unfairness to women of these practices are discussed constantly in the press and on political platforms by both regime and nonregime women; they seek an end to such practices. Stoning for adultery and lashings for violations of the dress code are still on the law books, but they are contested both in the public arena and in courts. Women politicians and women lawyers and journalists take the lead in attacking such measures. A handful of enlightened clerics are lending their support to the demands for further legal reform. Among such clerics are Mostafa Mohaqeq Damad and Mohsen Saidzadeh.[4] Women have yet to achieve equality under the civil and criminal codes.

On social issues, as on all issues related to women, the first two decades of the Islamic Republic have been full of contrasts and contradictions. The government has not succeeded in imposing the *hejab* universally. On the streets of Iranian cities one sees a variety of headdresses and clothing. The black *chador*, referred to as the "superior *hejab*," has become the official uniform of women in decision-making positions. The black *maghnae*, a kind of hood that fits tightly under the chin and covers a woman's head and hair, is required in government offices and universities both for female students and the teaching staff. Elementary schoolgirls under the age of puberty are allowed to wear a white *maghnae*. Colorful loose scarves and robes are worn by women of all ages on the streets and public spaces. Younger women do not hesitate to show a bit of hair from under their scarves or to wear makeup and nailpolish, violations punishable under the law. In these ways, young girls especially are constantly contesting the authority and the social codes that the *komitehs* and the morals police seek to impose on women.

Checkpoints at street corners are rare these days, but armed *Basijis* still stop cars driven by young people. The morals police still arrest people for

The Politics of the "Women's Question" in the Islamic Republic 85

not observing the dress code or the rules against mixing between the sexes. The *komitehs* still break into people's homes, confiscate satellite dishes, videos, and alcoholic beverages, and arrest people for partying, drinking, dancing, or for intermixing. Today, the fine for such violations is a large sum of money rather than lashing, as was the case in the early days of the revolution. Despite all these restrictions, women and men continue to defy the authorities by appearing in public places together, in cinemas, on scooters, or in cars. They walk together in city squares, on the outskirts of Tehran and other big cities, and they hike together in the mountains and picnic in public parks.

The number of women writers, translators, film and play directors, painters, and sculptors has multiplied in the last two decades. They express in their work the difficulties of being a woman in the Islamic Republic. These women have gained international recognition. A great number of novels and short stories written by women have been translated into Western languages. Almost every international screening of Iranian films includes films directed by women. Most art galleries in Tehran are owned or run by women. The number of women publishers is large, and there is now an annual book fair for women publishers.

Women have been very active in sports as well. Faezeh Hashemi headed the National Council of Women's Sports Organizations, and she has continued to run the organization since her election to parliament. Under her watch, women's sports gained public recognition. A woman served as the flagbearer for the Iranian team at the Olympic games in Atlanta. When women cyclists were attacked in a park in Tehran, Faezeh Hashemi publicly defended the right of women to ride bicycles in public, in effect disagreeing with the Spiritual Leader. He had declared cycling not suitable for women. Iran founded and sponsors the annual Islamic Games for Women. The event brings together women athletes from across the Islamic world for competitions. Women soccer teams were formed despite the ridicule and resistance of the conservative faction in the country.

The government, having initially dismantled the family planning program established under the old regime, determinedly reversed course in 1990. Birth rates had risen precipitously. The population had increased by almost 70 percent in just over a decade to 60 million. Half the population was under 20. Faced with the daunting task of having to provide schools, jobs, healthcare, and housing for this rapidly growing younger generation, the government launched a vigorous family planning program. It set up "Health Houses" in rural and urban areas to provide women with birth control advice and devices, offered men free vasectomies, put up billboards in cities encouraging families to have fewer children, and used clerics and the pulpit to preach the wisdom of family planning and birth control.

The Khatami Era

Women played a decisive role in the 1997 presidential elections when, for the first time, gender issues were debated in the election campaign. The women's vote helped secure victory for Mohammad Khatami, against the frontrunner, Majlis Speaker Ali Akbar Nateq-Nuri. But Khatami galvanized voters by campaigning on a platform of moderation, dialogue with the West, and tolerance for a variety of views. He also appeared particularly sympathetic to the problems of women, youth, and the underprivileged.

For example, during the campaign he gave an interview to the women's magazine *Zanan*.[5] He responded fully and frankly to the magazine's questions and did not exclude the possibility of nominating a woman to his cabinet. Unusual for clerics, he talked about his wife and daughters. He even joked that if his wife learned how to drive, he would let her do all the driving. Nateq-Nuri did not even bother to reply to *Zanan's* request for an interview, a fact that the magazine reported to its readers and that helped alienate women voters.[6] During the presidential campaign, when it became obvious that women, who normally did not participate significantly in presidential elections, would turn out in large numbers in the 1997 elections, Nateq-Nuri began to scramble to appeal to the women's vote. He denied a widespread rumor that he would impose the *chador* on women if elected. He reminded voters that he had speeded passage through parliament of a bill, pending since 1980, to establish a parliamentary committee on women, youths, and family. (The new committee ended up with eight female and seven male members, representing a wide spectrum of political views.)

In the months before the election, Nateq-Nuri also shepherded several bills of interest to women through the legislature, including a law that in certain cases allows surviving children to continue receiving the pension of their late mother and a second law that allows some women civil servants to work only three-quarters time but to receive full pay.[7]

Some women parliamentary deputies supported Nateq-Nuri's candidacy.[8] But the large majority of women across the political, social, and age spectrum voted for Khatami. These included educated, middle-class and working-class women, women from both Westernized and traditional households, and women in both large cities and small towns and villages. Younger women, like their male counterparts, actively campaigned for Khatami. They did so because they expected Khatami to end harassment of women by the morals police, give women more protection under the law, revise those parts of the Family and Civil Codes hostile to women, and facilitate access for women to senior and decision-making positions.

The position of women during the first two years of Khatami's presidency, however, remained full of contradictions. Politicians across the spectrum understood that they could no longer ignore women's issues or take the women's vote for granted. At the same time, the conservatives attempted to block the reforms pushed by the president. Despite expectations, Khatami, probably in deference to conservative opinion, did not appoint a woman to his Cabinet. Public opinion, however, would probably have supported such an appointment. A poll conducted by *Zanan* indicated that 78.6 percent of those polled had no objection to the appointment of women as ministers.[9] An earlier poll indicated that 41 percent of respondents would accept a woman as president, while 19.7 percent would not.[10]

Khatami, however, appointed a woman, Massoumeh Ebtekar, as one of his seven vice presidents, responsible for environmental affairs. Unlike ministerial appointments, vice presidents do not require parliamentary approval. Ebtekar, an immunologist, had served as official translator for the Iranian students who seized the American embassy in November, 1979, and was former editor of the feminist journal *Farzaneh*. She became the first woman since the establishment of the Islamic Republic to sit in on cabinet meetings. The president appointed another woman, Zahra Shojai, as his special advisor for women's affairs and the head of the Center for Women's Participation. The Cabinet voted an increase of 800 percent in the center's budget. Ms. Shojai also sits in on cabinet meetings. Khatami appointed Jamileh Kadivar, the wife of Minister of Culture and Islamic Guidance Ataollah Mohajerani, as his special adviser on press affairs. Ms. Zahra Rahnavard, a writer and commentator and wife of former Prime Minister Mir Hussein Mussavi, became chancellor of Al-Zahra University, a women's institution. She was the first woman in the Islamic Republic to head a university. Khatami's own wife, Zohreh Sadeghi, heads a special committee concerned with issues affecting rural women. Under Khatami's predecessor, there was one woman undersecretary, at the Ministry of Health; under Khatami there is also only one woman in a similar post, as parliamentary undersecretary at the ministry of Culture and

Islamic Guidance. The new president kept in place the offices for women's affairs established by his predecessor in each ministry and in provincial governors' offices. The number of women deputies in parliament increased to 14 in midterm elections in 1997, when Fatemeh Karubi was elected to the legislature from Tehran.

In December 1998, a group of women, the majority of whom had held senior positions in the bureaucracy, formed the *Majma-e Eslami Banovan*—the Islamic Women's Association. The founders described themselves as "activist, thoughtful Muslim women," dedicated to helping women realize their full potential in society. They named Fatemeh Karubi as their secretary-general.[11]

In the first two years of Khatami's presidency, parliament enacted several laws important to women, including a provision for readjusting the value of the *mahr* (monetary sum the husband pledges to his wife in the marriage contract and payable on divorce) in keeping with the rise in the cost of living,[12] and a law permitting women civil servants to retire after 20 years' service.[13] A conservative backlash against Khatami's reforms, however, also produced two laws in parliament that women regarded as retrograde. The first, an amendment to the Press Law, made it a punishable crime to print pictures or material "exploitative" of women, insulting to women, or encouraging women to "ornamentation," or that furthered friction between men and women. The second law mandated a segregated healthcare delivery system, with medical practitioners permitted to treat only members of their own sex. Both bills were approved against the opposition of Khatami's government, women activists, and women's magazines. These magazines criticized the proposals and those women members of parliament who helped to table and later on voted for them. In a sharply worded editorial, *Zanan* labeled these bills as "taking the roads of the Talibans," the extreme fundamentalists who had secured power in Afghanistan.[14] The medical bill, which also was opposed by many doctors, was originally sent back to parliament by the Council of Guardians on grounds that the government lacked the funds to create a two-track healthcare delivery system.

These bills were a throwback to earlier attempts at quasi-segregation of men and women. For example, in August 1996 the first women-only dental clinic was set up in Tehran. The clinic is run by women dentists and caters to women patients. A little earlier, the first all women's medical college was founded in the city of Qom. In June 1998, Khatami's government, by contrast, sought to further integrate women into public life. It announced it would set up the first women's police academy in the country. The graduates will serve in regular police units. In March 1999, the Ministry of Education barred women language teachers from teaching boys over the age of 10. Until then, private language classes were taught by men and women.

In 1998, seven women tried to stand for elections to the Council of Experts, a body composed almost exclusively of clerics and charged with selecting the Supreme Leader. The credentials of these women were uniformly rejected. Many women, however, stood as candidates for local council elections in February 1999. Some five thousand women were cleared to run for 220,000 local council seats in cities, towns, and villages across the country. To encourage large participation by women in the elections, the newspaper, *Zan,* offered to publish without charge the biographies of women candidates. Some three hundred women were elected to the local councils in many major cities. In some cities, women secured the highest number of votes. Among the 15 members of the Tehran city council were three women, including Jamileh Kadivar.

In the legal sphere, some greater role was permitted to women in the judiciary. Under President Rafsanjani, women had already begun to serve as consultants to the clerical judges presiding over the Special Courts that hear family cases. In 1997, the Chief of the Judiciary, Mohammad Yazdi, appointed a woman, Mahindokht Daoodi, as undersecretary to the office responsible for the implementation of rulings issued by the family courts. He named another woman to head administrative affairs division of the judiciary. The ban against women serving as judges was not lifted, but in 1997 four women were appointed as investigative magistrates. These "magistrates" cannot issue rulings but serve as investigative magistrates in the family courts. In 1998, the number of such women magistrates was given as 99. For the first time in Iran, seven women were given licenses to open and head notary offices, for generations a prerogative exclusively of men and, in earlier decades, especially of clerics.

Despite the pressure brought on the government and parliament by women activists, no changes occurred during Khatami's first two years in office in the Family Law, the inheritance law, or the law of retribution. In January 1998, parliament rejected by a large majority a bill amending the law of inheritance in favor of women. Under Islamic law, the daughter, or daughters collectively, inherit half the amount inherited by the son or sons. President Khatami has on several occasions alluded to discrimination and injustices suffered by women due to "certain prejudices upheld under the pretext of religion."[15] But women activists know that as long as the conservatives constitute the majority in parliament, it will be very difficult to change the laws supposedly derived from the s*hariah.* Even Ayatollah Khamenei's criticism of child marriage had little effect.

Khatami's emphasis on strengthening civil society and expanding freedom of expression and tolerance for opposing views also led to a burgeoning of new publications, among them women's newspapers and magazines. Faezeh Hashemi launched a new newspaper, *Zan.* Its first issue hit the newsstands in the fall of 1998. Intended as a daily for women, it has increasingly occupied a niche as a general interest, political newspaper, strongly supportive of President Khatami on social and political issues. *Zan* even overshadowed the daily, *Khordad,* which is published by former Minister of Interior Abdollah Nouri, and was expected to become the primary pro-Khatami newspaper in the country.

The monthly, *Hoquq-e Zanan* (Women's Rights), which came out in March 1998, was the first magazine devoted entirely to legal matters related to women. The publisher and editor, Ashraf Geramizadegan, was the former editor of the women's magazine, *Zan-e Ruz.* The magazine seeks to focus on women's affairs and to inform women of their legal rights.

While these publications thrived in the more open environment created by Khatami, the freer press also faced opposition from hardliners. *Tous* and *Jameeh,* initially the two most successful daily newspapers of the Khatami era, were closed down by the judicial authorities. In 1998, Ms. Sherkat, the editor of *Zanan,* and Ms. Hashemi, editor of *Zan,* were summoned to appear before the special press tribunal to answer charges, respectively, of slandering the Revolutionary Guards in the Caspian city of Salman Shahr and publishing allegedly false information regarding an attack on two of Mr. Khatami's cabinet ministers. Ms. Sherkat was found not guilty, but Ms. Hashemi was ordered to pay a monetary fine, and her paper was suspended for two weeks. In April 1999, *Zan* was suspended once again for publishing an allegedly offensive cartoon and news item.

Khatami's tenure also provided Iranians with a sense of liberation in the social sphere. Men and women felt freer to move about, to mix and mingle; university students of both sexes dared to address one another on campus without fearing the wrath of the Islamic committees set up to watch over them.

The streets became more colorful. Women wore makeup under their *chadors* and did not hesitate to expose a bare wrist, ankle, painted toe, or even a bit of bare neck. The conservative press admonished women for not observing proper *hejab,* but when Azad University required women students at most of its branches to wear the full *chador, Zan* criticized the

The Politics of the "Women's Question" in the Islamic Republic 91

imposition of the full Islamic dress, arguing that "*chador* is a choice, and must not to be imposed or devalued."[16] Zahra Shojai, the advisor to the president for Women's Affairs, added her voice to that of Faezeh Hashemi in suggesting that women should be free to choose the Islamic dress they wish to observe.

During the Islamic Conference in December 1997, Zohreh Sadeghi, the wife of President Khatami, appeared at her husband's side at Mehrabad Airport, welcoming the spouses of some of the visiting dignitaries. Although she was wrapped in her black *chador*, the presence of the president's wife on such an occasion was a first in the 20 years of the Islamic Republic. In the early years of the revolution, when the parliamentary Speaker Hashemi Rafsanjani took his wife along on a state visit to Japan, he was criticized for un-Islamic behavior. No Iranian official was after that occasion seen in the company of his spouse at official functions.

Women are now allowed to attend male sports events, such as soccer, volleyball, and tennis matches, although men and women still sit in separate sections of the stadium. This was a change in policy brought about, in part, by the women themselves. In June 1998, five thousand women crashed through the gates of Tehran's largest stadium, insisting on attending welcome ceremonies for Iran's victorious soccer team, just back from the Asian Games. The government subsequently decided to ease restrictions on women's attendance at sports events. The morals police and paramilitary *Basijis,* who also play a role in enforcing dress and moral codes, appeared less inclined, in the early Khatami period, to interfere in the manner in which people conducted themselves in public spaces.

By the end of 1998, however, infighting between the Khatami camp and the social and political conservatives led to reverses for Khatami's policies. Intrusion by the authorities into people's lives resumed; the morals police began once again to insist on the strict observance of the *hejab* and nonmixing of young men and women in public. These practices led, once again, to confrontations between the morals police and the younger generation. For example, the morals police started raiding pizzerias and coffee shops popular among the younger generation. Some conservative commentators went so far as to brand eating pizza, watching programs broadcast by satellite televisions, and accessing the Internet, as yet other signs of the Western "cultural onslaught." The first cyber-café was opened in the summer of 1998 in Tehran. Women and men are segregated, but they still get to eye each other.

Despite these setbacks, Iranian women have scored successes in the battle for rights that they waged over the last two decades. Iranian women have developed techniques of resistance, organization, lobbying, and steadfastness in pursuit of their goals. Some activist Iranian women have learned to use the language and teachings of Islam, others of international human rights, and women's rights to advance their agenda.

Thousands of others have had a powerful impact simply by "being there," in schools, in universities, in the workplace, in the arts, and on the streets. They have become a constituency that can influence Iranian politics and policies. They might differ among themselves on the methods to reach their goals, but they agree on the principle that discrimination against women must end.

Notes

1. See Haleh Esfandiari "The Majlis and Women's Issues in the Islamic Republic of Iran" in Mahnaz Afkhami and Erika Friedl, eds., *In the Eye of the Storm: Women in Postrevolutionary Iran*. (Syracuse, NY: Syracuse University Press, 1994).
2. For a detailed description of the status of women in pre-revolutionary Iran see Haleh Esfandiari, *Reconstructed Lives: Women and Iran's Islamic Revolution*. (Washington, D.C.: The Woodrow Wilson Center Press, and Baltimore and London: Johns Hopkins University Press, 1997).
3. For a detailed description, see Haleh Esfandiari, *Reconstructed Lives: Women and Iran's Islamic Republic*. The book also contains a select bibliography of books and articles on Iranian women.
4. In virtually every issue of *Zanan*, there appears an article by Mohsen Saidzadeh, sometimes writing under a pseudonym, on these issues.
5. *Zanan*, April-May 1997.
6. Ibid.
7. *Zanan*, June-July 1997.
8. *Zanan*, April-May 1997, statement by Nafiseh Fayazbakhsh,
9. *Zanan*, August-September 1997.
10. *Zanan*, June-July 1997.
11. *Zan*, December 1998.
12. *Zanan*, June-July 1997.
13. *Zanan*, July-August 1997.
14. *Zanan*, March-April 1998.
15. Iran Weekly Press Digest, August 8–14, 1998.
16. *Zan*, November 1998.

5

Iran's Economy: Twenty Years after the Islamic Revolution

Bijan Khajehpour

Introduction

The Islamic Revolution of Iran was the root of a number of dramatic social and political changes in Iran. Probably the most significant ingredient of revolutionary processes that have unfolded since the revolution is the ideologization and politicization of all aspects of politics, society, and economy. As far as the Iranian economy is concerned, it is valid to say that the economy has experienced an eventful two decades since the 1979 Revolution. Events such as the revolution itself and its social and political consequences, the 1980–88 Iran–Iraq War, as well as economic sanctions, emigration of experts, and flight of capital have all had their impact on the country's economic development. It is, therefore, impossible to examine Iran's economic performance since the revolution without discussing the interrelation of economic phenomena with domestic as well as foreign policy areas.

The objective of this paper is to identify the actual and structural changes in Iran's economy as well as economic policy directions over the past two decades. While the paper will look at quantitative issues and will evaluate the government's policies or rather lack of policies in different stages, the emphasis will be on qualitative changes since the revolution. Furthermore, the paper will discuss the future perspectives of economic development in Iran.

The First Postrevolutionary Decade: 1979 to 1989

The immediate aftermath of the Islamic revolution in Iran translated into one of the most severe shocks to the Iranian economy. The mass nationalization of industries and economic entities, initially under the name of "confiscation of assets of the Royal family and its affiliates," but later clearly derived from the revolution's economic philosophy, put some 60 to 80 percent of the economy under the government's control—either directly through the ownership of ministries, banks, and government institutions, or indirectly through a number of "revolutionary foundations"—changed the ownership structures of economic activity dramatically. This behavior, which was a product of anti-capitalistic sentiments during the revolution, manifested itself in the country's new Constitution. Article 44 of the Constitution states:

> The economy of the Islamic Republic of Iran is to consist of three sectors: state, cooperative, and private, and is to be based on systematic and sound planning.
> The state sector is to include all large-scale and mother industries, foreign trade, major minerals, banking, insurance, power generation, dams, and large-scale irrigation networks, radio and television, post, telegraph, and telephone services, aviation, shipping, roads, railroads, and the like; all these will be publicly owned and administered by the state.
> The cooperative sector is to include cooperative companies and enterprises concerned with production and distribution, in urban and rural areas, in accordance with Islamic criteria.
> The private sector consists of those activities concerned with agriculture, animal husbandry, industry, trade, and services that supplement the economic activities of the state and cooperative sectors.
> Ownership in each of these three sectors is protected by the laws of the Islamic Republic, in so far as this ownership is in conformity with the other Articles of this chapter, does not go beyond the bounds of Islamic law, contributes to the economic growth and progress of the country, and does not harm society.
> The [precise] scope of each of these sectors, as well as the regulations and conditions governing their operation, will be specified by law.

Despite the legal existence of three economic sectors, the scope of the state sector that was defined by this article was meant to limit the private sector to small economic enterprises. Although in practice this law was never fully implemented, the very existence of it has been one of the key obstacles to sound economic development in Iran—an issue that will be discussed in later sections.

Furthermore, the revolutionary sentiments also included an article in the Constitution in regard to foreign investment. Article 81, which was damaging in the long run, states: "The granting of concessions to foreign individuals and companies is prohibited." Although the law never elaborated what it meant by concessions, it was clear that the authors of the Iranian Constitution[1] wanted to avoid a repeat of oil concessions that Iran had offered to foreign companies early in the twentieth century. Besides other factors, however, this very notion in the Constitution has had a limiting effect on foreign investment activity in Iran.

Another major shock to the economy in the aftermath of the revolution was the commencement of the Iran-Iraq War in 1980. Not yet settled in its new role as the "patron of the economy," the government had to deal with the huge challenges of the war, which required a shifting of financial and manufacturing attention in the country. Furthermore, the war mainly took place in the country's oil-rich province, Khuzestan, limiting the government's access to oil export income. On top of the already critical situation, as a result of the hostage-taking in the American Embassy in Tehran in 1979, the country was sanctioned by Western countries, especially the United States, putting additional pressure on Iran, which was heavily relying on American products for its industry, military, and oil sector.

Consequently, faced with the heavy responsibilities assigned to the government through the Constitution, the war and economic sanctions by the West, Iran's economic policy in the 1980s was a catalogue of steady government intervention in economic affairs. At the same time, as the majority of interventionist policies were politically motivated, fluctuating policies became a normal phenomenon in revolutionary Iran—another damaging factor for the Iranian economy.

Crisis management and, at times, mismanagement of government budgets led to enormous deficits within the government's financial structure. Although it is impossible to put the entire blame on the government as it was handling the war crisis, the way budget deficits were covered, was the government's doing, that is, almost unlimited borrowing from the Central Bank. Both these factors—namely continuing budget deficits and government borrowing from the Central Bank—led to serious inflationary pressures on the economy. The only factor that was controlling the inflation (held at about an annual average of 18 percent in the first decade) were tight subsidies that the government had introduced on basic foodstuffs, fuel, and a number of services. The subsidies were the key instrument of the government to hold on to its "social justice" pledge and also to maintain a degree of living standard amid deteriorating economic conditions.

Another source of pressure for the economy came about by the official insistence on maintaining the exchange rate which Iran had inherited from the prerevolutionary period. Some experts believe that that exchange rate (about 70 Rials to the dollar) was even unrealistic before the revolution, but the most damaging element was the fact that the government and Central Bank of Iran maintained that rate as the country's official exchange rate until the early 1990s. As a result, the gap between the official exchange rate and the real value of the Rial (at times reflected on the country's black market) widened enormously. The extent was so bad that in the first official devaluation of the currency in 1993, the Rial was devalued 20 times.[2]

Both as a result of the artificial official rate, as well as a number of social and economic restrictions, an increasing section of the country's economic activity moved into black market underground activities. In fact, even governmental entities were more engaged in how to benefit from the disparity between the official exchange rate and the black market rate than in their actual economic objectives. The phenomenon of the underground economy is one of the most serious parameters disturbing sound economic policy to date.

As a result of all the above parameters, between 1979 and 1989, the country's gross domestic product (GDP) had virtually experienced no growth. In the same period, due to another area of postrevolutionary intervention, that is, the country's initial postrevolutionary population policy (complete rejection of birth control), Iran's population grew at a pace of 3.5 to 3.9 percent per year. The clear consequence was that every year the real per capita income of Iranians fell—a phenomenon that has continued constantly in the past two decades.

Postwar Economic Development

The decision to end the Iran–Iraq War in 1988 through the acceptance of a cease-fire brokered by the United Nations had different motivations, but many analysts believe that deteriorating economic conditions were among the top reasons to end the war. Indeed, the immediate impact of the decision on the economy was enormous. The black market value of the U.S. dollar collapsed from about Rials 1,400 to Rials 500 overnight, which is an indication of the positive psychological impact of the cease-fire.

Clearly, the decision to end the war was the first major decision by the

Islamic regime which underlined the inset of a degree of pragmatism that had triumphed over revolutionary fundamentalism. This new pragmatism was steered by then Majles (parliament) speaker, Ali Akbar Hashemi Rafsanjani. Rafsanjani also became the key figure in determining the direction of Iranian politics when, in June 1989, the Leader of the Revolution, Ayatollah Ruhollah Khomeini, died. Rafsanjani was elected president in August 1989 and promised a new era of economic policy, this time based on so-called five-year plans that would determine the framework of economic policy and development and attempt to introduce a medium-term consistency in economic policy. Below, the two five year plans that have been drafted and executed since 1989 will be briefly discussed in order to evaluate the new approach to economic policy.

The First Five Year Development Plan
(March 1989 to March 1994)

The era that started with the first five year plan is known in Iran as the "Era of Reconstruction." Clearly, for the regime, the reconstruction of the economy and the war-damaged regions was a high priority. Furthermore, 10 years of revolution and war had left a number of social and economic scars on the Iranian society that were difficult to repair. It seems that the planners and policy makers of the time saw a fast economic growth period as a key to calming the damaging effect of the previous decade.

A brief evaluation of the first five year plan (First Plan) indicates that the main objective of the planners in Iran's Plan and Budget Organization (PBO) was to get the Iranian economy out of the negative growth of the first postrevolutionary decade. To achieve that growth, the government planned to liberalize the economy through partial privatization of industries and services, utilize the economy's idle capacities (which had prevailed throughout the war) and, most important, increase the ratio of capital formation to the GDP from about 13 percent in 1989 to a predicted 25 percent in 1993/94. Consequently, the economic growth rates that the First Plan predicted were very ambitious. Table 5.1 compares the predicted and the actual growth rates in the different economic sectors between 1989 and 1994. Interestingly, the main economic activities in which the actual growth stayed behind the projected growth rate were manufacturing and mining as well as construction. Studies on this matter indicate that the main reason for the lack of parallel growth in these sectors was the absence of the private sector. In other words, the growth that was generated in the ambitious First Plan was mainly due to a concerted effort by the government. This fact is well reflected in the fully government run energy sector, which experienced a higher growth than projected. Furthermore, the government played the main role in increasing the capital formation ratio from 13 percent in 1989 to 17 percent in 1994, but a deeper look at the actual performance indicates that the government achieved this at the rate of heavy borrowing from domestic and foreign sources. Although in the initial phase (1989/90) the Iranian government did not obtain major loans from abroad, through a payment crisis of Iran's short-term debts to foreign creditors (mainly accumulated in the form of delayed letters of credit), Iran managed to receive a number of medium-term foreign loans, which were in fact a rescheduling plan for Iran's short-term foreign debts.

Table 5.1: Growth of GDP by Economic Sectors (constant prices)

Sector	1988	Average Annual Growth 1989 to 1994	
		Projected	Actual
Agriculture	-2.5	6.0	6.0
Oil	9.7	9.5	8.6
Manufacturing & Mining	1.3	15	9.1
Electricity, Gas, & Water	-3.6	9.1	12.7
Construction	-21.2	14.5	5.3
Services	-7.1	6.7	7.3
GDP	-7.8	8.1	7.3

Source: Central Bank of Iran

Consequently, it is valid to say that the growth between 1989 and 1994 was mainly financed through the accumulation of some $30 billion in foreign debt. In 1993, the ratio of Iran's foreign debt to the country's GDP reached 38 percent, which was alarming. Although this issue has been contained since, the emergence of this problem had a negative impact on the degree of interest of foreign companies in the Iranian market, an additional factor that constrained the Iranian economy in later stages. Also in the same period, the Iranian government and CBI devalued the Iranian Rial, introducing the single exchange rate of Rials 1,450 (in March 1993), correcting the rate to Rials 1,750 within two weeks. The monetary shock of this decision was enormous, especially as suddenly the entire oil income was converted into Rials at a rate almost 25 times higher than previously.[3] The inflationary pressures were obvious, so that the average official inflation rate in the five year period reached 18.7 percent per year. The

First Plan had forecast an annual inflation of 14.4 percent. As a result of the introduction of the new exchange policy, the country's money supply exploded, growing by more than 25 percent annually in the plan period. Notwithstanding the economic difficulties, the plan also included a number of steps in human and social development. Iran was facing a severe challenge through the country's demographic structures. The baby boom of the 1980s meant that almost one-third of the population was under the age of 10 in early 1990s. One of the first positive steps in this regard was the introduction of birth control policies in 1989, which happened with the blessing of religious authorities. The country's demography meant that special attention was needed in the creation of schools as well as educational and vocational facilities for the youth. In this regard, the government achieved quantitative success. In the plan period, the number of school pupils increased by 6.2 percent per annum, and the number of university students increased by 19.4 percent a year. The annual increase in university lecturers was almost the same, forcing the government to reintegrate a large number of university lecturers who had been pushed out of their jobs in the early stages of the revolution for ideological reasons. Technical and vocational training opportunities also showed considerable increase, reaching an annual growth rate of 56.1 percent. In addition to the quantitative growth, the fact that in the light of the developments, the Iranian authorities privatized a number of educational facilities and also legalized the establishment of private schools and universities, led to some qualitative improvement, though a real measure of this factor has been difficult. These moves happened in response to social and demographic pressures, proof that the regime was capable of pragmatic thinking—although sometimes too late.

The Second Five Year Development Plan (March 1995 to March 2000)

In 1993, when the then administration introduced the bill for the second five year development plan (Second Plan), the composition of the Iranian parliament had changed dramatically. For the first time in postrevolutionary history, Islamist conservatives had taken the majority of the parliamentary seats,[4] and they wanted to impose their own views on administrative politics. Therefore, the bill for the Second Plan, which was introduced in 1993, became a piece of factional confrontation, and to underline the differences, the commencement of the plan was postponed from March 1994 to March 1995, which gave the factions more time to iron out differences.

Eventually, the actual law for the Second Plan was passed in late 1994, with a number of major changes from its original version. It is not within the scope of this paper to discuss the details of the factional disputes in regard to economic planning, but it can be said that the differences between the leading factions of the country, that is, the Moderates, the Conservatives, and the Revolutionary Leftists, have been a main obstacle to prevailing economic policies in Iran.

The good aspect of the long review of the second five year plan bill was the fact that the experiences of the First Plan were taken into account in order to draft a more practical and balanced approach to economic policy. Figure 5.1 summarizes the objectives of the Second Plan.

Figure 5.1: Objectives of the Second Five Year Development Plan
The key objectives and policies of the plan relate to three sectors: external, financial, and fiscal. They are defined as follows:

External Sector
Adopting a managed unified floating exchange rate;
Maintaining the convertibility of the Rial for current-account transactions;
Streamlining customs procedures; and
Setting tariffs at an "appropriate" level, defined as "taking into account the need to protect domestic producers and consumers as well as maintaining comparative advantage for Iranian goods in the international market."

Financial Sector
Providing greater incentives for savings, through rationalizing bank "profit rates" (i.e., interest rates) and ensuring a positive real return on bank deposits;
Issuing "long-term partnership and investment certificates" (the Islamic legal equivalent of Treasury bills);
Supplying the specialized development banks with funds "commensurate with the government's development objectives";
Stimulating the participation of the private sector through nonbank financial intermediaries; and
Keeping monetary growth at noninflationary levels.

Fiscal Sector
Increasing the share of taxation in total government revenue;
Increasing the share of direct taxes (except on wages) in total taxation;
Eliminating tax exemptions to "various" sectors other than agriculture;
Replacing other indirect levies with value-added tax;

Iran's Economy: Twenty Years after the Islamic Revolution 101

Establishing indirect tax rates based on the value of commodities;
Channeling oil revenue toward development spending;
Granting tax exemptions or rebates to infrastructure investment, investment in the production of strategic goods, activities generating foreign exchange, the development of deprived regions and job-creating activities;
Reforming the tax system, including the improvement of its administration; and
Reducing subsidies overall, while increasing them for vulnerable groups and making them more transparent in the budget.

Most of the stated objectives made sense even based on an international standard. Some Iranian economists even commented that the key stated objectives of the Second Five Year Plan could have been drafted by the International Monetary Fund (IMF) or the World Bank. Notwithstanding, the reality looked very different. Continued struggle between the factions, initiation of short-term responses to economic crises, and a number of external factors (such as intensified U.S. sanctions introduced in 1995, as well as unfavorable developments on international oil markets) have put pressure on the Iranian economy and practically deteriorated economic structures of the country.

A brief evaluation of the government's success or failure in different areas indicates the following: As table 5.2 underlines, the projected growth figures for different economic indicators in the Second Plan were more realistic than those in the preceding development plan. Nonetheless, the evaluation of the actual performance of the economy in the first three years of the Second Plan indicates how poorly the government has performed in achieving its own goals. Indicative of Iran's problems are the liquidity (money supply) growth. The Second Plan correctly identified the liquidity volume growth as a source of inflation and set an annual growth of 12.5 percent as the target for the five years. The fact that in the first three years of the same plan the money supply grew by almost 30 percent annually underlines the inability of the government to implement its own plans. Other missed targets also speak for themselves.

Financial Sector Developments

As seen above, one of the key reform areas in the Second Plan was the financial sector. Although the success in this regard has been modest, Iran-

Table 5.2: Economic Indicators in the Second Five Year Plan compared to the average of First Plan and the Projected Valued for the entire Second Plan (all figures in percentages)

	ACTUAL First Plan	Year between the two plans				Projected Second Five Year Plan	
Iranian year (years start on 21 March and end on 20 March)	1368–72 1989/90– 1993/94 (Annual average for five years)	1373 1994/95	1374 1995/96	1375 1996/97	1376 1997/98	1374–1376 1995/96– 1997/98 (Annual average for three years)	1374–1378 1995/96– 1999/2000 (Annual average for five years)
GDP Growth	7.3	1.6	4.5	5.8	2.9	4.4	5.1
Liquidity Growth	25.1	28.5	37.6	37.0	15.2	29.9	12.5
Inflation (rate)	18.7	35.2	49.4	23.3	17.3	30.0	12.4
Imports (FOB)- GDP ratio	20.8	11.9	11.2	11.1	9.1	10.7	15.4
Exports – GDP ratio	18.5	18.5	17.0	16.6	11.5	15.0	16.8
Per Capita Income Growth	4.3	-0.5	1.4	3.5	1.5	2.1	3.0
Investment Growth	13.3	3.4	3.7	7.4	-1.5	3.2	6.2

Source: Compiled through different statistical sources.

ian officials managed to reform some of the areas that were creating serious problems for the Iranian economy. Among such reforms were:

Introduction of bank interest: Fixed bank interest was forbidden based on a 1983 law on Islamic banking. According to that law, every bank and financial institution had to share its profits with the holders of savings accounts after it had been determined how much profit had been made. In reality, for most of the 1980s, Iranian banks offered interest free savings accounts with limited draws in which the customers could win a material gift. Realizing the extent of damage through the fact that national saving was very low, however, the officials in the CBI and in the government developed a compromise solution through which fixed bank interests could be introduced. The compromise solution created the notion of "advanced payments," which refers to the bank's prepaid interest in anticipation of future profit. Consequently, fixed interest rates were introduced. Currently, the bank interests for savings stands at 15 to 18 percent per annum depending on the type of savings account. Although the actual interest is below inflation, the new policy has attracted some private saving into the banking system.

Introduction of municipality bonds: Another major breakthrough for the country's financial sector was the introduction of municipality bonds in 1994 by the Municipality of Tehran. To limit the political resistance against this scheme, the former Mayor of Tehran, Gholamhossein Karbaschi, secured the approval of a number of Grand Ayatollahs in the Holy City of Qom, who lifted the religious ban on municipality bonds. Once again, in order to avoid further criticism, municipality bonds were dubbed "participation certificates," which were sold by state owned banks and carried a 20 percent guaranteed interest. Using this new instrument, over the past four years, state-owned institutions have attracted large sums of small investor capital into municipal and other projects.

Activation of the Tehran Stock Exchange: As one of the institutional instruments needed for the privatization process, in the early 1990s, the government put some effort behind promoting the Tehran Stock Exchange (TSE). The local exchange experienced a period of enormous growth between 1992 and 1996, but then was flawed as a result, especially, of its institutional and legal deficiencies. Currently, the TSE is in a phase of decline, and unless strong laws and regulations are introduced to guarantee the interests of small and big investors as well as introduce continuous supervision and reporting about the activities of listed companies, the exchange will not attract serious private capital.

Process of Industrialization

Interestingly, despite the quantitative discrepancies within both five year plans, one important qualitative aspect of postrevolutionary, and especially postwar, economic development of Iran has been the process of industrialization. The inward looking policies of both five year plans hand-in-hand with the diminishing financial base of the government have evidently led to a degree of development of domestic manufacturing that Iran had not experienced before. The introduction of a law in the early 1990s that protected domestic producers by forbidding the import of all products that were produced domestically in sufficient amounts had a direct effect on encouraging domestic industries to invest in manufacturing. Although this approach of import substitution favored a number of state monopolies and secured them against foreign competition, it also led to the establishment of a number of small- to medium-sized manufacturing companies that have grown based on the growing domestic market. Evidently, as a result of a combination of socioeconomic factors, the nature of Iran's domestic market also has changed. While in the 1970s and 1980s domestically manufactured products had a very limited market, the growth of a new and confident urban middle-class population that demands modern products but cannot afford to pay for foreign-made items has led to a new demand for domestically produced manufactured goods. Furthermore, the emphasis of both five year plans on promotion of nonoil exports and the various policies in this direction, helped improve the quality standards of Iranian industrial products. Although industrial production is still lagging behind international quality and management standards, the general development in this regard can be considered one of the qualitatively positive processes in Iran's postrevolutionary economic development.

Foreign Trade, Balance of Payments, and Exchange Rates

Another area of examination of Iran's economic performance since the 1979 Islamic Revolution is the country's external trade. Clearly, the trade figures in the case of Iran have traditionally been dependent on the amount of exported oil and the actual international oil price. This is very clearly reflected in the sharp decline of exports in the 1990s when, because of the war, Iran's capacity to export oil was reduced heavily. The lowest figure was reached in 1986, when the country only exported $7.8 billion. Compared to the prerevolutionary performance or even the peak of $23.2 billion in 1982, the decline in the second half of the 1980s was a heavy burden on the government, especially in light of the growing population. Iran's imports have usually been fully dependent on the volume of exports; however, the picture changed dramatically in the period between 1989 and 1992, when in the aftermath of the war, the new administration of President Rafsanjani attempted to impact the country's economic mood by flooding the market with imported goods. The consequent payment

Table 5.3: Balance of Payments (million US dollars)

Fiscal Year	EXPORTS Oil & Gas	Nonoil	Total	Imports (FOB)	Trade Balance	Services NET	Transfers	Current Account Balance	Capital Account (NET)	Changes in International Reserves
1992–93	16,880	2,988	19,868	23,274	-3,406	-5,094	1,996	-6,504	4,699	-166
1993–94	14,333	3,747	18,080	19,287	-1,207	-4,508	1,500	-4,215	5,563	232
1994–95	14,603	4,831	19,434	12,617	6,817	-3,059	1,198	4,956	-347	921
1995–96	15,103	3,257	18,360	12,774	5,586	-2,224	-4	3,358	-774	2,808
1996–97	19,271	3,120	22,391	14,989	7,402	-2,633	463	5,232	-5,508	2,346
1997–98	15,464	2,910	18,374	14,598	3,776	-2,489	288	1,575	-4,817	-3,705
1998–99 first quarter	2,629	573	3,202	3,714	-512	-397	NA	-909	-887	-533

Source: Central Bank of Iran

problems and the debt crisis led to a series of fluctuating trade policies throughout the 1990s. Table 5.3 summarizes Iran's balance of payments since 1992/93, indicating the fluctuating nature of trade policies.

Clearly, in the past few years, the main emphasis of the government and the CBI has been to produce a positive balance of payments to be able to repay Iran's foreign debts. This has mainly been achieved through a sharp decline in official imports, but the result has been that part of the country's necessary imports are being realized through semiofficial (Free Trade Zones) and illegal (smuggling) channels. Notwithstanding, low oil prices have changed that trend dramatically, and in the current fiscal year (ends on March 20, 1999), Iran is facing a huge current account deficit (up to $5 billion), which will worsen the economic situation and lead to inflationary effects. In order to contain the pressures, Iranian officials have sought some $3 billion in bridge financing from the country's main trade partners (Germany, France, Italy, and Japan)—the latest reports indicate that $2 billion of such bridge financing has been secured through yet another rescheduling of the same amount in foreign debts.

As far as the profile of Iran's foreign debt is concerned, it is valid to say that the worst years are over and that the country is able to manage the repayment of its current debts in the next few years (see tables 5.4 and 5.5), although some further rescheduling and bridge financing might take place.

One of the biggest failures of the Iranian government in regard to managing the economy has been experienced in the exchange rate policy. As mentioned above, the government developed an ambitious plan of unifying the exchange rates in 1993, which collapsed after one year, and Iran

Table 5.4: External Debt (*million US dollars*)

Fiscal Year	Short–Term	Medium and Long-Term	Total	Debt / GNP (percent)
1993–94	17,616	5,542	23,158	38.0
1994–95	6,707	16,030	22,737	31.7
1995–96	4,536	17,392	21,928	21.0
1996–97	4,557	12,278	16,835	12.5
1997–98	3,287	8,828	12,117	7.6
1998 first quarter	3,196	8,113	11,309	

Source: Central Bank of Iran

Iran's Economy: Twenty Years after the Islamic Revolution 107

Table 5.5: Planned External Debt Payments (*million US dollars*)

1998–99	1999–2000	2000–01	2001–02	2002–03	2003 onward
5,567	3,742	885	500	276	562

Source: Central Bank of Iran

It should be noted that due to low oil prices in 1998/99, Iran rescheduled some $2 billion of its foreign debt. However, the surge in prices in the second half of 1999 and through 2000 put Iran in a better financial position, so that in August 2000, the country's hard currency reserves with foreign banks reached $5 billion. This fact has promoted Iran's credit-worthiness in international markets.

Table 5.6: Different Exchange Rates in Iran

Exchange Rate	Parity of Rial to the Dollar	Comment
Floating Rate (official)	Rials 1,750	This rate is used for the conversion of oil export income into Rials and also for the import of subsidized goods into the country by state institutions.
Export Rate (official)	Rials 3,000	This rate was originally used as a basis for nonoil export earnings, but it is currently being phased out and replaced by the TSE rate.[5]
Tehran Stock Exchange (TSE) rate (official)	Rials 8,150[6]	This rate was introduced as an attempt to control black market activity. It failed in that sense, but it is now being used for nonoil exports, which makes Iranian products cheaper on international markets and should promote nonoil export activity.
Black Market (unofficial)	Rials 8,450[7]	The black market is a speculative market that follows free market rules. This market feeds all demand that is not covered by the official channels.

was back at a multitiered exchange rate system by introducing the so-called export rate in 1994. In the meantime, the country has four different exchange rates, and once again the large disparity between the rates (see table 5.6) creates the opportunity for economic gains to be sought in black market activity.

Roots of Current Problems

In light of the above list of missed economic targets, the challenge is to identify the roots of current problems in the country's economic management. Prior to the election of President Khatami in 1997 Iranian officials were readily offering external shocks and factors as the main source of the problems. Although external factors such as fluctuating oil prices, economic sanctions, and so on have an impact on Iran's economic development, they are not the only source of disturbance of economic development in Iran. In this regard, the issues mentioned below should be borne in mind:

Multiplicity of Economic Decision Makers

Economic policy in Iran is not the product of an authoritative decision maker who sets the targets and implements policies accordingly. The government, or in fact, the Plan and Budget Organization (PBO), which used to be the powerful arm of the government in planning and budgeting has certainly lost its authority in postrevolutionary Iran, and today a number of different-minded institutions are mingling in Iran's economic policy or are responsible for the failure to implement and achieve policy objectives. The most important such organizations are:

> The government, that is, PBO, but also all ministries and large state owned companies;
>
> High Council of Economy;
>
> Central Bank of Iran (CBI);
>
> The Parliament;
>
> Revolutionary and religious foundations that are responsible to the Supreme Leader and follow their own agenda;
>
> Traditional merchant associations, which have close ties with the conservative faction in power.

In order to underline how each of the mentioned power centers influence policy making and implementation, one can elaborate on the government's failure to control the economy's money supply.

When the targets of money supply growth are set for each year, the CBI defines the amount of loan facilities that the banks are permitted to offer to the public and the private sector. When the large public sector and the foundations face financial pressures, however, they force the state-owned banks to extend more facilities to them than planned. Eventually the banking sector, under political pressure from different power centers, overextends the facilities and explodes the money supply. Consequently, political bargaining and power play undermine economic policy. The same can be said about trade policies, foreign exchange policies, and so on.

Social and Political Considerations

The issue of "social justice" was one of the key slogans of the Islamic revolution. In fact, as mentioned earlier, the instruments that the Iranian government used in order to achieve social justice (i.e., subsidies, rationing methods, etc.) were among the most significant tools of the government to contain the economic hardship in the 1980s. Clearly, the legacy of that thinking has remained, especially in the form of subsidies. Both the former administration and the current administration have tried to cut the huge amount of subsidies in order to reduce the financial burden on the government. Currently, the actual and opportunity cost of the subsidies paid on all oil derivatives, basic foods (i.e., rice, cheese, flour, sugar, cooking oil, tea, and a number of other agricultural products) is estimated at $10 billion per year. Notwithstanding, the interplay of the different political power centers and ideologies have so far prevented a sensible approach to subsidies, so that the bulk of subsidies have remained in place, though a step-by-step cut has been introduced in the Second Plan.

Iran's current labor law is probably another perfect example of misplaced social and political consideration in Iran. The rigidity of the law and its proemployee nature are a main obstacle to creation of new employment opportunities and also to privatization. Many private sector investors have voiced their concern about the question whether they would be able to rationalize the staff of a privatized state owned entity. The current law does not allow mass redundancies. In mid-1999, an attempt to review the labor law and exempt all small enterprises with three or fewer employees from the labor law provisions failed in the face of pressure from different political power centers. The Iranian parliament had no choice but to put the law on hold for six months in order to create a greater consensus for the law. This example underlines the obstacles that a potential economic reform program faces in Iran as a result of overemphasis of social justice and socialist ideals in the postrevolutionary era.

Another damaging factor is the politicization of economic and trade decisions in Iran. The revolutionary ideology and also the constraining foreign relations of Iran have limited Iran's options in foreign trade, which has its impact on the economy. Although the Khatami administration has attempted to undo some of the limiting factors in foreign trade through improving ties with Europe as well as Iran's neighbors, serious obstacles remain in place.

Institutional and Management Deficiencies

Another key obstacle to implementation of economic policies is the prevailing deficiencies in management and also in institutional realities.

The postrevolutionary prioritization of ideology in appointing economic managers was a harmful process for Iran's economic efficiency. Mismanagement and corruption have certainly damaged the economy and business mentality in Iran. Interestingly, the issue of management deficiencies was admitted by former President Rafsanjani in the early 1990s; however, the political realities of the country did not allow a complete restructuring of management structures and the introduction of expertise into this area. The best Rafsanjani's administration was capable of was to ask the state managers to "re-educate" themselves—a process that has had little real effect on management realities. President Khatami has had a different approach and has on many occasions called for rethinking in the issue whether "ideology" was more important than "expertise." Khatami has also left no doubt about the fact that he gave the priority to "expertise," but it is too early to judge whether his approach will improve the country's management patterns.

Also, institutional deficiencies are an important obstacle. For example, the deficiencies of the TSE as a capital market and the absence of modern laws and regulations in this market have been a constraint in the government's attempt to privatize its entities through the TSE. Other shortcomings are felt in the country's banking system and in institutions such as customs, and so on. Clearly, a number of recent initiatives by the government address these issues, which will be discussed later.

Lack of Transparency

Another issue is clearly lack of transparency among economic activities in Iran. The existence of huge revolutionary and religious foundations, such as the *Bonyad Mostazafin va Janbazan* (Foundation for the Deprived and the War Veterans—MJF), or of the religious entity in Mashhad called *Astane Qodse Razawi* (entity managing the assets of Imam Reza's Shrine), and the fact that they are only accountable to the supreme leader, are a discomforting reality for any player in the Iranian economy. Furthermore, even registered government entities are irresponsible in providing correct and transparent information about their activities. The result is that even the government itself has to base its economic policies on guesswork rather than an expert and informative approach to economic directions.

Ambiguities in laws and regulations and the motivation of the government in introducing new laws are another source of problems, especially for private sector activity. Although the new administration has taken important steps to address the ambiguities in the legal context, it takes time to create the necessary confidence among the private sector players.

Status Quo of the Economy

Current Trends

Iran is in an enduring stage of stagflation. High inflation (although the current levels of around 30 percent are lower than the 50 to 60 percent inflation of the mid-1990s), a stagnant market, and an economic recession worsened through low oil prices and political and factional struggling in the country have worsened the economic conditions. As a result, the Iranian economy experienced a negative growth in the Iranian year 1377 (ended March 20, 1999) for the first time in a decade. Unemployment is set to rise and all other economic indicators are unfavorable. Almost all sectors are hard hit by the current recession—most significantly the construction sector, which had traditionally been a growth sector in postwar Iran. There are different current sources for the continuing recession in Iran. Current solutions to the problems will be discussed later.

Fluctuating Oil Income: As a result of fluctuating oil prices, the government has not been capable of continuing the role it has played in the past, that is, both provider of wealth and also source of capital formation. This was clearly felt in 1998/99, when oil prices dropped to about $10 a barrel. Despite a reverse trend in oil prices since mid-1999, it is valid to say that the oil export income in Iran will mainly be sufficient for the basic expenditure of the government on subsidies, salaries of civil servants, and basic infrastructure. In the absence of a functioning taxation system, the financial situation of the government will clearly have a negative impact on capital formation and also on the level of contract work that the government can offer to the economy as an instrument to reverse the recessionary trends. Although international oil prices relaxed to Iran's favor in the second half of 1999, the Iranian government is not in a position anymore to provide a financial backbone for the Iranian economy.

Factional Infighting: Interestingly, the factional infighting that intensified after the 1997 presidential elections has had a direct impact on the economy. It is evident that access to large-scale economic and commercial activity has been mainly available to figures and institutions close to the core of the political establishment. Therefore, economic activity has always been overshadowed by political wrangling between factions.

Failure of Social Engineering: Another important shift in economic realities has come about as a result of the new administration's correcting attitude to the policies of former President Rafsanjani. Iranian analysts have called the approach by the former administration the era of "social engineering," whereby the government believed that through the introduction of vast infrastructure projects, the country's basic economic ills would be cured. Today, it has become clear that those investments have been a waste of Iran's economic potentials in many areas. To underline the extent of the damage, it should be noted that in 1997 President Khatami instructed all state institutions to stop the infrastructure projects where less than 10 percent of the project had been completed. It is estimated that some 10,000 such projects were put on hold, which is currently a major source of recession. The vast investments associated with these projects will only be partly revived, where and if the government manages to transfer some of the projects to the private sector.

Limitations of the Middle Class: For the past two decades, while the Iranian economy has been stagnating, one phenomenon saved the relative income situation of Iran's growing middle class: The majority of the families had accumulated some assets from the prerevolutionary boom between 1973 and 1978. Over the postrevolutionary period, the majority of the middle-class families sold off their assets to survive economically. Recent surveys indicate that the average family is not in a position to use any other assets for economic survival, which leads to an additional pres-

Iran's Economy: Twenty Years after the Islamic Revolution

sure on the economy, that is, lack of consumer spending in the absence of sufficient income. Unfortunately, the situation had led to a tendency among the population to tend to underground economic activities, which are on the rise. According to official statistics, in the Iranian year of 1375 (March 21, 1996 to March 20, 1997), the expendable monthly income of an average Iranian family was Rials 620,000—in the same year the poverty line was set at Rials 1,000,000 per month.[8] This comparison indicates the insufficiency of official income and the need of average families to create other sources of income, usually through underground economic activity.

Current Challenges

In addition to the recessionary developments, the Iranian government is currently facing the following challenges:

Demographic pressures: Iran's young population (about 50 percent of the population is below the age of 20, 70 percent below the age of 30) is the most serious challenge to the government, especially with regard to job creation.

Underground economy: The existence of an underground economy is another damaging fact about the Iranian economy. There are different estimates about the volume of underground economic activity; however, the most serious and reliable estimates believe that 25 to 40 percent of economic activity in Iran is underground activities. These are not necessarily all illegal activities, but also a number of activities are legal but conducted outside visible economic structures. Smuggling and also trade in prohibited goods are clearly the largest such activities. A recent study has shown that some $4 to $8 billion worth of goods are smuggled into Iran annually. According to the same study,[9] an institutionalization of smuggling in legal goods would create some 200,000 job opportunities in the Iranian economy.

Need for Investment in the Oil Industry: As mentioned earlier, the oil sector is Iran's most important economic sector, especially with regard to hard currency earnings. Years of disinvestment and neglect, in which the oil industry was treated as a "cash cow" for the government, have led to an immediate need for large-scale investments and transfer of technology into Iran's oil sector in order to sustain the export capabilities of the country. The government is aware of the need and has also introduced a new policy in regard to foreign investment in the oil sector (in form of buy-back agreements); however, it is clear that the current developments in the oil sector will limit the financial resources of the government over the next few years, as a considerable section of the oil income will need to cover the rent of foreign companies that are investing in Iran's oil and gas sector.

Where Are the Solutions?

Having discussed the deficiencies and problems of the Iranian economy, below we will discuss the solutions to the current problems, evaluating the stated plans of the government, as well as other solutions that are being debated.

Government Approaches

The Economic Recovery Plan
The new administration's main response to the economic challenges came in the form of an "Economic Recovery Plan," which President Khatami presented on August 3, 1998, exactly one year after taking office. The recovery plan is rather general, but it identifies the main problems of the economy with special attention to the issue of unemployment. The plan forecasts that Iran will need some 15 million new jobs in the next two decades, and it envisages that the bulk of these jobs have to be created by the private sector.

Probably the plan's most encouraging element is the fact that it pays attention to needed political reforms in order to achieve economic objectives. Its pledge for observance of law, reviewing of all current laws and regulations in order to improve economic conditions, attention to transparency as well as its focus on the promotion of civil society institutions in the economic sector (i.e., trade unions, associations, etc.) are all important pillars of the plan. Another significant issue is the plan's pledge to "break monopolies." How far the new administration is prepared to go in this issue will depend on many political developments, but the stating of the objective is clearly an important step.

Another important element in the plan is the attention to the mobilization of investment sources. The plan refers to three sources, that is, domestic funds, funds of Iranians residing abroad, and also foreign investment. It pledges to introduce laws that guarantee the security of investment in Iran—laws that have partly been initiated in the past few months.

Once more, this plan puts an emphasis on the promotion of non-oil exports. In the meantime, the government has introduced the so-called High Council of Non-oil Exports, which is entrusted with introducing reforms that would increase Iran's non-oil exports in the future.

The detailed approaches of the government will have to be evaluated in future steps and initiatives, but it is valid to say that the general directions are rather positive and that the main problem areas have been identified.

The Third Five Year Plan
Another important document in regard to the government's approach to solving the economic ills of the country is the third five year development plan (Third Plan), which was debated in the Majles in the second half of 1999 and then passed by the parliament as well as the Guardian Council in March 2000. The main principles of the third development plan, which sets the overall framework for development policies in Iran from March 20, 2000 to March 20, 2005, are as follows:[10]

Regulating macroeconomic policies (fiscal, monetary, trade, exchange) to achieve sustainable growth and development;

Removing production and investment obstacles (encouraging domestic and foreign investment);

Reforming the public administrative system, reducing the public sector's economic responsibilities, private sector development, and privatization.

Reforming the structure of the market, regulating monopolies, and increasing competition in economic activities;

Institutional and structural reforms (regulating financial markets . . .);

Management of the resources and efficient utilization of the existing capacities;

Development of human resources, job-creation policies, and improvement of productivity;

Outward orientation (reaching foreign markets);

Non-oil export promotion;

Special planning (regional development and deregulation);

Environmental considerations (pollution control and recycling policies);

Research and Development, establishing databanks, evolving and applying information technology;

Social welfare and security;

Regulating foreign policy (detention, development and national security . . .);

Social, cultural, and political development (judicial security, establishing civil society, and the rule of law).

The above list is a combination of many old and a few new objectives that the government is setting. As past experiences have shown, however, the main issue is the successful implementation of policies and not the actual drafting of them. The same will go for the third five year plan when it is passed by the parliament. To guarantee a successful implementation, Iran will need to address issues such as management and institutional deficiencies and the interference of political consideration into economic decisions.

Qualitatively, there are a number of interesting issues in the Third Five Year Plan. These include: The country's main cultural tendency leans towards educational improvement of the young generation, reform of public beliefs, and vision of the status and role of women, promoting the notion of public participation emphasizing the principle of the rights of citizens and creating an appropriate environment for innovative minds to flourish; the government's principle in governing the country includes the growth of civil establishments for the purpose of developing national participation and supervision of the nation's various matters, institutionalizing general rights and privileges as stipulated in the Constitution, protection of civil rights, observation of the rights of freedom of thought, and speech and the rule of law; preparation of foreign policy for the purpose of strengthening the country's economic power through effective support from foreign trade development and attraction of foreign investment, and the supply of foreign resources and transfer of technology; promoting the culture of observance of law and order as the basis for national and individual security and social stability, and bringing about necessary conditions for the general public to benefit from judicial facilities; strengthening the power of overall national defense; privatization with an emphasis on its benefit and use of society's human and monetary resources and minimizing the government through cession of nongovernmental affairs; strengthening and development of a comprehensive social security system to reduce poverty, to target subsidies through a series of government-supported movements; decentralization in organizational and executing departments and transfer of power to local councils; reorganization and deregulation of government companies within the framework of commercial laws in order to eliminate cumbersome and unnecessary procedures; remedy of investment barriers, promoting production and trade, creating free market conditions and competition, revision of current regulations and creating equal conditions and opportunities for the government's financial infrastructure through a realistic national budget and avoiding increases in the government's public expenditures (stabilizing rates); reorganization of financial markets through establishment of competitive, motivated, deregulated, and unrestricted standards, and private sector cooperation; establishment of economic security through guarantee of private ownership and profit generated from economic activities within a legal framework and establishment of necessary infrastructure to attract and support direct foreign investment; unified exchange rates except in cases related to essential goods, medicine as well as services and commodities, the production and supply of which are exclusive, or that major portion of its expenses that supports low-income families; development of productive areas of employment with emphasis on creation of production related jobs especially through support of small- and medium-sized industries; promotion of non-oil exports, especially in the increase of industrial exports; establishment of suitable means for identification, support, and guidance of talent and innovation and the growth of creative and innovative mentality; emphasis on use and development of information technology in governmental and non-governmental organizations; augmenting the importance of science and technology in national development by participating in the global science/technology process and the creation of targeted connections between education, research, and technology; focus on the principles of sustainable development and environmental protection when considering investments and economic activities, bearing in mind the proportionate level of output from regenerating sources with recycling ability, reduction of pollution and wastes during production, protection of the ecosystem, and retaining environmental balance.

The important issue in the Third Plan is the fact that qualitative aspects and also the interrelation between different policy areas (especially foreign, domestic, and economic policy) have been recognized.

Quantitatively, the overall framework of the Third Plan is reflected in table 5.7:

Table 5.7: **Quantitative targets of the Third Plan (20 March 2000 to 20 March 2005)**

(five years accumulated)	Second Development Plan	Third Development Plan
Non-oil exports	Less than $17 billion	$34.5 billion
Imports	$82 billion	$112.5 billion
Inflation (annual)	26.5%	15.9%
Creation of employment opportunities	1,350,000	3,500,000

Clearly, some of the quantitative aspects of the Third Plan seem to be difficult to achieve, especially in the field of inflation. It is clear that in a time of economic adjustment and liberalization, it will be very difficult to keep inflation down. The experience of early 1990s when the liberalizing impulses of the First Plan (such as unification of exchange rates) led to inflationary results, should serve as a warning to the current government. Another quantitative target of the plan, namely an investment growth of 7.1 percent per annum, with a private sector annual investment growth of 8.5 percent, are also difficult to achieve, unless major reforms pave the way for sufficient private sector investment.

One interesting principal of the Third Plan is the planned utilization of oil export income. According to oil minister Bijan Namdar Zanganeh,[11] the Plan foresees a new approach to expending oil revenues through the Iranian government. According to Zanganeh, there will be an upper limit to the annual oil export income for the treasury. In other words, oil revenue for the government treasury will be limited to a fixed figure of US$12.50 per barrel of crude oil. Any excess income will be injected into a special account entitled the Stabilization Fund. The objective is to turn the country's underground capital into working capital for the Iranian economy, especially promoting non-oil sectors. The new approach will certainly take fuel out of those critics who argue that the Iranian government is wasting Iran's key asset by not generating new income sources for the country.

As can be seen from the above outline of the plan, the Third Plan has addressed some of the issues and has focused on institutional and legal reform, which will clearly help the economy, if correctly implemented. In the meantime, the Third Plan has been subject to severe criticism from the major political faction. On the one side, conservative forces have criticized the Third Plan as a bill that lacks any logical structure and is merely a collection of new laws and regulations; and, on the other side, leftist forces (such as the Islamic Labor Party) have criticized the Third Plan for its dedication to privatization and liberalization of the economy. Such criticism could be anticipated; therefore, it was important that the Third Plan had the initial approval of the Supreme Leader as well as the Expediency Council.

Probably the most valid critique of the Third Plan is that many proposed acts within the plan, such as privatization of entities such as the telecommunications company, certain section within the oil sector, the railways organization, and so on, are actually against the Iranian Constitution. Clearly, the Khatami administration will not earn enormous credibility for its slogan of "observance of law," if its own proposed actions are against the current Iranian Constitution. Consequently, it is clear that eventually the country will require a constitutional amendment before any major economic reforms can take place. Whether such a constitutional amendment is politically feasible will depend on the dynamics of political change in Iran. Although the recent parliamentary elections (held in February 2000) have given the majority of the Majles seats to the reformist camp, it is believed that a constitutional amendment will only be possible in Khatami's second term in office (beyond August 2001).

In the meantime, the government, strengthened through a favorable parliament, will try to find compromise solutions to achieve the objectives of the Third Plan. A good example of such compromise is the recent law passed on the establishment of private banks. Although such entities are clearly forbidden by Article 44 of the Iranian Constitution, a recent law passed by the Majles and approved by the Guardian Council has legalized private banking in Iran, which is among the key objectives of the Third Plan. Until a constitutional amendment has clarified some of the ambiguities, the government will require such additional laws to pave the way for a more liberalized economic structure.

The Key Solutions

While all the above mentioned plans and solutions are valid, the combination of economic problems and future challenges in Iran can be solved through two pillars, which are connected, that is, privatization and development of a functioning private sector on the one side, and attraction of foreign investment and technology on the other. To show the extent of the actual economic challenges, it is noteworthy that according to Deputy Foreign Minister on Economic Affairs, Mohammad Moussavi, the Iranian economy requires an investment of $100 billion in the next seven years just to keep the unemployment rate at the current level. Undoubtedly, such investment volumes can only be achieved through increased involvement of the domestic private sector and foreign investors. Clearly, the success in both these areas will depend on domestic and foreign policy developments.

The privatization process and also the consolidation of a really independent private sector will only be achieved through massive domestic policy reforms. Undoubtedly, the Khatami administration has taken important steps in this regard, not only through introduction of reforms and the promotion of civil society institutions but also through the planned decentralization of power through local council elections. The local council elections, which were held on February 26, 1999, and the consequent decentralization of the power structure, will have an enormous effect on private sector activity in Iran. Although the responsibilities of the local councils are still limited, it is expected that with time a real transfer of power from the center to the provinces will take place, which will make the relationship between the private and the public sector more transparent. Parallel to this, the government has to break the enormous state-owned enterprises, which also should be privatized or at least decentralized. Initial campaigns to restructure the huge revolutionary foundations into smaller and more targeted entities are currently being discussed. In fact, the largest such foundation, *Bonyad Mostazafin va Janbazan* (MJF), is undergoing reforms as a result of which the conglomerate will withdraw from all light industrial activities and only focus on areas that are strategic for the country and where its presence does not threaten the private sector prospects (heavy industries, petrochemicals, etc.).

The attraction of foreign investment and technology on the other side will fully depend on Iran's foreign relations. It is clear that the Khatami administration also has made significant progress on this front, especially through improved relations with the European Union and the regional countries. Iran-U.S. relations and the future of U.S. sanctions still remain an important obstacle, but analysts agree that over time this issue also will be solved. The key element for Iran will be internationally responsible behavior, which will pave the way for better relations. This, in turn, will depend on the outcome of domestic political struggles and developments; however, despite many upheavals, the trends are positive, unless one is very pessimistic.

Conclusion

The above outline has indicated that economic development in postrevolutionary Iran has been a very difficult process. The postrevolutionary economic structure and thinking had evolved around the concept of "providing for the basic needs of the society." Notwithstanding, probably because of the revolutionary approaches, the thinking has failed and today the need for a more liberalized economic structure is felt more than ever before. Evidently, the average Iranian is much worse off today that he or she was 20 years ago. Economic hardship is undoubtedly the main source of discontent with the Islamic revolution; however, as the presidential elections of 1997 indicated, the people are aware of the interaction between political and cultural reforms and economic wealth. When President Khatami was elected in 1997, he clearly had no economic plan, but within a year he produced the so-called economic recovery plan, in which he stated that the Iranian economy was "sick." This ill economy is facing huge challenges and is now waiting for a serious cure, which can only be achieved through political as well as structural and legal reforms in Iran. While the majority of the problems and potential cures have been identified by the government and other players, it is expected that the real recovery will take a few years. Before that, the country will be engaged in the process of political and cultural reforms that will need to establish the different institutions that are needed to successfully implement new economic policies. In the meantime, Iran and Iranian officials will continue the path of the past, that is, fire-fighting on different fronts and finding short-term solutions (such as debt rescheduling, bridge financing, buyback projects, etc.) in which, one has to admit, the Islamic government has been relatively efficient. In the medium to long run, however, Iran will need the real changes that will be achieved through a real privatization and the establishment of an independent private sector as well as through increased interaction with the rest of the world in form of foreign investment and technological exchange. The long-term path of development will certainly be hazardous, but Iran and Iranians have the potential and the needed resources to embark on a sound path of economic development. Economic miracles and a fast recovery from the current critical state of affairs will not be realistic, but a medium- to long-term recovery is within reach if the needed domestic and foreign policy reforms take place.

Notes

1. The Iranian Constitution was drafted by the first "Assembly of Experts," which was elected in 1979, and later approved by a public referendum in 1980.
2. In March 1993, the government devalued the Rial from Rials 70 to Rials 1,450 to one US$.
3. The official exchange rates prior to the introduction of the single exchange rate in 1993, were: official rate: Rials 70 to the dollar; and export rate: Rials 600 to the dollar. The single exchange rate, which was introduced, was close to the black market rate, which stood at Rials 1,800 to the dollar at the time.
4. In the 1992 parliamentary elections, the conservative faction had managed to win 150 out of the 270 seats in the Majles.

5. According to the Third Five-Year Plan, this rate will be phased out as of March 20, 2000.
6. Rate as of end of March 2000.
7. This rate fluctuates strongly. The rate given here refers to early April 2000.
8. For a detailed discussion of this topic, please see "Iran-e Emrooz," by Hossein Azimi, published by Daftar-e Nashr-e Farhang-e Eslami, 1378, pp. 15 to 28.
9. The results of this study were published on February 4, 1999 in the newspaper *Emrooz*.
10. Source: Ahmad Azizi, *Iran's Economy*, paper presented at Chatham House on December 3, 1998.
11. Quoted by *Iran Energy Focus*, Vol. 1, No. 16, September 1, 1999, p. 8.

6

The Rule of the Religious Jurist in Iran

Abdulaziz Sachedina

In our discussion of the doctrine of *wilayat al-faqih* (Farsi, *velayat-i faqih*)(the rule of the religious jurist) in Iran since the Islamic Revolution of 1979, we will not be concerned with the content of the doctrine, or with those proofs that had been used to support it, or, except perhaps in passing, with its exposition by Shii jurists before Ayatollah Khomeini. Our concern here will be rather with the political context in which the doctrine has been enunciated and developed in Iran since the revolution, and the political and legal consequences of its elaboration. I have made every effort to be as objective and neutral as possible on the subject, but inevitably value judgments will creep in if only through what I have selected as the pertinent facts.

Following the landslide victory of Sayyid Mohammad Khatami in 1997, Iranians enjoyed an unusual sense of political achievement. A cartoon in the Arabic-language daily *Al-Hayat* depicted Khatami standing in front of a large open window, suggesting that fresh air from outside had brought Iran's political isolation to an end. By electing Khatami president, the Iranian people had sent a message to the religious establishment that they were determined to exercise their democratic right to elect a person of their choosing—albeit from among an officially approved list of candidates—even though it meant ignoring the endorsement of another candidate by the spiritual leader of the country.

Khatami's election was in no way a vote against Islam as the source of the nation's spiritual and moral values. On the contrary, he, too, had been on the approved list of candidates drawn up by the Council of Guardians, which meant that his Islamic credentials were unquestioned. Nonetheless, his victory did mean the defeat of the candidate favored by the establishment, so the immediate concern at Qom was to find a face-saving device to explain that defeat and to consider how to deal with the election of a relatively liberal member of the religious class. It was almost two weeks following Khatami's victory that Ayatollah Javadi Amoli, the influential *imam juma* of Qom, used the Friday sermon to express Qom's satisfaction with the outcome of the election and congratulate Khatami publicly for his stunning political victory.

Qom was fully aware of Khatami's relatively liberal views: His campaign promises had included policies that were bound to raise opposition from the conservative camp, including appointing women to high public office and improving relations through dialogue rather than confrontation between Islam and the West. Moves like these were bound to meet with opposition from the conservative members of parliament, including its reconfirmed speaker Nateq-Nuri.

There were two reasons for concern over Khatami's ability to handle the opposition and avoid constant challenges to his power. The first was that Khatami did not—Hashemi Rafsanjani did—have the political acumen needed to run a complex government. The second was that Khatami's relationship with the religious establishment in Qom was cool. The message of congratulation following the elections was a tactical maneuver to put to rest any fears that a power struggle might ensue over ideological differences between the president and the seminarians, but it was not meant to warm up relations. There were serious doubts that Khatami could muster the necessary support for his non-isolationist foreign policy and liberalization projects at home.

The struggle between the two would have a long-term impact on the direction Iran would take as a modern Islamic state, and it needed to be resolved if Khatami's proposed transformation of Iranian political society into a truly civil one was to be successful. The major ideological power was in the hands of the constitutionally mandated post of *vali-e faqih* (ruling jurist) who had unlimited authority; he could nullify any act that he considered to be contrary to the interests of Islam. Since Ayatollah Khomeini's death in 1989, however, insurmountable difficulties had kept that position vacant.

Religious Leadership in Shii Islam

Unlike the Sunni Muslims, the Shii look to their religious leaders for political and social as well as religious guidance. Until the Islamic Republic of Iran came into being in 1979, they also had a procedure for determining who the so-called governing jurist, this most learned authority and source of guidance, was to be, but after the revolution the position[1] had been incorporated into the constitution and determining what qualified Shii *mujtahid* (jurisconsult) would occupy the post entangled the selection process in politics by making it an ideologically defined position.

In the last decade, in particular, controversy over the religious leadership of the ayatollahs at the international level and the spiritual leadership of the Iranian nation under its governing jurist has flared up more than once. The death one after the other of the senior members of the Shii religious establishment, including, in addition to Ayatollah Khomeini (d. 1989) himself, ayatollahs Khoie (d. 1992), Golpaygani (d. 1993) and Araki (d. 1994), has left the community to fall back on candidates from among the succeeding generation of scholars whose leadership, for mostly practical reasons, has yet to be approved by the authorities who represent the various interest groups in the worldwide Shii community.

The traditionally recognized criteria for determining whether a *mujtahid* was qualified to assume the position of the *marja-i taqlid* (supreme legal authority) are dictated by the conservatives in the Shii centers of religious learning in Qom and Najaf (in Iraq). Among them, vision about the future of the widely dispersed Shii community is totally lacking. The same conservative spirit has also prevented the religious centers from producing a set of objective criteria and a well-defined mechanism that would allow for the smooth transition of religious-juridical authority from one ayatollah to the next in the highly technocratic world of today.

A further complication in determining the *marja* has arisen, since the Iranian government formally placed the position under the rule of religious jurist (*velayat-i faqih*), as defined by the Ayatollah Khomeini, in the Iranian national constitution. Consequently, whether the government of Iran likes it or not, the choice of the *marja* has become enmeshed in Iranian national politics, undoubtedly because the government has a stake in who assumes the supreme religious authority. The *marja* was instituted to provide the necessary Islamic legitimacy to the Shii nation-state of Iran. In addition, it is in large measure responsible for providing the cohesion needed to maintain the spiritual, moral, and sociopolitical identity of the Iranian Shiis. It is precisely the nationalistic orientation of the *marja* that is at odds with the generally held belief among Shii Muslims that it is a universally recognized position. To exacerbate the situation further, Iranian efforts to obtain worldwide Shii acknowledgment of "the rule of religious jurist" as defined by Ayatollah Khomeini have not been supported by other leading ayatollahs and their followers among the Shii community at large.

For the Shii community around the world, the question is not merely who is next in line to be *marja*, but more practically how to avoid the decision's being determined by politics in Iran or, for that matter, Iraq. The community has had a long history of living under unfriendly governments and at times as a persecuted minority, and of safeguarding its religious autonomy against pressures to have a particular *marja* accepted. Shii leaders, whether in Iran or elsewhere, are fully aware that selection of the *marja* is a religious duty imposed upon the believer as a matter of conscience; it is not an obligation that can be enjoined by the collective decision of the government or of community leaders.

When the supreme religious office of the *marja* was incorporated into the national constitution, both the Iranian government and the Shii community had to fall back on an inadequate and mostly unwritten traditional system of transferring religious authority to the next *marja*. Its inadequacy has not crippled the everyday religious lives of the Shii community, but it has posed an urgent national problem in the long run. Iran cannot afford to continue the present inevitable division of the *marja* into political and religious functions, as has been done since the death of Ayatollah Khomeini. This division not only threatens to destabilize the delicate consensus supporting Iran's integrated politico-religious administrative system; it also has the potential of dividing its citizens into different religious camps, each holding its own uncompromising position on the question of the "rule by the religious jurist."

In the absence of traditionally admitted criteria for filling the supreme juridical office of the *marja* since Khomeini's death, Iran has acknowledged, albeit tacitly, the constitutionally promulgated position held by Khamenei, in addition to the traditional and mostly ceremonial position, as far as the government's day-to-day functioning is concerned, of the *marja-i taqlid*, held successively by the late ayatollahs Golpaygani and Araki. Neither Khoie nor his disciples have conceded the legality of the political power vested in the *marja* through the concept of the governance of the jurist.

To understand the present crisis faced by the Shii community, it is important to understand Sunni-Shii aspirations in matters of religious leadership, which is central to Islam in general and to Shiism in particular. The founder of Islam was not only a spiritual head of the community; he also was the political head of its public order. Islam could, therefore, never recognize anything resembling the Western principle of the "separation of church and state" in its constitution, because both religious and temporal authorities were vested in the single person of Muhammad the Prophet. This dual role of the Prophet was at the root of the crisis of leadership that followed his death in 632 C. E. The division of the Muslims into Sunni and Shii factions was the direct consequence of the way prominent members of the early community defined the role of the leader, the caliph/imam, once the Prophet's divinely sanctioned dual authority had ended.

The consensus that gradually emerged among Sunni theologians denied the extension of the Prophet's religious authority to the caliphs. Instead, the caliph or imam was to be the political head of the state; specialists, collectively known as the ulama, were to provide religious leadership. This solution to the *fait accompli* in community leadership in practice led to the separation of religious and political authorities in Sunni Islam, with the former being institutionalized as part of the administrative structure of the caliphal state.

The Shii understanding of the Prophet's mission, in contrast, was based entirely on religious idealism. If the purpose of appointing a prophet for a community is to establish an ideal public order, can the community afford to overlook the qualifications of the Prophet's successor? Ensuring qualified leadership for the religious community was central to Shii belief. The Shii imam in theory was invested with the dual—spiritual and temporal—authority of the Prophet. It was unthinkable, Shiis argued, that God would require Muslims to build an ideal community without providing adequate guidance through the Prophet's successors. They believed that God had actually appointed a series of qualified imams through the Prophet, but that the community at large had rejected them. The last, the Twelfth, of the Imams, according to Shii belief, has been living an invisible existence since the tenth century. He is the ideal ruler of the Muslim community, the Mahdi who will come at the end of time when God invests him with the final command to establish the ideal government on earth.[2]

Shii Leadership during the Post-Occultation Period

Shiism offers the modern world with a rare glimpse of the dynamics of religious ideology that postulates active divine intervention into human history to enable humanity to build an ideal public order.[3] Shii legal theologians have at different times in history undertaken to interpret the parameters of divine intervention for the construction of this new polity.

One of the major questions that arises in the minds of pious Muslims is how to explain the existence of injustice in society and what the obligation of the community is in dealing with it.[4] The response to the question depends upon the circumstances of a given time and is conditioned by the precedents set by the imams whose answers to similar situations are treated as binding precedents for their followers.

Historically, the guidance of Shii scholars, whether leading to radical political action or not, has turned on their interpretation of the two basic doctrines intrinsic to an authoritative perspective or worldview that organizes the mundane existence of the Shii community. These two doctrines are the justice (*al-'adl*) of God and the leadership (*al-imma*) of righteous individuals in upholding and promulgating the rule of justice and equity. In the highly politicized world of early Islam, there were numerous ideas and conceptions about God's purpose on earth and the leadership of human society. The swift conquest of vast territories and the supervision of these conquests and of the affairs of the conquered peoples not only demanded strong and astute leadership; it also required a system that would ensure stability and prosperity. Central to this social, political, and economic activity was the promise of Islamic revelation that only through obedience to God would believers create a just and equitable public order embodying His will.[5]

From its inception, Shii religious thought has given a central position to the question of religious leadership. The question assumed critical importance during the absence of the theological leadership of the imams from among the Prophet's descendants. This is reflected in the debate among the Shiis regarding the propriety of religious scholars assuming the leadership of the Shii community as the specifically designated deputies of the Twelfth Imam, who disappeared in 874 and would reappear at the end of time. Regardless of the importance attached to the continuation of religious and moral guidance, the Shiis needed to survive under the prevailing governments of their times; not just anyone could guide the community.

The position of the jurist as the guardian of the community became definitively institutionalized and centralized in the eighteenth century, when the jurists writing under the Qajar dynasty formulated their notion of the supreme legal authority in Shiism. The centralization of the juridical authority came about through the legal doctrine of *taqlid*. *Taqlid*, meaning "following or emulating a religious authority in matters of *shariah*," was regarded by classical scholars of law as a way of providing some kind of uniformity of practice within each school of legal thought.

The Shii jurists extended the function of *taqlid* by requiring their followers to abide by the rulings of the most learned among their class. The *mujtahid* then became the source of emulation (*marja*) in the matters of legal prescriptions. This was the idea behind the *marja-i taqlid*. It is important to bear in mind that from then until this very day, the *marja-i taqlid* has always been conceived in terms of guardianship and not of governance.

With the weakening of the political authority of the Shii rulers, the *marja-i taqlid* as governor became a viable alternative, as in the popular Shii perception that he was the designated deputy of the Twelfth Imam, authorized to assume the duty of guiding and governing the community during the imam's absence. The *mujtahid*, who held the position of *marja-i taqlid*, then came to be entrusted with the job of rationally interpreting (*ijtihad*) the sources of Islamic jurisprudence, the Quran and the Sunna, in terms of contemporary sociopolitical exigencies. His rulings in all matters were binding. Through a process of deductive reasoning, the jurists were able to legitimize their authority in the community and make it obligatory for all the Shiis to follow the *marja-i taqlid* in religious practice.[6]

The loyalty of the Shiis to the *marja-i taqlid* depended on his reputation.[7] His standing as the most learned was established through his publications on religious subjects and the training of disciples. His character was established by his piety, which qualified him, among other things, to receive the religiously ordained taxes for distribution among the needy.

The emergence of the *marja-i taqlid* as the supreme leader of the community was a gradual process. Although the Shii popular belief today is that an ayatollah whose knowledge and moral probity are beyond question functions as the deputy of the hidden Twelfth Imam, exercising the latter's spiritual-juridical authority in the community, there is nothing in the classical tradition about it. On the contrary, tradition clearly points to the collective responsibility of the Shii community to ensure its religious well-being by investing in the training of talented minds to discover the divine purpose for the community in the elaboration of the *shariah*. These "specialists" can then manage the community's religious affairs by providing it with legal and moral guidance through the interpretation of the Quran and the teachings of the Prophet and the imams. They also supervise its financial affairs through the collection and distribution of religious donations—*zakat* (alms) and *khums* (a 20 percent tithe on income). In due course, these supervisory and managerial roles became institutionalized in *velayat-i faqih*, but its scope was strictly limited to applied Islamic law and spirituality. Governance by the jurist at this point suggested a collective responsibility that could be shared by several well-qualified *mujtahid*s. It was understood as a kind of general deputyship on behalf of the Hidden Imam without any specific designation of a leading specialist in religious matters.

The lack of specificity regarding how the community leader should be chosen was detrimental to the community's sense of religious autonomy and unity, especially when the Shii dynasties that ruled Iran beginning in the sixteenth century came to power. The Shii rulers manipulated the religious leadership, and followed the Sunni state policy in reducing its once independent religious leadership to an officially appointed administrator. Not all *mujtahid*s succumbed to this stagecraft, but the only way to preserve their independence was to keep the community loyal to the religious leaders by engaging in a fresh interpretation of legal doctrines. It was time for reform.

The Centralization of the Shii Religious Leadership

Reforms began in the procedures used to determine the most qualified scholar capable of exercising juridical authority in the absence of the last Imam. If the religious leadership and the community were to steer clear of the menace of the Shii rulers, then some legal mechanism requiring the Shiis to declare their allegiance to the *mujtahid* was necessary. Hence, the ruling requiring the emulation (*taqlid*) of a well-qualified *marja-i tailid* was made part of the believer's religiously ordained duty.[8] Without such a declaration, the Shiis were taught, their religious acts were invalid. This process of *taqlid* allowed a specific Shii *mujtahid* to emerge as the supreme religious leader without interference from the Shii rulers.[9]

The presumption that the Hidden Imam had a deputy was the cornerstone of the emerging institution of *marja-i taqlid,* which was, again in the popular imagination, more than merely the "supreme legal authority accepted for emulation." The *marja* symbolized the supreme religious authority, but in function he resembled the Hidden Imam himself. Such an elevation of the *mujtahid*'s position was inevitable in a community that had come to believe that the Hidden Imam was in constant communication with the leading *mujtahid*s, protecting them from committing errors of judgment. The importance of these popular beliefs in their overall influence on the formation of Shii political culture in Iran cannot be overestimated. The loyalty that binds the popularly acknowledged religious leader to the community is unique to Shii Muslims. Without such *marja*

The Rule of the Religious Jurist in Iran 131

(loyalty), the Iranian revolution would probably never have gotten off the ground in the late 1970s.[10]

"The Rule of the Religious Jurist" since the Islamic Revolution

The elaboration of the doctrine of *velayat-i faqih* has frequently been determined in the history of Shiism by the political context and even by the changing outlook and application of the jurists themselves. Ayatollah Khomeini's treatment of the principle of *velayat-i faqih* corroborates this changing perspective. There is a noticeable and significant difference between his prerevolutionary and postrevolutionary position vis-à-vis one controversial aspect of the political authority of the jurist, namely, whether or not it is all-comprehensive and absolute like that of the infallible imam. Khomeini's earliest public statement regarding the "governance of the Jurist" appeared in the work entitled: *Kashf-i asrar* (Unveiling the Secrets),[11] a detailed response to an anti-religious tract that included criticism of claims to political power by a *mujtahid*. The concept of *velayat-i faqih* in *Kashf-i asrar* is presented in the cautious, traditional terms used by prominent jurists of the Qajar and post-Qajar era. He remarks that the doctrine has been controversial from the beginning, as jurists disagree among themselves on the "fundamental question of whether [a jurist] possesses the *wilayat,* and [if he does] the extent of *wilayat,* [and] the scope of its jurisdiction [which happens to be a matter related to the juristic practice]."[12] He makes it clear that just because jurists possess both *hukumat* (the authority to administer justice) and *wilayat* does not mean that they are simultaneously "king, vizier, and general." Khomeini proposes the establishment of an assembly made up of the qualified, God-fearing jurists to replace the corrupt assembly (*majles*) under the Shah. This new body can then elect a just ruler (*sultan adil*) who will not resist divine laws and will not rule unjustly and tyrannically.[13] If the consultative assembly (*majles-i shura*) is composed of the pious jurists or is kept under their supervision, as required by the constitution, then the state will achieve its goal of preserving justice and promoting the general welfare. In other words, Khomeini's proposal does not rule out the possibility that a just ruler could be the executive arm of a legitimately established Majles of jurists.

His concluding observation deals with the peaceful role played by the *mujtahids* in the Islamic world. They, Khomeini notes, did not oppose their countries even when they encountered unjust conduct by rulers and recognized the unjust system they perpetrated. This pacifist attitude of the *mujtahids* means that when they speak about the limits to their right to administer justice (*hukumat*) or to exercise their *wilayat* (Persian *velayat*), they do not go beyond the few functions specified in the jurisprudence, including "the authority [*wilayat*] to issue judicial decisions, to adjudicate, and to intervene in protecting the property of a minor or of a legally incapacitated person. They never mention political authority (*hukumat*) or political power (*saltanah*) as being among their functions, though they are fully aware that, except for the law of God, all other legal systems [which originated in Europe] are invalid and ill-suited [to the Muslim peoples]. They respect these ill-suited laws and do not reject them, believing that they should be tolerated so long as the system does not improve."[14]

This hesitant attitude in *Kashf-i asrar* changed to a more activist attitude in the celebrated Najaf lectures of 1970 regarding the authority of the jurist in the Shii nation, which culminated in the present doctrine of *velayat-i faqih*. The title he gave to these lectures, *al-Hukumat al-Islamiyyah* (Islamic Government), suggests that the principle of *velayat-i faqih* was changed into a form of government that required the subordination of political power (*saltanah*) to the divine norms elaborated in Islamic jurisprudence. In other words, an Islamic government is one in which the religious-moral authority of the jurists prevails in all its branches—legislative, executive, and judicial. The lectures accordingly stressed how urgent it was for jurists to assume positions of responsibility and actualize the goals of divine governance.

Ayatollah Khomeini then introduces *velayat-i faqih* as a "subject that in itself elicits immediate assent and has little need of demonstration to anyone who has some general awareness of beliefs and ordinances of Islam." He attributes the controversies surrounding it to the "social circumstances prevailing among the Muslims in general and in the teaching institution (*hawza-yi ilmiyya*) in particular," in Iran.[15]

Undoubtedly, the single most important question that still dominates the controversy over the *wilayah* among religious scholars is that of the scope of the jurist's political authority in a modern nation state that has invested ultimate authority in a constitution. Relatively few jurists are ready to concede that the *wilayah* of a jurist constitutes more than what Khomeini regarded as his legitimate functions, as enumerated in his *Kashf-i asrar*.[16] Although he expressed general agreement with traditional judicial opinions even in the Najaf lectures, in spite of his assertion that the jurist had the ability and the right to assume broader political powers in a Shii state, Khomeini did not claim that the *wilayah* was absolute (*mut-*

The Rule of the Religious Jurist in Iran 133

laqah) and comprehensive (*ammah*) for the *mujtahid*, as he was later to maintain in his *fatwa* of January 7, 1988.[17]

Following the overthrow of the Shah's regime and the institution of the Islamic Republic, but before he issued his *fatwa*, Ayatollah Khomeini rarely referred to the principle of *velayat-i faqih* in his declarations. In line with his Najaf lectures, he constantly referred to the "Islamic government" (*hukumat-i islami*) and, following the establishment of the republic to the "Islamic Republic" (*jumhuri-yi islami*) in the place of *velayat-i faqih*. This silence on the subject of *velayat-i faqih* led Professor Hamid Algar in the early 1979 to ask a prominent member of the Revolutionary Council, who at that time was visiting the United States, whether in his opinion the form of government to be established after the revolution would incorporate the principle of *velayat-i faqih*. The visitor replied with a categorical denial, saying that "Imam Khomeini had not been heard to speak about *velayat-i faqih* for a long time; and it was highly unlikely that he himself still believed in the necessity or the legitimacy of this principle."[18] Even during the drafting of the constitution, according to Bani Asadi, who was the Minister of Justice in the provisional government under Mehdi Bazargan, when the draft constitution had been presented to Khomeini, he had made no notable objections to it nor had he insisted on the insertion of the concept of *velayat-i faqih*.[19]

Judging from the statements regarding the role of the *mujtahid* in the Shii state in *Kashf-i asrar* and the Najaf lectures, however, the notion of the *wilayat* was not only still present in Khomeini's mind when he assumed power in 1979, it was also the only valid juridical source for legitimating his own as well as his provisional government's authority, once he had named Mehdi Bazargan as the prime minister. In his statement following Bazargan's appointment Khomeini declared:

> "By virtue of the governing authority (*wilayat*) that I have from the sacred legislator (*shari-'i muqaddas*), I have appointed him [Mehdi Bazargan] and it is therefore necessary to obey him."[20]

The implications of this statement delegating authority are important. First, by virtue of the *velayat-i faqih*, Khomeini saw himself as possessing the juridically conferred authority to designate Mehdi Bazargan to head the government of Iran. Second, because of the religiously ordained nature of his authority as the "general deputy," representing the infallible Imam, obedience to Khomeini's decree, and, more immediately, to his appointee, was obligatory. This statement should therefore be regarded as the logical conclusion of Khomeini's adumbration of the juridical authority in his *Kashf-i asrar,* where he explicitly maintains that God's government cannot be established without the *mujtahid*'s direct supervision,[21] and which antedates the terms of its enshrinement in Chapter 8 of the Constitution of the Islamic Republic, which is entirely devoted to *velayat-i faqih.*[22]

As Khomeini's proclamation indicates, the broad interpretation of the principle had implications for the doctrine of the theological imamate. In some ways, it is argued by those who were suspicious of such an arrogation of the infallible Imam's authority on the part of the jurist, the ideological confusion over the power of the jurist has beset Iran ever since.[23] This confusion stems from combining the constitutional principle of the sovereignty of the people as exercised through their elective representatives in the modern state and the principle of religiously invested sovereignty, which, if implemented absolutely through the office of *vali-e faqih,* can render the constitution invalid.[24] In other words, some kind of tension or even contradiction was built into the imperfect compromise worked out between the principle of religiously ordained absolute sovereignty of the person holding the *wilayat* and the constitutionally founded sovereignty by the people.

Because the confusion and the problems that arose in postrevolutionary Iran in the exercise of power by the various branches of government, especially the legislative and the executive, can be traced back to the new political system under the *velayat-i faqih,* it seems paradoxical that no attempt was made to undertake a serious theoretical consideration of this central principle before the January 7 *fatwa* was issued.[25] In the centers of Shii learning, the religious establishment had misgivings about the claim to all-inclusive *wilayat* by the jurists in the light of their perceived role as the protectors of the people's sovereignty and independence, but they were understandably silent on the subject, because the official position stated by Khomeini in the most explicit terms was that "opposition to *velayat-i faqih* is denying the imams and Islam."[26] Unquestionably, the triumph of the revolution under the religious leadership was assumed, at least by those in the government, as the government of the deputy of the Hidden Imam, the functional imam, Ayatollah Khomeini.

This clarification of the scope and meaning of the *velayat-i faqih* in 1988 had to await the crisis created by the failure of the government after the revolution to resolve important problems of society and the economy in accordance with Islamic laws and criteria. In the meantime, unresolved questions about a number of legislative measures caused the reappearance of the never-ending debate between those religious scholars who take the prohibition of human prerogative to legislate in the narrow and literal sense and those who, on the contrary, would permit further legislation on the grounds that to use traditional jurisprudence as guidelines was insufficient for solving the complex problems faced by a modern society.[27] The question of the Islamic propriety—that is, the legal validity—of measures passed by the parliament and the important figures in the government indirectly cast doubt on the assertion of the religious class that in the modern age Islam, as a way of life, had its own distinctive solution to the main problems of humanity, and it challenged the ability of the jurists to provide coherent responses to concrete questions such as the redistribution of land for public benefit, or intervention into relations between the employer and the employee to attain some measure of justice for which traditional jurisprudence had no solution.[28]

The dichotomy between human legislation in a modern parliament and the Islamic propriety of undertaking such an activity was apparently the reason behind the establishment of the Council of Guardians, which was formally appointed to ensure that legislation was in conformity with the *shariah*. On several occasions, the parliament encountered opposition from the Council of the Guardians for passing measures contrary to traditional jurisprudence. A number of matters dealing with urban real estate, environmental protection, nationalization of foreign trade, and so on were held up because of unresolved differences of opinion between the Majles and the Council.

These persistent deadlocks in determining the scope of the power of the state to intervene in matters that assured some measure of justice in the society served as the background to Khomeini's *fatwa* asserting the supremacy of the Islamic state under the *velayat-i faqih* for preserving the welfare of its citizens. The *fatwa* was issued in the form of a letter to the then President Ali Khamenei, whose Friday sermon had touched upon a sensitive matter in the Prophet Muhammad's mission on earth. Apparently, Khamenei had concluded that the Prophet's function was to deliver the religious message and that the creation of a state had not been within the scope of his primary mission. Khomeini published his response, which, after some preliminaries, went as follows:

> It appears from your excellency's statements at the Friday prayer that you do not regard government to be equivalent to the absolute governance (*wilayat-i mutlaqa*), which was bestowed on the most noble Prophet (peace be upon him and his progeny) by God, and which is the most important part

of the divinely ordained position, and which has preponderance over all other ordinances that are dependent upon his position (as *wali-yi mutlaq*). Your interpretation of what I have said—that the government is empowered to act only within the framework of the existing [secondary] divine ordinances [preserved in the *shariah*]—runs entirely counter to what I have in fact said. Were the powers of government to lie only within the framework of secondary divine decrees, the designation of the divine government and of absolute deputed guardianship (*wilayat-i mutlaqa-yi mufawwada*) to the Prophet of Islam (peace be upon him and his progeny) would have been in practice entirely without meaning and content. Let me refer to some of the consequences of such a view—consequences which no one could accept.[29] For example, the laying of roads that necessitates the confiscation of houses or of the land on which they stand is not provided for within the framework of the secondary divine ordinances. Military conscription and the compulsory dispatch of soldiers to the front; forbidding the import or export of foreign currency, or of various kinds of goods; the prohibition of hoarding; customs duties, taxation,[30] the prohibition of exorbitant pricing, price regulation; the prohibition of narcotics and addiction, with the exception of alcoholic drinks; the prohibition against bearing all kinds of arms; and hundreds of similar measures, none of these, according to your interpretation, are among the powers of the state. *I must point out, the government which is a branch of the absolute governance of the Prophet of God is among the primary ordinances of Islam, and has precedence over all secondary ordinances such as prayer, fasting, and pilgrimage* [my emphasis].[31]

This last statement is the key passage of the *fatwa*, and it has been interpreted in a variety of ways, both in Iran and among the scholars of Middle Eastern studies in the West. The apparent sense of Khomeini's declaration is that political considerations can override the tenets of the *shariah*, and this is the sense in which most Western scholars have taken it; such an interpretation finds support in the political history of Islam as well, as those in power, whether the Sunni caliphs or de facto sultans, did in fact overrule the dictates of the *shariah* whenever political expediency required it.

When examined in the context of Shii rational theology, however, the statement is the reassertion of a fundamental belief among the Shiis and the Mutazilites of the essential interrelationship between the divinely ordained absolute, infallible religious leadership (the Prophethood or the Imamate), and the creation of the divinely sanctioned order. The existence of the government under the Prophet or the imams is regarded as a fundamental prerequisite to the performance of the secondary divine ordinances elaborated in the *'ibadat* (the God-human relationship) and *mu'amalat* (the human-human relationship). Accordingly, the existence and consolidation of the government belong to the divinely mandated institutions that have priority over secondary ordinances such as prayers, fasting, and so on in the *shariah*. In other words, the primary expression of the Islamic belief system is not the conventional fundamental pillars of the Islamic faith, but rather the comprehensive relationship of the Muslim community to the legitimately constituted authority in Islamic public order. This is the meaning of the cardinal doctrine of *wilayah,* and it is the sole criterion for judging true faith in Shiism.[32]

Thus, there are no grounds for claiming a doctrinal breach in a *fatwa* when the Islamic government is declared to be so all-inclusive that it can decide all matters pertaining to the welfare of the people, even if it means overriding secondary ordinances if necessary. Investing this deputized absolute *wilayat* of the Prophet and the imams (protected by infallibility [*isma*] against committing acts of injustice) to the government headed by a jurist (regarded as being in possession of sound belief, knowledge, and character [*adalah*]), however, raises the ever-present suspicion in the Shii juridical writings as to the legitimacy of anyone claiming the absolute, all-powerful authority of the infallible leader during occultation.

More indicative of this transformation to all-powerful *velayat-i faqih* was Khomeini's statement (in the same *fatwa,* following the key declaration) that the Islamic "government can unilaterally abrogate legal (*shari*) contracts it has concluded with its own people whenever the contract is contrary to the interests of the country and of Islam." In other words, the government under the governing jurist can exercise unrestricted power over matters that have traditionally been part of the *mu'amalat* (interpersonal, human-human relationship) section of the jurisprudence in the—undefined—"interest of the country and Islam." The constitution that served as the protector of people's sovereignty subjected to the absolute power of Islamic leadership under the aegis of *velayat-i faqih*—the only entity qualified to define the parameters of the "interest of the country and Islam." The Islamic government, hence, was empowered to

> prevent any act performed as part of one's relationship to God (*abadi*) or otherwise in nature, the fulfillment of which runs counter to the interests of Islam, as long as it continues to be harmful to Islam. For example, it can temporarily forbid the performance of annual pilgrimage (*hajj*), one of the most important duties decreed by God, whenever a pilgrimage is contrary

to the welfare of Islam. What has previously been said or is now being said on the subject [of the *velayat-i faqih*] derives from an inadequate knowledge of the *wilayat-i mutlaqa* (absolute governance).

What was in fact said at that time was that all jurisprudence in its classical formulations would be rendered null and void, because of the powers that the Islamic government could claim in the interest of the country and Islam.

Khomeini's innovative exposition of *velayat-i faqih* in this *fatwa* was intended to provide solutions to the practical socioeconomic problems at the legal-theoretical level by empowering the Majles to enact legislation. Ever since the establishment of the Islamic Republic, it had been faced with fundamental questions about the propriety of enacting laws for a modern nation-state. It was also meant to confer on the Majles the religious legitimacy to allow the execution of its decisions in conformity with the "interests of Islam and society." This was predictably reflected in Khamenei's interpretation of Khomeini's *fatwa* when in its support he declared that the jurist who holds the *velayat-i faqih* should be obeyed because his command is "the command of God. and, it is, therefore, religiously incumbent [upon the people] to obey (*wajibu'l-ita'at*) him."[33] In addition, Khamenei asserted that the *vali-e faqih* was the only source of religious authorization not only for the Majles but also for all branches of government, and even of the constitution of the Islamic Republic,

> which provides the criteria and framework for all legislation [and] derives its consideration (*i'tibar*) from being accepted and confirmed by the *wali-yi faqih*. . . . The validity of all organs of government depends on the *wali-yi faqih*. To oppose it [government] is prohibited (*haram*) and a major [cardinal] sin, because it is being instituted by the *vali-e faqih*, with the permission of God.[34]

Such absolute interpretation of the *fatwa* by the then President of Iran meant elevating the *marja-i taqlid* (the most learned juridical authority in the Shii community) to the absolute ruler of the Shiis, whose unrestricted authority allowed all governmental institutions to function. It also marked the permanent breach between the office of the *marja*, however, which also included the limited *wilayah* (guardianship) traditionally conceived in jurisprudence, and the virtually unrestricted *wilayat* expounded by Khomeini in his position as one of the *marja*, and promulgated in the modern constitution of Iran.

These ramifications became obvious when Imam Khomeini died in 1989, leaving his position as *marja* to be filled by other leading jurists. But his position as the *vali-e faqih*, in theory at least, could not be assumed except by another *marja* of similar status in learning and piety. To accommodate this vacuum in the constitutionally ratified leadership of the Shii polity, the Council of Guardians was forced to abandon a well-established tradition in Shii Islam, namely, the recognition of the juridical excellence of the *mujtahid* before declaring one's allegiance to that authority as the *marja-i taqlid* and *vali-e faqih*. There was no provision in the traditionally expounded principle of *velayat-i faqih*, even in its limited form, for a non-*mujtahid* to assume the position of the Guardian Jurist. It was only through a constitutional provision that Hojjatolislam 'Ali Khamenei could be elevated to the position of an ayatollah. The assumption of the position of *vali-e faqih*, however, as with Ayatollah Khomeini, for someone without the qualifications required of a *mujtahid*, was not possible without circumventing the well-known prerequisites.[35] This was probably gotten around by substituting the more political, even Sunni, title of *vali-e amr-i muslimin* (the person in whom authority to manage the affairs of the Muslims has been invested[36]) for Ayatollah Khamenei, as religious leader in the Islamic Republic of Iran. Whereas traditionally, loyalty and devotion to the religious leaders in Shiism had always been a matter of individual consent, now loyalty to the Ayatollah Khamenei, as the holder of the office of the *vali-e faqih*, was prescribed by the Constitution of Iran.

Velayat-i faqih in the Post-Khomeini Era

Ayatollah Khomeini's reinterpretation of the concept of the "governance of the jurist" went beyond the function of providing guardianship to a community deprived of the Hidden Imam's guidance. Under Khomeini, the concept emerged as the source of legitimate sovereign authority in the modern Shii state. This innovative extrapolation and its concretization in the modern nation state of Iran to provide for an Islamic republic under "the governance of the jurist" was problematic in three ways. First, there was nothing in Shii jurisprudence to rule out there being more than one governing *marja*. Thus, there could be more than one qualified *mujtahid* to exercise authority in the Shii state, giving rise to the problem of deciding which *marja* was the most acceptable to the state.

Second was the problem of "nationalizing" a transnational Shariah-based position of the *marja* that bound the Shiis together, regardless of the believer's national or ethnic affiliations, in a state that was bound by the norms of international public order. By ordaining a constitutional position to the supreme religious authority, Iran was indirectly engaged in appropriating the loyalty of the entire Shii community for the nation-state of Iran. It overlooked the religious implications of creating a modern territorial state under the inherently transnational and transcultural Khomeini concept of "the governance of the jurist," which claimed that together with the obligation of acknowledging the supreme holder of that position was attached the God-given right of the Shii Muslims to live under his rule. The Shii right to Iran, then, would be on the same principle as the one that allowed the Jews in the Diaspora to claim a divinely ordained right to Palestine. Such an oversight on the part of the Muslim religious leaders is not surprising. Even now, the *ulama* continue to think in terms defined by an Islamic legal tradition that never imagined such a thing as a world made up of a community of nation-states. The *shariah* always spoke in terms of the Ummah, the religious-political community under God's representative on earth, whereas the presuppositions that govern the establishment of a modern sovereign state regard territorial integrity as the fundamental principle of its claim to independent statehood.

Third was the problem of promulgating the position of the *marja* as a state functionary, which required the government to fill this position with a qualified *mujtahid*. By using the model of leadership provided by the Ayatollah Khomeini, who was able to fill in both the traditional and the constitutional roles of the state *marja*, the government of Iran was inadvertently laying the foundation for the future division of the Shii religious leadership. Careful examination of Ayatollah Shariatmadari's criticism of the constitutional deliberations in the early 1980s reveals that he was aware of the problem when he raised a critical question about the continuity of "the governance of the jurist" in the post-Khomeini era. Both he and other leading ayatollahs at that time predicted that the traditionally independent position of the *marja* was bound to be compromised when it was established as an arm of the state under the concept of "the governance of the jurist," leaving the community to continue to choose its own *marja*.

Institutionalizing the *marja* through the constitution was meant to overcome the problem of plurality of the *marja* in the area of "the governance of the jurist," without which the smooth functioning of the state was impossible. The conventional juridical individualism and resulting independence enjoyed by the *mujtahid*s in discovering the divine purposes for the Muslim community could and did create an explosive situation, as was affirmed in Ayatollah Montazeri's public criticisms of the political conduct of the Islamic government, with its far-reaching impact on the future of the Islamic republic under an ayatollah.

It was to minimize the occurrence of such episodes that, according to the doctrine of the "governance of the jurist" as formulated by Ayatollah Khomeini, if and when such a qualified person existed, then the entire community was under the religious obligation to accept his authority both as a religious and a constitutional leader and obey him in all his directives in the interest of Islam and Muslims. What that interest might be, of course, had to be defined by the holder of that office. Such extrapolations regarding the political authority of the *marja* as the "guardian of Muslim affairs" (*vali-e amr-i muslimin*) were clearly based on the Islamic legal assumption that this governance would be exercised in a transnational Shii polity where all believers would enjoy equal rights of settlement. Hence, promulgation of the notion of the "governance of the jurist" in a modern nation-state, regardless of its being part of the legitimate constitution of Iran, runs into direct conflict with the transnational character of the *shariah*-based institution. This has led to exactly the opposite result from the one Imam Khomeini intended with his integration of civil and religious authorities in Iran.

Political and juridical problems aside, the institution of the *marja* in the modern history of the worldwide Shii community has been plagued by the two fundamental problems: The irrelevance in the modern world of many of the traditional religious directives that govern interpersonal human relations and of the laws that result, and the self-serving attitudes that beset the immediate family members and close associates of the leading ayatollahs, whose regular sojourns in the Western capitals are observed by many Shiis with a shock and dismay. The loss of confidence in the institution that has been known for its austere and puritanical lifestyle, in addition to the death of several leading members of the religious establishment in the first half of this decade, has brought to the fore the age-old question of the reforms needed to make the *marja* relevant in the most challenging times for the community around the globe.

The leading ayatollahs on the Iranian Council of Guardians during the Friday prayer meetings and at other times in the aftermath of Ayatollah Araki's death on November 29, 1994, besides pointing to the viability of Ayatollah Khamenei's candidacy for the supreme leadership, pointed to the crisis in Shii leadership. The situation was aggravated by the Iranian government's insistence on a consensus on the new vision of a centralized leadership under the Khomeini concept of the governance of the jurist, which, as articulated by the most intelligent voice in the Council of the Guardians, Ayatollah Ahmad Janati, resembled the papacy. None of the prominent *mujtahid*s from among the disciples of the Ayatollah Khoie, all of whom were in disagreement with the Khomeini concept, were regarded as viable alternatives for the post by the Iranian government and its religious arm, the Council of Guardians, and at least one of them happens to be in Najaf, Iraq. Although Ayatollah Khamenei continues to be addressed as both the leader (*rahbar*) and the universal Muslim ruler, *vali-e amr-i muslimin* (the guardian of Muslim affairs), it is doubtful if he will ever be acknowledged by the public as *vali-e faqih*.

It is probably correct to say that the constitutionalization of *velayat-i faqih*, in its broader interpretation, was only possible because of the leadership of the Ayatollah Khomeini, who combined the authority of the *marja-i taqlid* and the *vali-e faqih*. Since his death, the *velayat-i faqih* has been assumed by the Council of Guardians, who, for political reasons, have restricted it to the political dimension similar to that assumed by the *vali-e amr* of the Sunni Muslims, while retaining its juridical dimension within the jurisdiction of the council, until further progression in the political history of the Shii community could accommodate another *vali-e mutlaq* (absolute governing authority) in Iran. The present status of the principle of the *velayat-i faqih* underscores the culmination of its gradual particularization in the Iranian Shii context, because it has ceased to be relevant beyond its geographical boundaries. In all probability, its relevance in Iran has been overshadowed by the complex practical problems facing a nation confronted by the immediate concern of reinstating itself as a credible member of the modern international order, which is more important than being regarded as the hope of "the downtrodden" for the establishment of an international Muslim order under the *velayat-i faqih*. Nevertheless, the religious experience of the Shiis has nurtured uneasiness at the injustices inflicted by those in power. It will be hardly surprising if we witness yet another revolution of the downtrodden under their religious leaders in the name of the Shii messianic aspiration for the rule of justice and equity on earth.

Concluding Remarks

When Khatami took over the presidency, the question of the powers of the institution of the "governance of the jurist" in its new form was taken up by the Council of the Guardians. In several discussions and panels on the subject, the central questions seem to have been the identification of the "governing jurist" and the extent of the power he could exercise in the context of a modern nation state. Some leading legal experts in political jurisprudence believe that the office of governing jurist, in the absence of a Khomeini-like *mujtahid,* should be invested in a collective leadership of qualified *mujtahid*s under the "governance of Islamic jurisprudence" (*velayat-i fiqahat*). The debates and resolutions are realistic, insofar as they recognize the need to institutionalize the traditional concept in a modern state that cannot afford to depend on a personality cult for its day-to-day operations. Social and economic problems have to be resolved in line with the relevant Islamic norms, and these still await adequate retrieval and reinterpretation to fit the needs of a modern society. This institutionalization of the "governance of Islamic jurisprudence" could very well become the major source for Khatami's intended reforms in Iran's domestic as well as foreign policy. The process of building consensus among the political and ideological forces has been underway since he took his office, and there is a reasonably good chance that he will find support for his proposed reforms among the conservative elements in Qom. But the bifurcation of the political power between the liberal wing of the religious establishment under Khatami and the conservative wing under Khamenei can undermine the ability of the present government to deliver its campaign promises. Khatami is constantly defending his liberal stance on issues related to foreign policy as well as civil society. It is hard to imagine how he can build the necessary political consensus if the conservative wing of the religious establishment is unwilling to entertain anything that smacks of compromise with the West. In predicting the politics of a nation with a powerful religious establishment, however, I tend to be cautiously optimistic, while adding a sincere expression of *inshallah,* God willing.

Notes

1. In this paper, I have used *wilayah* or *wilayat* in its broad sense of "authority to govern"; the person who holds it has the right to demand obedience. The word also denotes "guardianship," however, and it is in this sense that it is used in the juridical texts. There it entitles a qualified person in the position of a guardian (*wali*) to assume the custody of a person or property (or both), of a minor, an insane person, or anyone else legally incapable of managing his/her own affairs.
2. In Abdulaziz Abdulhussein Sachedina, *Islamic Messianism: The Idea of*

Mahdi in Twelver Shiism (Albany: State University of New York, 1980), I deal with the Shii idea of what the public order under the leadership of the last, the Hidden Imam will be.
3. In Abdulaziz Sachedina, "Activist Shiism in Iran, Iraq, and Lebanon," in *Fundamentalisms Observed* (Chicago: University of Chicago Press, 1991), pp. 403–56, I discuss Shii ideology in detail and the implications of activist radicalism or quietist authoritarianism among the Shii movements in Islamic history.
4. Bernard Lewis, *The Political Language of Islam* (Chicago: University of Chicago Press, 1988), Chapter 5, discusses the language that was developed by the radical and quietist responses to injustices in the Muslim polity.
5. In Abdulaziz Sachedina, *The Just Ruler in Shiite Islam: The Comprehensive Authority of the Jurist in the Imamite Jurisprudence* (New York: Oxford University Press, 1988), I relate theological doctrines to juridical development in Shii jurisprudence.
6. Chibli Mallat, *The Renewal of Islamic Law: Muhammad Baqer as-Sadr, Najaf and the Shii International* (Cambridge: Cambridge University Press, 1993), p. 44.
7. These three requirements for the *mujtahid* are derived from the juridical sources that specify the qualifications for serving in this official capacity. In Shiism, sound belief implied upholding the Imamate of the Twelve Imams; sound knowledge meant learning acquired from the teachings of the imams, and sound character was the moral probity (*adalah*) required of all those individuals who served as the leaders of congregational prayers, judges, witnesses, and so on.
8. Abu al-Qasim al-Khu'i, *al-Masa'il al-muntakhaba: al-'ibadat wa al-mu'amalat* (Beirut: Dar al-Andalus, 1971), p. 2.
9. The need for *taqlid* led to a growing influence of the leading *mujtahid* in the community, to the extent that in the popular belief of the Shii masses the *marja al-taqlid* functions as the deputy of the infallible Imam, sharing in the latter's infallibility when making any decision pertaining to religious matters. Needless to say, such a popular assessment of the *mujtahid*'s position has led to an uncritical approach to the practical relevance of the institution in modern times. Apparently, the imams themselves foresaw the danger of the growing influence of some of their deputies and warned the community not to fall prey to such exaggerated adoration of the scholars or their teachings. (See *Just Ruler*, p. 211–13.)
10. Loyalty to the imams is characteristic of *tashayyu'*, or early Shii loyalty to Ali b. Abi Talib. "Alid-loyalism" is M. G. S. Hodgson's term for this ear-

lier form of Shiism (*Venture of Islam* [Chicago: University of Chicago Press, 1974], vol. I, p. 260.). Because the *mujtahid*s are regarded as general deputies of the last imam, I have extended the term to them, as they shared the leadership of the community and their loyalty to these deputies through *taqlid*.
11. The edition I have used in this paper has no date or place of publication, but it must have been published soon after the removal of Reza Shah Pahlavi by the Allied Forces, and the installation of his son, the last ruler of the Pahlavi dynasty in 1941. See Hamid Algar, "Development of the Concept of *velayat-i faqih* since the Islamic Revolution in Iran," paper presented at London Conference on *Wilayat al-faqih*, in June, 1988; see also his "Introduction to Islam and Revolution," p. 41.
12. *Kashf-i asrar*, p. 185.
13. Ibid.
14. Ibid., p. 186.
15. *Islam and Revolution*, p. 27. The situation in the centers of Shii learning to which Khomeini is referring pertains to the quietist posture adopted by a number of leading *mujtahid*s, some of whom also held the position of *marja-i taqlid*, who had misgivings about assumption of political power by the religious leadership.
16. As I have shown in *Just Ruler*, pp. 226–229.
17. This famous *fatwa* has been widely reported and commented upon in different contexts.
18. Algar, "Development of a Concept."
19. Ibid.
20. Ibid.
21. *Kashf-i asrar*, p. 222.
22. *Constitution of the Islamic Republic of Iran*, trans. Hamid Algar (Berkeley: Mizan Press, 1980), pp. 66ff.
23. One of the most profound critiques of the growing chaos and the distribution of power in the period following the constitutionalization of the *velayat-i faqih* within Iran was undoubtedly the late Ayatollah Kazim Shariat-madari. He believed in sharing power equally among those who would collectively share the "guardianship" and would become the Council of Elders, like the justices of the Supreme Court in the United States, instead of the all-powerful "guardianship of the jurist" that was constitutionalized with Khomeini serving as its personification. See Shariat-madari's "Exclusive Interview" in *The Middle East,* January, 1980, following the downfall of Mehdi Bazargan's government.
24. This fear was expressed by Shariat-madari, who firmly believed that the

only limitation on the absolute authority of the jurist was the recognition of the fact that the people were sovereign. He saw the role of *velayat-i faqih* as protecting the country's independence by remaining loyal to the sovereignty of the people and Islam ("Exclusive Interview," in *The Middle East*, January 1980, p. 33).

25. There were others outside Iran who undertook to evaluate Khomeini's earlier opinions on the subject critically and even offer their own interpretation of the *velayat al-faqih*. See, for instance, Muhammad Jawad Maghniyya, *al-Khumayni wa dawlat al-islamiyyah* (Beirut, 1979) who undertook to challenge Khomeini's conclusions that limit the *wilayah* to the jurists. Muhammad Baqir Sadr also undertook to elaborate on the principle in his lectures entitled *Islam yaqudu al-hayat* (Tehran, 1983). Ayatollah Montazari's three-volume work, *Wilayat al-faqih wa fiqh al-dawlat al-islamiyyah* (Qom, 1408 H/1988), is a detailed study reiterating the official Khomeini line on the authority of the jurist, tracing it back to the Prophet through textual study and relating it to the conception of leadership and government in Islamic juridical thought.

26. Algar, "Development of the Concept."

27. See Abdul-Hadi Hairi, *Shiism and Constitutionalism in Iran* (Leiden: E. J. Brill, 1977), for a discussion on the problem of human prerogative to legislate among the jurists during the Constitutional Revolution of 1907; also, Said Amir Arjomand, *The Turban for the Crown: The Islamic Revolution in Iran* (New York: Oxford University Press, 1988), pp. 50 ff.

28. The criticism of the absolute claim to government authority in a modern state at the expense of the people's right to sovereignty by the jurist offered by the Nihdat-i Azad-yi Iran in their publication entitled *Wilayat-i mutlaqa-yi faqih* (Tehran, 1368 Sh./1989) seems rather anachronistically to suggest that divine law is timeless and comprehensive, but not to be tampered with by suggesting (as Khomeini does in the introduction to his *fatwa*) that it does not have solutions to all human problems faced in a modern society.

29. That is, consequences of the view that the Islamic government can act only within the framework of existing ordinances of the *shariah*.

30. By *maliyat* obviously non-shari taxes are meant.

31. I have used Algar's translation as it appears in his "Development of the Concept," with minor changes.

32. *Islamic Messianism*, p. 6.

33. As cited by Algar, "Development of the Concept." Khamenei, the president of Iran at the time, held the title of *hojjatolislam* ("proof of Islam"). He was not yet elevated to his present position of ayatollah and the *vali-e*

amr-i muslimin (the authority invested with the power of guardianship over Muslim affairs).
34. Ibid.
35. These prerequisites are well documented, even in Khomeini's *Kashf-i asrar* and his Najaf Lectures.
36. The de facto Sunni rulers were regarded as such by the Sunni jurists.

7

Iran's Foreign Policy Toward Russia, Central Asia, and the Caucasus

Mohiaddin Mesbahi

Twice in the last two decades, events of historical proportion have dramatically affected the shape and direction of Iranian foreign policy. The February 1979 revolution was the most significant development affecting the prism through which foreign policy values, motivations, ideals, priorities, and commitments were defined. The perception of Iran as a revolutionary state carried with it a historically unprecedented burden on Iran's foreign policy. The revolution internalized by the international system had as much to do with the shape and scope of Iran's foreign policy as the revolution externalized by the new custodians of Iran's foreign policy. The construction of Iranian foreign policy identity took place not only in the hands of the revolutionaries or the new elite, but, and more so, in the hands of international actors responding to the revolution, regionally and globally.

The December 1991 collapse of the Soviet Union, a superpower bordering the northern frontier of Iran, was the second seminal event that fundamentally altered the scope and dimension of Iran's foreign policy. The collapse of the Soviet Union not only changed Iran's policy toward Russia and the remnants of a once-powerful empire, but reactivated a totally new set of dynamics, affecting Iran's domestic national security on ethnoterritorial lines.

The encirclement of Iran's regional security framework is now complete. The instability of the East (Iraq), West (Afghanistan), and South (the Persian Gulf), has now been complimented by the North. The collapse of the Soviet Union and the emergence of new independent states, catapulted Iran, largely unprepared, to engage unknown prospects or regional competitions, pressures, and opportunities in the new northern frontier.

This study explores the crucial elements in the conceptual framework of the Iranian vision, which underlies Iranian policy toward the new frontiers of Iranian foreign policy, namely, Russia, Central Asia, and the Caucasus. The study is not designed to detail bilateral ties, but rather to provide key generalizations regarding Iran's policy in the region.

Iranian Foreign Policy: Conceptual Frameworks

Iran's view of its new northern frontier, that is, its place in the Iranian foreign policy framework and objectives is generally affected by the interactive dynamics of four issues: first, the role of Russian-Iranian relations or *Russian-centric* aspects of Iranian foreign policy in Central Asia; second, the *Islamic factor* or the geopolitics and geocultural role of Islam; third, the global factor, namely the constant presence of the *United States* in shaping Iranian regional policy; and, finally, a vision of *Iran's centrality* in shaping Central Asian and Caucasian developments. Iran's bilateral ties and multilateral policies and initiatives, while in micro level are issue/country-specific, they will nevertheless be influenced, on macro level, by the uneven symbiosis of these four dynamics.

Geopolitics and Balance of Power: Relations with Russia

Iran embraced the collapse of the Soviet Union with "mixed emotion." The collapse of the Soviet Union relieved Iran in one stroke from the threats of both the military presence of a superpower and the ideological challenge of Marxism as a historical universalist rival claimant in the Muslim world. For more than a century, Iran's geopolitical calculation had been informed by the threat of Russian/Soviet imperialism pressing its considerable weight against its long Iranian border. Iran's historical gravitation toward alliance with distant powers, like the British Empire up to 1945 and the United States in the postwar years, was a result of this historical vulnerability and the perception of Russian expansionism. Iran became the buffer state between the presumed Russian southward thrust and the Western powers' historical geopolitical and economic interests (i.e., British India, and Persian Gulf oil). Iran's territorial integrity was to a large extent dependent on the great powers' implicit understanding of its position as the buffer state.

The Iranian revolution of 1979, and the subsequent hostility between

Iran's Foreign Policy Toward Russia, Central Asia, and the Caucasus   151

Iran and the United States, signaled the beginning of change in the historical fixation of the "buffer" concept and the balancing context of Iranian geopolitics. Somewhat unique in its foreign policy consequences, the anti-Western orientation of the Iranian revolution did not translate into a pro-Soviet stand. In fact, Iran, especially in light of the Soviet presence in Afghanistan and Moscow's support for Iraq, remained distant from and critical of the Soviet Union through most of the 1980s. Iran's independent position vis-à-vis the superpowers, beyond its ideological motives, was calculated to emphasize a message of nonalignment and thus recast Iran, not as a buffer, but rather as a neutral zone.

Viewed from this perspective, Iran has had a stake in the maintenance of a certain balance in the regional and international structure and distribution of power. Given the increasing hostility between Iran and the United States in the 1980s, and the gradual and thus decisive consolidation of U.S. power in the Persian Gulf, the presence of the less aggressive, yet functioning, "Gorbachevian" Soviet superpower would seem to have served Iran's overall geopolitical interests. The fear of a U.S.-led unipolar world system was thus the underlying reason behind Iran's cautious and subdued attitude toward the unfolding process of the Soviet collapse in the 1990–91 period. A major editorial in the *Tehran Times,* the semiofficial mouthpiece of Iran's Foreign Ministry, assured the Soviet leadership that Iran, in contrast to other countries in the region, had a stake in the territorial and political integrity of the Soviet Union and would not utilize Soviet vulnerability.[1]

This consideration of Iran's vulnerability in a U.S.-dominated regional/international order is the key underlying factor in the development of Iran's Russian-centric policy toward the new independent states of Central Asia and the Caucasus in the post-Soviet period. To have a correct, if not warm, relationship with Russia remains critical to Iran's regional foreign policy.[2] This Russian-centric policy is designed to respond to three sets of Iranian concerns and objectives: namely, the importance of bilateral Russian-Iranian relations; the impact of Russia on Iranian-Central Asian relations; and the impact of the emergence of new states for Iran's domestic, that is, territorial, integrity.

First, bilaterally, Russia has been and will continue to be a source for purchasing arms and technology and for economic, trade, and political cooperation.[3] The Russian-centric policy, however, is not based on single issues or purely bilateral considerations, but also reflects Iran's concern over multilateral and bilateral relations with Central Asian states.

Second, this Russian-centrism reflects Iran's recognition of Moscow's geopolitical influence in the former republics and its impact on Iranian-Central Asian relations. An anti-Russian policy in Central Asia on the part of Tehran will not serve Iran's immediate and long-term interests. Such a policy would create impediments to regional receptivity and further pave the way for more intensive regional coalitions against Iran.

Third, Iran's vulnerability against regional conflicts in Central Asia and the Transcaucasus, and its needs for regional stability, demand a closer cooperation with or understanding of Moscow. This is particularly important in view of the prominence that Iran has attached to its own role as a peacemaker and mediator.

This regional perspective does not exclude conflicts of interest and competitive policies, as has been the case in Tajikistan, but illustrates the continuous attempt by Tehran to accommodate the Russian factor, to minimize Moscow's obstructionism, and to solicit its acquiescence or cooperation. Furthermore, the multiplicity of issues concerning the Russian-Iranian-Central Asian triangle does not lend itself to a uniformity of interests in all situations. Conflicts of interest between Iran and Russia in Tajikistan, for example, are simultaneously accompanied by the relative convergence of interests of the two countries on the issues concerning the geopolitics of the Caspian Sea, Iran's "second Persian Gulf," the sovereignty over Caspian Sea energy and food resources, and, especially, the long-term and very serious impact of the Caspian environmental crisis on Iran's northern provinces.[4]

The nature and impact of Russian-centrism in Iran's regional policy will be decided at the nexus of the bilateral and multilateral dimensions of Russian-Iranian relations, and the nature of relations with the other key emerging actors, namely, the United States. This latter factor has a particularly enormous implication for Russian-Iranian relations.[5] Russia has decidedly elevated the Iranian factor in its regional policy, giving a high profile to this relationship in the domestic politics of foreign policy, and demonstrating its willingness to seriously test its relations with the United States, especially in view of Washington's serious concerns over transfer of nuclear and missile technology to Iran.[6]

Russian-Iranian nuclear cooperation has been the most important testing ground of Russian-Iranian relations and a focal point of U.S.–Russian negotiations since 1995, when Russia and Iran signed a protocol for the completion of the Bushehr nuclear power plant.[7] The Israeli stake in the Iranian nuclear project has pushed the Russian nuclear deal with Iran to the top of the U.S. policy agenda toward Russia and Tel Aviv's bilateral relations with Moscow. The nuclear issue has been subjected to the ebb

Iran's Foreign Policy Toward Russia, Central Asia, and the Caucasus 153

and flow of Iran's economic limitations, Russia's hesitation, and, above all, the impact of the U.S. carrot[8] and stick[9] policy to limit Russian-Iranian nuclear and military ties.

The Russians have not been completely consistent in their promises of nuclear cooperation with Iran, and have been responsive to U.S. pressure.[10] Nevertheless, the nuclear and military cooperation with Iran will continue not only because of economic incentives, but the political symbolism attached to these ties. For Russia, they are symbols of an assertive and independent foreign policy, and for Iran, they are a critical barometer of Russia's intentions, and Moscow's desire to maintain Iran as a potential strategic partner in the face of NATO's expansion, both in Europe and the Caucasus.[11]

The controversy over Iran's nuclear and missile capability, like many other issues related to Iran, has acquired a life of its own. Independent from Russian-Iranian relations, it now serves the interest of a complex web of military industrial and special interest groups who wish to reinvigorate the American strategic defense projects, previously known as SDI, to safeguard the United States against nuclear missiles from "rogue" states such as North Korea and Iran. The debate over Iran's nuclear and missile capabilities has provided an opportunity to revisit and revise a sacred strategic cow in U.S. and Russian relations, namely the 1972 Anti-Ballistic Missile (ABM) Treaty. The longevity of the nuclear missile problematic in Russian-Iranian relations is now guaranteed.[12]

Russian military ties with Iran are not significant in terms of the overall volume of the Russian global arms trade, almost three-fourths of which is accounted for by China and India.[13] Yet, the nuclear component of these ties remains significant. The ongoing Iranian nuclear project, peaceful or not, may not enhance Iran's security, as perceptions, real or imagined, matter most. In the absence of a comprehensive nuclear and missile nonproliferation regime in the Middle East and Southwest Asia, which could include not only Iran and Iraq, but also Israel, India, and Pakistan, Russian-built nuclear facilities in Iran would remain a realistic target of preemptive military strikes by the United States, and especially Israel. Russia's interests and prestige will be tied to Iran's physical vulnerability.

In spite of the military ties, Russian-Iranian relations are subjected to unpredictable and unforseen challenges and pressures. Iran, for example, will continue to be concerned with Russia's manipulation of the Nagorno-Karabakh problem, its ambiguous policy toward the Caspian legal regime,[14] its continuous domination of Tajikistan, and its abrupt maneuvering of different aspects of the nuclear trade. The policy differences, in fact, have gone beyond the Caucasus and Central Asia and now include regional differences, especially on developments in the Balkans.

Iran and Russia differed on the Bosnian crisis, where Iran played a relatively important role in helping the Bosnians resist Serbian domination. Iran's military aid to Bosnian Muslims, in the midst of international sanctions against the warring factions, was not welcomed by Moscow. As in Bosnia, the Kosovo crisis also highlighted Iran's paradoxical relations with Moscow. The mutual condemnation of NATO's intervention could not overshadow Iran's disagreement with Moscow concerning the Serbian atrocities against Kosovar Albanian Muslims. As the self-proclaimed custodian of the Muslim *ummah* on the one hand, and the avid critic of Western intervention on the other, Iran found itself in an awkward position. Handicapped by its fear of the precedent-setting NATO intervention,[15] and the psychological and ideological inability to support the U.S.–engineered policy in Kosovo,[16] Iran's Islamic credentials were threatened, both domestically and internationally, as the general Muslim public sympathy lay with NATO's actions against the "Muslim-killing Serbs." The perceptions of Iran as siding with Pan-Slavic Russia against Muslims, could potentially be very damaging, as the Muslims of the North Caucasus in Chechnya, Dagestan, Tatarstan, and to a lesser extent, Central Asia, saw in the Russian pro-Serbian policy an expression of the well-entrenched historical animosity of the Slavs against the Muslims.[17]

Identification of Iran with an "anti-Islamic Russia" could severely complicate Iran's self-image in the region. This is particularly important as the type of activist Islam increasingly emerging in the former Soviet territory, especially in the North Caucasus, is characterized by a new breed of "Talibanism" that, both theologically and politically, has opposed Iranian Islam, and Shiism.[18] Historically, Soviet Islam, although belonging predominantly to the Sunni tradition, was not particularly hostile to Iran, due partially to the significance of Sufi *tariqahs* in the North Caucasus and to a lesser degree in Central Asia, and their spiritual connections with Iranian and Shii saints and Imams. Iran's relative silence toward the Russian intervention in Chechnya had already begun to question the Islamic image of Iran.

Moscow's attitudes toward Kosovo, its clear ethnoreligious flavor, and its reluctance to condemn Serbian atrocities against Kosovo Albanian Muslims[19] tested the limitations of the civilizational/religious dialogue that the Iranian clergy and seminaries have initiated with the Russian Orthodox Church in the last several years. Russia's increasing concern over its own Islamic problem in the North Caucasus and the objections of the Muslim world in general,[20] voiced increasingly by Iranian officials,[21] will continue to force Moscow to modify its Balkan policy.[22] In view of Western problems with the Muslim world and Iran, Moscow clearly remains concerned over further loss of prestige in the Muslim world and the potential Islamic backlash at home and abroad. Russia will continue to be watchful over the evolution of Iran's position toward the Balkans. Iran's Bosnian policy had unintentionally but tellingly coincided with the U.S. position. Kosovo, underlined again another area of Russian-Iranian tension and, not by accident, an unacknowledged area of political convergence of U.S.–Iranian interests.

Iran now occupies an important place in Russian foreign policy, not only in Central Asia and the Caucasus, but also in the Middle East, particularly, in view of the alarming implications of NATO expansion, and possible militarization of the Caspian basin early next century. Thus, Russia will carefully watch the extent and the scope of the thaw in U.S.–Iranian relations under Khatami.[23] Although the logic of security dilemma and strategic balance dictates Iran's partnership with Russia, Iran's acquired postrevolutionary identity, as a uniquely independent country, along with historical mistrust of Russia will continue to make Iran, at best, a reluctant balancer.

Islamic Geopolitics

The second factor in Iranian-Central Asian relations is the impact of Iran's particular characteristics as an Islamic state, specifically one with a revolutionary/revisionist ideology perceived by a host of regional and international actors as destabilizing and threatening. This particular image of Iran has been the central and defining element in shaping its opportunities and constraints, and affects Iranian foreign policy behavior. It is this uniformity in the Iranian image in the eyes of both friends and enemies that has created an inescapable context for Iranian foreign policy in its bilateral or multilateral dimension.

Iran's foreign policy, pragmatic or revolutionary, will be measured within the confines of the level of sensitivity of other actors toward the geopolitics of the Islamic factor. Central to these geopolitics is, of course, the attitude of the great powers, above all the United States and Russia. U.S. attitudes toward the "Islamic threat" and its containment in the Persian Gulf, the Middle East, and North Africa, now includes Central Asia and the Caucasus as well. Russia will increasingly look to the Islamic factor as the cornerstone of its policy formulations, options, and strategies, vacillating between the historical fear of encirclement, thus temptation for domination, or coexistence, tactical alliances, and manipulation. Given the Islamic character of Central Asia and its linkage with the Middle East and Iran's geographical location, it will be an important consideration in shaping Iran's position in Central Asia as well.

A discussion of the role of Islam in Central Asia and the Caucasus is beyond the scope of this paper; what is important here, however, is the role of the "threat" of Islam in shaping the attitudes of multitudes of actors with divergent interests who usually converge on the issue of "containment" of the Islamic, and by association, the Iranian threat. Whether Islam is a real "threat" in Central Asia, or whether it is conveniently imagined as such, remains largely irrelevant, as regional and international actors act upon the "Islamic factor" as one of the key threats to their domestic and external security in the post-Soviet period.

Whereas the general culture and religious characteristics of Central Asia may point to areas of opportunity and influence for Iran, the same factors are nurturing resistance and obstacles—a dichotomy that has characterized Iran's policy in the Middle East and the Islamic world in general. This dichotomy originates from the divergent impact of Iran's bilateral relations with other states on the one hand, and Iran's real or perceived impact or influence on social movements (i.e., Islamic activists/ groups, etc.) on the other. In Central Asia (in Tajikistan in particular), and as is the case in Iran's relations with Islamic states elsewhere, the inherent tension between state-to-state relations and state-to-social movement relations will be a continuous source of challenge and opportunity for Iran. This is notwithstanding Iran's repeated assertion of noninvolvement in revolutionary Islamic movements or lack of interest in exporting the revolution.

Iran's policy toward the role of Islam or Islamic movements in Central Asia is fundamentally pragmatic. Its pragmatism reflects Tehran's appreciation of the underdeveloped nature of both political and orthodox Islam in Central Asia, the strength of the Soviet secular legacy, and above all, the strength of the local and regional coalition that fear of Islam generates. This coalition not only targets Islam as a domestic challenge, but, more importantly, targets Iran and attempts its isolation. Iran's pragmatism is challenged by a combination of interdependent and mutually reinforcing dynamics, including: (a) the inertia of a self-proclaimed Islamic metropolis in Iran (Umm al-qora), (b) domestic ideological pressure, and above all, (c) an absence of international and regional mechanisms willing to acknowledge Iran's pragmatism. The absence of any "reward structure" erodes support and legitimacy at home, while resulting in the loss of credibility with potential friends abroad.[24]

Cognizant of its own limitation in exporting its "revolutionary" model and aware of the supersensitivity of all regional actors, Iran has emphasized the cultural rather than the political aspect of its Islamic credentials. A survey of the content of Iranian-Central Asian relations indicates a marked emphasis on cultural ties and activities, which are devoid of a direct political dimension.[25] It is hoped that the emphasis on "cultural Islam," will reduce the anxiety of Central Asian states, while reinforcing Iran's uniqueness as an Islamic state.[26]

In the short run, this shift may not solve the Iranian dilemma; a dilemma that is compounded by the ambiguity of the *reward structure* of pursuing a pragmatic moderate foreign policy. Pragmatic or revolutionary, Iran continues to have difficulty in reaping the benefits of the former, while it still feels the overwhelming weight and the baggage of the latter. A pragmatic Iran will still be perceived and treated as revolutionary. The Iranian/Islamic threat is an instrumental force for building consensus, overcoming differences, and making strange bedfellows a political normalcy. Yet, a persistent policy of pragmatism and insistence on culture and dialogue as a serious instrument of foreign policy, especially under Khatami, is believed to overcome the ideological baggage of the 1979 Revolution.

The U.S. Factor

U.S.–Iranian hostility, itself a function of the complexity of the Islamic factor, has played a major role in shaping the international relations of Central Asia. In fact, the tension in U.S.–Iranian relations that has engulfed the politics of the Persian Gulf/Middle East since the 1979 Islamic Revolution has been extended to Central Asia and the Caucasus. Concern over the Islamic/Iranian threat has now become the conceptual and the policy bridge linking security discussions of Central Asia and the Caucasus with those of the Persian Gulf/Middle East. In a nutshell, through U.S. "agency," Iranian foreign policy has been globalized since the revolution, and especially in the 1990s.

The degree to which U.S. preferences and displeasure can decide or influence regional choices, that is, advocating distance from Iran, will depend on parallel threat perceptions as well as the level of expectations and realities of rewards for following the U.S. lead. Promises of U.S. direct or indirect "economic" support can play a major role. As the Azerbaijan oil deal indicates, Washington will not hesitate to go beyond generating atmospheric pressure to overtly intervene politically to undermine or contain Iranian interests and influence. U.S.–Iranian hostility would also affect relations between Iran and Azerbaijan, and will be an important element in affecting Iranian policy in the Caucasus as a whole. If Azerbaijan is perceived as pursuing a Washington-inspired policy vis-à-vis Iran, Iranian-Azeri relations could become the most complex, if not explosive, in the region.

As the most outspoken critic of Iran, Uzbekistan perceives its ambiguous, if not hostile, attitudes toward Iran both as an instrument of domestic control against the opposition—which has been branded "religious extremist"—and a useful vehicle for rapprochement with the United States.

The U.S.–Uzbek relations, which had been frozen because of Washington's dissatisfaction over slow economic reforms and political repression, have shown marked improvement since the early months of 1995. The tension in Uzbek-Iranian relations, which followed the reports of President Karimov's support for the U.S. trade embargo against Iran,[27] was just another indication of continuous difficulty between Tashkent and Tehran, and the enduring impact of U.S.–Iranian relations on Iranian foreign policy in Central Asia.[28] The possible normalization of U.S.–Iranian relations, prompted by the recent "thaw" under President Khatami, could have a significant impact on Iranian relations with the Central Asia states.

Such "normalization" demands a new political discourse that does not equate "normalization" with friendship, let alone with "alliance;" a normalization that reflects convergence of national interests at least on selective but important issues, if not on long-term structural dynamics. The discussion of the nature of U.S.–Iranian relations and the problems of its normalization is beyond the scope of this paper and has been dealt with elsewhere in the book. Suffice it to say that a key element of two decades of hostility has been the ideological nature of the conflict; not just the Iranians, but the seldom discussed role of the "ideational" in deciding U.S. policy toward Iran, especially in the post-Soviet world. The U.S. self-image as a triumphant neoliberal entity bent upon seeing and reinventing the world in its own image has, especially under the Clinton team, played a critical role in shaping U.S. foreign policy toward particularly vulnerable countries with "revisionist/rogue" ideologies who either have lost the battle of ideas and are struggling with transition, that is, Russia, or those like Iran who still harbor the illusion of hanging on to "antiquated" non-Western ideas.

Iran's Foreign Policy Toward Russia, Central Asia, and the Caucasus 159

The United States has shown remarkable propensity toward believing in and acting on the assumption that normalization with former and current ideological enemies cannot take place on the basis of a pragmatic national interest—of realist argument varieties—but, rather, is predicated on sustained and verifiable signs of the "transition" of identity of the enemies, mirror imaging of the U.S. self. "Transition is a notion rooted in the U.S. ego," noted Stephen Cohen commenting on U.S. policy toward Russia.[29] Morganthau's "autonomous" state has acquired an identity that does not easily lend itself to a rational historical definition of national interest. At the altar of this ideational approach, pragmatic U.S. political and economic interests are being sacrificed.

No other case is more illustrative of this than U.S. policy in the Caspian, where preoccupation with the ideational, rather than the pragmatic, transitionology rather than accommodation drives Washington's policy. While the U.S. domestic constituencies such as oil companies, the multinationals, and their political and "academic" lobbies have pushed for the most pragmatic and economically feasible policies, that is, to include Iran in the networks of pipelines,[30] the U.S. administration has opted for exclusion of Iran at all cost. In addition to frustrating the U.S. oil companies,[31] the policy has not only generated fantastic and economically unfeasible alternative pipeline scenarios, but has more seriously set in motion a geopolitical dynamic that perhaps unintentionally would lead to a new East-West fault line and the reemergence of a new "great game" in the former Soviet South. Increasingly, political and military patterns of U.S.–NATO interests, such as expansion of military ties with the region through the Partnership for Peace Program, joint military exercises, and naval visits, have been complimented with the clear gravitation of Azerbaijan and Georgia toward closer politicomilitary ties with NATO. This emerging lineup has been gradually supplemented by Israeli-Turkish "minialliances," thus connecting the Middle Eastern geopolitical dynamics with equally complicated security systems in the Caucasus.[32] In Central Asia, the seeds of closer politicomilitary ties between NATO/U.S. and Uzbekistan has been planted through peace-keeping varieties and schemes.

The symbiosis of pipeline geopolitics and geoeconomics with ideology has provided the context for the emergence of a new "great game." This context reveals the paradox of official U.S.-stated policy toward the Caspian Basin—a policy that conceptually was designed to prevent the new great game but, ironically, operationally is constructing one. Commenting on the new great game, Strobe Talbot, U.S. Assistant Secretary of State, argued,

Our goal is to avoid and actively to discourage that atavistic outcome. In pondering and practicing the geopolitics of oil, let's make sure that we are thinking in terms appropriate to the twenty-first Century, and not the nineteenth. Let's leave Rudyard Kipling and George McDonald Fraser, where they belong—on the shelves of historical fiction. The Great Game which starred Kipling's Kim and Fraser's Flashman, was very much of the zero-sum variety. What we want to help bring about is just the opposite. We want to see all responsible players in the Caucasus and Central Asia be winners.[33]

In the post-Soviet world, and on the eve of the twenty-first century, Iran has yet to qualify for membership in the U.S.–defined "club of responsible players," and, as such, and notwithstanding the "mixed signals" of the last three years,[34] is dealt with as nineteenth century fiction!

Iran's Centrality

The fourth factor shaping Iran's policy in Central Asia and the Caucasus is Iran's self-image as a central player in the region's international dynamics.[35] This self-image is rooted in Iran's perception of its assets and liabilities. Iran's unique assets include its geographical contiguity with the former Soviet Union (Iran has land borders with Azerbaijan, Armenia, and Turkmenistan, and sea borders with Russia and Kazakhstan); its natural role as the key transit link between Central Asia and the Middle East, the Persian Gulf, and the open sea; and its political importance as a major actor in the Middle East and Southwest Asia. Iran, thus, sees itself as a nexus and center of regional economic and political activities. This centrality, in addition to Iran's other assets, also reflects appreciation of its resultant vulnerabilities.

Concern over territorial integrity, a traditional preoccupation, has now been strongly reinforced by the emergence of surrounding states with active and significant ethnoterritorial problems—problems magnified by the multiethnic nature of Iran itself. A prime regional refugee hub, Iran hosted more than four million refugees, 14 percent of its population in the 1980s and early 1990s, as a result of conflicts on its western border (Iraq) and on its eastern border (Afghanistan). More recently, Iran received refugees from the North (Azerbaijan and, to a lesser extent, from Tajikistan). Regional conflicts are a major challenge to Iranian security and a direct consequence of its central location. This centrality has generated certain perspectives and attitudes in Iranian foreign policy toward Central

Iran's Foreign Policy Toward Russia, Central Asia, and the Caucasus 161

Asia, which are not very different from those adopted toward the Persian Gulf. These attitudes and perspectives include an anticontainment strategy (a desire to undermine any attempt at Iran's isolation) and proactive diplomacy to enhance Iran's political, security, and economic strength and leverage. Iran's self vision of centrality is best reflected in its determination to expand *bilateral ties* with the new independent states as well as constructing and participating in *multilateral* regional initiatives.

Bilateral Ties

The dynamics of Iran's bilateral ties with the new states of the Transcaucasus and Central Asia are characterized by variations in propensity, interests, and accomplishments indicating differentiations in priorities, opportunities, and constraints.

The geographical contiguity and ongoing and seemingly intractable ethnic conflict in Nagorno-Karabakh, the crossborder ethnic makeup of Azerbaijan and Iran, Azerbaijan's increasing tendency for closer relations with states unfriendly to Iran, and the issue of energy (i.e., Caspian oil), make Iran's relations with Armenia, and especially with Azerbaijan, potentially the most explosive. The ethnic and religious affinity between Azerbaijan and Iran has not been enough to prevent the increasing difficulties in bilateral relations and a warmer relationship between Iran and Armenia. Mutual suspicions and accusations (i.e., Iran's security anxiety over Azerbaijan's interests in developing close ties with the United States, and especially Israel, the exclusion of Iran from the Caspian oil deal, and ethnic ambitions in Iranian Azerbaijan on the one hand, and the Azeri accusations of Iran's support for an Islamic movement and Armenia's military effort, on the other) have overshadowed occasional attempts at improving the relationship.[36]

Relations with Armenia remain in much better shape, especially in view of Azeri-Iranian tension, Russian-Iranian partnership, and Iran's historical ties with the Armenian community. Iran remains concerned over the territorial integrity of Azerbaijan and, therefore, has opposed full self-determination for Armenians in Nagorno-Karabakh. (In the conference of Organization of Islamic States in Tehran, 1998, Iran pushed for a resolution that emphasized Azerbaijan's territorial integrity.) An Armenian hardline position pushing for full independence of Nagorno-Karabakh may complicate Iranian-Armenian relations.[37] Iran's opposition to the independence of Nagorno-Karabakh is predicated on Iran's concern over precedent-setting territorial changes on the Iranian frontier along ethnic lines.

The United States' and Iran's position on a realistic solution to the Nagorno-Karabakh problem are similar, although they may differ on the monitoring mechanism. Iran would prefer a regionally organized, or U.N. peace-keeping force, to NATO's peace-keeping forces modeled along the Dayton option in Bosnia.

Of all Central Asian states, Iran-Turkmen relations have been the most expansive and successful, as the two states have adapted a policy of accommodation and security neutrality. Iran takes comfort in Turkmenistan's "neutral" security policy, and its hesitant attitudes toward the CIS, in spite of long-term ties with Russia. Economic ties, especially in the areas of energy, pipelines, and strategic transportation links have underscored these relations. The fact that Khatami chose Turkmenistan as the first country to visit only underscores the significance of Ashkabad-Tehran ties. Iran, nevertheless, will remain sensitive toward any significant changes in the Turkmen neutrality doctrine, especially in view of the U.S. pressure in Ashkabad to look for alternatives other than Iran for its pipeline projects. In this context, Turkemenistan's connection with Afghanistan and Pakistan will potentially be of great significance.[38]

Tajikistan, for reasons of both ideology and culture, has occupied a unique place in Iran's Central Asian policy, and as such will continue to remain a permanent fixture.[39] Iran not only sees Tajikistan as the only Persian/Iranian enclave in the Central Asian Turkic milieu, and thus worthy of attention, but it has been a relatively successful showcase for Iranian *mediation* strategy and attempts at *centrality*. Iran's success, however, is tamed by the continuous Russian monopoly of domination,[40] the ambiguity of the attitudes of the current regime toward Tehran, and Iran's own hesitation about a deeper emotive, cultural commitment to its civilizational brothers. Although cultural cooperation, especially in the area of language, has been expanding, the economic and security assistance has been limited. The recent "defense agreement" between the two countries is probably more symbolic than substantive.[41] A more substantive politicosecurity link between the two countries may have to wait for a diminishing Russian presence and a more unified Tajik leadership, which may look into Iran as an important source of security support against its powerful neighbor Uzbekistan.

Early Tajik expectations for an idyllically close relationship, ethnoculturally and politically, with Iran, have not materialized. The Tajik civil war, immediately after independence, deprived Iran from an opportunity to deal with its civilizational brothers in a "normal" setting. Iran had to take sides in the civil war, supporting the opposition against the Dushanbe

Iran's Foreign Policy Toward Russia, Central Asia, and the Caucasus 163

regime since 1992.[42] In view of Iran's increasing emphasis on its own culture as a prevailing content of its domestic and foreign policy identity, Tajikistan could have a much more significant place in future Iranian regional policy. The prerequisite for such a prominent role for Tajikistan requires a more serious intracivilizational discourse.

Iran's relations with Kazakhstan and Kyrgyzstan are underlined by a gradual and patient improvement since 1992, overcoming the earlier ideological political barriers of "the Islamic threat" (especially during the intense period of the Tajik civil war). The gradual acceptance of Iran as an important player, especially in view of mediation in Tajikistan, and new concerns over the Taliban's influence in Central Asia,[43] has been complimented by gradual improvement in trade relations with Iran as a source of affordable consumer products for both republics, and above all as an important outlet to access to the open sea, especially for oil-producing Kazakhstan. And it is interesting to note that Kazakhstan's Caspian oil was among the first to find its way to external markets, namely Iran itself![44]

Iran's relations with Uzbekistan are among the most complicated, if not difficult. Uzbekistan's regional ambitions (viewed in Tehran as "instinctively imperialist"), its increasingly close relations with the United States (viewed by Washington as "the island of stability"), and its "championing" of the containment policy have overshadowed occasional improvements in diplomatic ties with Iran. Closer ties between Uzbekistan and the United States have inadvertently contributed to an improvement of relations between Russia and Iran in Central Asia, and more specifically in Tajikistan.

Multilateral Response

Two themes in Iran's anticontainment and proactive diplomatic posture are essential to its foreign policy in Central Asia and the Caucasus, namely, *regional multilateralism* and *diplomacy of conflict resolution and mediation*. Iran's multilateral policy is reflected in its promotion or creation of regional organizations such as the Economic Cooperation Organization (ECO) and the Caspian Sea Littoral States Organization, and multilateral economic projects focusing on transit and energy.[45] Building transit linkages with Central Asia through an expanding shipping line in the Caspian Sea, and more significantly through the railroad with Turkmenistan (Sarakhs-Tezhen), will be a significant component of Iran's multilateral and regionalist approach toward Central Asia. This policy is also reflected in regional cooperation in the areas of energy and the transport of oil and gas to Europe via multilateral pipeline projects such as the one involving Turkmenistan, Iran, and Turkey.[46]

This multilateralism also has been expressed in Iran's initiative and participation in several regional "triangulations," such as Iran-Turkmenistan-Armenia, Iran-Greece-Armenia, Iran-Turkmenistan-India, Iran-Georgia-Armenia, Iran-Ukraine-Turkmenistan, and so on. These multilateral relations are designed to: (a) provide a regional cross-current network that will hopefully provide Iran with economic benefits; (b) solidify Iran's role as an integral part of the regional community; and (c) confront attempts to isolate Iran, thus complicating the establishment of anti-Iranian security alliances, thus making containment unlikely or unworkable. Iran's interest in multilateralism and triangulation mechanisms is designed also to serve Iran's geopolitical calculation in balancing potential regional challenges. For example, closer ties with Greece and India is hoped to leverage Iran's position vis-à-vis Turkey and Pakistan.

Iran's *regional rivalry* with Turkey is usually viewed as a significant factor shaping Iranian foreign policy and Central Asia's international relations. What is not clear, however, is the operational or real significance and substance of this competition. Although both Ankara and Tehran have jockeyed for a position in the region, given their limitations and enormous needs of Central Asia and the Caucasus, the region has so far accommodated both, and avoided the stark choice of choosing between the two. At times, the competition seems more ethereal than detrimental, and more the reflection of the anxiety of two regional newcomers that the new states willingly manipulate.

Geopolitically, the exaggerated sense of self-importance of both countries has been modified or tamed by the reality of their practical limitations, and the more salient roles of Russia, and, increasingly, the United States, in the region. Ideologically, although the issues of "competitive Turkish and Iranian models" do have certain relevance, the impact of the ideological competition remains limited. The Central Asian states are not eager to embrace a new "Big Brother" model. Nor do either of these two countries successfully exemplify what they preach; secularism and Islam are not the exclusive domain of either Turkey or Iran.[47]

Iran's regional rivalry with Pakistan, although more subtle, has thus far had a more significant regional implication. Pakistan's attempt to present itself and its allies in Afghanistan as a primary source of Western access to energy in the region led to its support for the Taliban in Afghanistan (a policy tacitly approved by Saudi Arabia and the United States). Whereas this policy has jeopardized Iran's border security in the East, and has weakened its influence in Afghanistan, it has ironically benefited Iran in Central Asia. The crisis in Taliban-dominated Afghanistan helped shift the nature of the ideological threat from Iran to the Taliban's "extremist Islam" (i.e., "Saudi-type," "Wahabbi"). It contributed to Russian-Iranian rapprochement in Tajikistan and weakened the hand of the Uzbeks in their anti-Iranian posture. Iran's fluctuating relations with Turkey and Pakistan has prompted Tehran to opt for closer relations with Greece and India (crossing the Huntingtonian civilizational divides!), and in the process involving several regional states, such as Turkmenistan and Armenia, in tripartite fashion.

Multilateralism also reflects Iran's beliefs in its own geographical centrality for extraregional actors interested in access to Central Asia and the Caucasus. Finally, it reflects Iran's insistence in projecting a nonideological foreign policy, as indicated by emphasis on closer ties with countries of different civilizations and cultures, that is, Greece, India, Armenia, Georgia, and so on. The latter point will be further reinforced in the future as Iran looks into cross-cultural civilizational dialogue and ties as a serious instrument of its foreign policy.

The Iranian strategy of conflict resolution and mediation diplomacy in Central Asia and the Caucasus is designed to: (a) safeguard against regional conflicts affecting Iranian security, and their propensity to invite great-power intervention; (b) enhance Iran's prestige and its regional leverage, thereby contributing to Iran's *centrality* in regional affairs; and (c) develop a positive image that neutralizes the complex or negative impact of the "Islamic factor." Iran's continuous mediation in the two major regional conflicts in the Caucasus and Central Asia, that is, Nagorno-Karabakh and especially Tajikistan, is underscored by the significance of *mediation* as a method in promoting Iran's security and political relevance to important regional dynamics. (It is interesting to note that Iran's "functionalist/neofunctionalist" approach to overcoming the constraining political and ideological environment of Central Asia has been driven to some extent by the infusion, in recent years, of fresh policy analysis in Iranian official circles inspired by Western functionalist literature.[48])

Conclusion

An overview of Iran's foreign policy toward its new northern frontier since the collapse of the Soviet Union points to several fundamental themes. The key preoccupation of Iran in the region has been and will remain regional stability. The implications of "ethnoterritoriality," and the inviolability of existing regional borders, including those of the new states, have become an important consideration in Iranian foreign policy thinking.

The desire for stability is accompanied by a determination to avoid deliberate or imposed isolation, and to remain involved in regional politics affecting the key dynamics of the region's interstate relations, which have a direct impact on Iranian interests; Iran's centrality will be emphasized.

The concern over U.S. domination and pressure, along with contiguous geopolitical realities, will continue to make Russia a significant player in Iran's foreign policy towards the new frontier. The attempt at strategic partnership with Russia, however, will continue to be tested by deep-seated historical mistrust and the largely tactical nature of the friendship between Moscow and Tehran, in spite of strategic claims. U.S. regional policy will be a major factor affecting Iran's policy and position, especially in the Caspian Basin. The degree of success and difficulties in Iranian foreign policy will be to a significant measure a function of the overall atmospherics of U.S.–Iranian relations.

As it stands, the Caspian has been at best a mixed blessing. The potential for gain has been balanced by multiple challenges: no significant economic benefits, potential environmental disaster of colossal proportions, securitization of its northern border, and unnecessary commitment of national energy to prevent or play in a new "great game" of little positive consequence. In this context, the growing pessimism regarding the economic feasibility of the Caspian energy projects, along with the modified projections of its available resources, and thus the diminishing significance of the Caspian, might ironically be Iran's saving grace.[49]

Iran's Islamic identity will continue to have a major place in shaping its opportunities and constraints. The effort to deideologize its Islam and culturalize its foreign policy will continue to inform the ideational dimension of Iran's foreign policy. As the new independent states dig into their past to construct a history for their present, the Iranians hope that a genuine archeology will lead to discovery of a significant Iranian cultural heritage and contribution and, thus, embracement, not containment of Iran.[50]

Although the Persian Gulf has traditionally preoccupied Iranian foreign policy makers, Central Asia and the Caucasus have gradually gained equal significance for Iranian leaders. While in the south smaller weak states, oil, great power presence, and ideology have made Iran a significant country in the Persian Gulf, the emerging weak nation-states in Central Asia and, the Caucasus, the new gold rush for Caspian oil, the inevitable great power competition, and again, ideology also have made Iran a significant player in the north. Squeezed between the two significant subregions of the Caspian and the Persian Gulf, Iran's foreign policy in the next century, like that of so many other actors in this region, will be decided at the crossroads of three intermingling dynamics: the international political economy of access to energy, the geopolitical balance of power, and the geocultural interaction of Islam, modernity, and post-Soviet legacy.

Notes

1. *Tehran Times,* January 8, 1990, p. 2. The Iranian press was replete with warnings to Gorbachev about the trappings of too close relations with the United States and the danger of the disintegration of the Soviet Union.
2. In the words of the then Iranian U.N. Ambassador, and current Foreign Minister, Kamal Kharazi, "Our relations with Russia are excellent and are of a strategic nature." Cited in "Iran's Caspian Policy," *Statement of Ambassador and Permanent Representative of Iran to the United Nations at the First International Conference on Caspian Oil, Gas, and Pipeline: Seizing Opportunities: The Second Persian Gulf,* New York, May 29, 1997.
3. In this context, the issue of Russia's arms sales to Iran and the transfer of so-called dual use technology, especially in the area of nuclear technology, given U.S. sensitivity, will remain a complex one; it is an issue shaped by the interaction of multiple factors and dynamics such as its impact on U.S.–Russian relations, its financial and political utility for Russia, and, perhaps above all, the level of Iran's sensitivity. Iran's reaction to President Yeltsin's announcement of no more sales of arms to Iran during his trip to Washington in October 1994 was remarkably low key.
4. Iran's coastal regions will be among the most affected by the current environmental problem in the Caspian, and a potentially disastrous zone in the event of an oil-related environmental crisis. See Rory Cox and Doug Norlen, "The Great Ecological Game: Will Caspian Sea Oil Development Lead to Environmental Disaster?" *Pacific Environment and Resource Center,* January 1997, in *Turkistan Newsletter,* Vol. 3, March 5, 1999.
5. See Mohiaddin Mesbahi, "Iran's Emerging Partnership with Russia," *Middle East Insight,* Summer 1995.
6. While media reports, especially since the mid-1990's, have on occasion indicated that the United States and Russia have reached serious agree-

ments to block Russian technology transfer to Iran, Russia's commitment to uphold all of the promises has usually remained uncertain. For a report on U.S.-Russian negotiations regarding Iran in 1998, see *New York Times,* January 23, 1998, p. A6.
7. For reports on the Bushehr plant, see "Russia-Iran Protocol Provides Evidence of Discussions, but no Firm Agreement on Sale of Centrifuge Plant for Uranium Enrichment," *National Resources Defense Council, News Release,* May 10, 1995; *Izvestya,* January 13, 1995, p. 3; "Iran, Russia Agree on $800 Million Nuclear Plant Deal," *The Washington Post,* January 9, 1995, p. 18; "In Russia," *Post-Soviet Nuclear and Defense Monitor 2,* January 16, 1995, p. 12.
8. During the meeting between Vice President Al Gore and Russian Prime Minister Victor Chernomyrdin on March 10, 1998, the United States proposed an increase in Russia's quotas for commercial launches using Russian missiles, booster rockets for foreign satellites with U.S. components in exchange for Russia "axing the Bushehr power plant" and the Russian guarantee of terminating missile technology transfer to Iran. The Russian Prime Minister reportedly had argued "that Russia has cooperated and will continue to cooperate with Iran.... We are clean in this respect. We never overstep any limits with regards to missile technology and nuclear matters.... Everything we do in the spirit of cooperation with Iran, we do within the framework of what is permissible." For this and a discussion of the Russian view on the U.S. attempt to offer incentives to Moscow for abandoning nuclear cooperation with Iran, see the article by Valeriya Sycheva, "A Bird in the Hand, Is Worth Two in Outer Space," *Segdnya,* March 11, 1998, p. 6.
9. U.S. pressure on Russia, which has been intensifying through a sustained lobby, especially on the congressional level by the Israelis, has included repeated threats of U.S. congressional disapproval of aid to Russia and the administration's economic and financial sanctions against Russian research and manufacturing companies with militarily related ties to Iran. See "Clinton Penalizing 7 Russian Enterprises," *New York Times,* June 29, 1998, p. A14.
10. Russian research and technical institutes such as the Scientific Research and Design Institute for Power Technology (known as Nikiet) and Mendeleyev University of Chemical Technology have been the focus of U.S. pressure and Russian concessions. Yevgeny Adamov, Russian Minister for Atomic Energy and former director of Nikiet, announced that the Institute had abandoned the plan to sell Iran the research reactor and Mendeleyev's contact had been limited to delivery of unclassified infor-

mation regarding heavy water technology. This, the Russian Minister hoped, would clear the way for lifting of U.S. sanctions against Russian research institutes; although he was not sure the deal would bypass "some narrow-minded" and "angry people in the Department of State." See Michael Gordon, "Russia to Offer U.S. Deal to End Iran Nuclear Aid," *New York Times*, March 17, 1999, p. A12.

11. "Even without NATO's expansion, it is probably unlikely that Moscow and Washington would be working in lock step, to thwart Iran's nuclear ambition." Michael Gordon, "Russia Remains Uneasy over NATO's Expansion," *New York Times*, March 14, 1999, p. 10.

12. A bipartisan commission headed by former U.S. Defense Secretary Donald Rumsfeld concluded in 1998 that "rogue" states such as Iran and North Korea are much closer to developing a ballistic missile threat than the CIA had predicted. The House and the Senate, over the objections of the Clinton administration, and its threat of veto, overwhelmingly approved a bill supporting an antimissile system project. Eric Schmidt, "House Joins Senate in Voting for System to Defend Against Missiles," *New York Times*, March 19, 1999, p. A14.

13. For an overview of the Russian arms trade, see Igor Khripunov, "Russia's Weapons Trade: Domestic Competition and Foreign Markets," *Problems of Post-Communism*, vol. 46, no. 2, March-April 1999, p. 42.

14. Whereas Russia and Iran have displayed a common approach toward the legal regime of the Caspian Sea, nevertheless, Iranians are not certain about the level of the Russian commitment to the principle of "equal sharing" of the resources of the Caspian and, thus, fear midcourse abandonment and manipulation of the legal regime for tactical advantages by the Russians. For a report on attempts by both sides to solidify cooperation in the Caspian in the face of the increasing isolation of both, see "Iran and Russia Unite over Caspian Hydrocarbon Export," *Izvestiya*, April 22, 1999, p. 6, and a report by Demetry Zhdannikov, "Russia, Iran, in New Energy Initiative," *Reuters*, April 23, 1999.

15. For an Iranian expression of concern over the global meaning of NATO's intervention in Kosovo, see English language daily, *Keyhan International*, April 6, 1999, pp. 1–3.

16. Iran's condemnation of NATO's intervention was not uniform. Although the Foreign Ministry was careful to question the intervention's legal base as being outside of the U.N. framework, others, such as Ayatollah Khamenei, were much more directly critical. "Iranian Criticizes NATO," *New York Times*, April 6, 1999, p. A 11.

17. For an account of Muslim reaction in the North Caucasus toward Russian

policy toward Kosovo, see "Kazan's Tatars Oppose Union of Slavs," *The Irish Times*, April 24, 1999, p. 6.

18. Although one has to be very skeptical about the pejorative label of Wahabism used by official circles in the Caucasus and Central Asia to oppress the Islamic and secular opposition, it is clear that the traditional Islamic tendencies, both official and underground, have increasingly been complimented or challenged by the emergence of "Taliban-type" Islamic groups in Central Asia and the North Caucasus. See Sanobar Shermatova, "Said Amirov Will Shave Off His Beard: Will Daghestan Stay in Russia or Follow Chechnya's Example," *Moskovskiye Novosti*, May 8–15, 1998, no. 9, pp. 6–7 and Nabi Abdulliev, "Daghestan's True Believers," *Transitions*, March 1999.

19. The Russian Ambassador in Iran, Konstantin Shubalov, irritated Iranians when he attributed reports of Serbian atrocities largely to NATO's propaganda. For this interview, see the English language *Daily Iran*, April 7, 1999, p. 1–2.

20. For a reflection of Russia's concerns over a Muslim backlash at home and abroad over Moscow's Balkans policy and rise of pan-Slavism, see Michael Winer, "Russia's House Betrothes Belarus and Yugoslavia," *New York Times*, April 18, 1999, p. 10.

21. Iran's frustration and concern was highlighted by the fact that it also had to carry the burden of being the President of the Organization of Islamic Countries, and thus had to be more openly vocal in demanding Moscow's diplomatic intervention. Celestine Bohlen, "Russia Seeks to Mediate Kosovo Crisis," *New York Times*, April 21, 1999, p. A14.

22. Ibid. For Iran's view on the necessity of the Russian role in solving the Balkan crisis, see "Iran's Foreign Minister's Interview with BBC," in *Hamshahri*, April 22, 1999, p. 1.

23. For a discussion of the general outlines of Khatami's foreign policy, see Ziba Farzin-nia, "The Seventh Iranian Presidential Election and Its Probable Impacts on the Islamic Republic of Iran's Foreign Policy," *The Iranian Journal of International Affairs*, Vol. IX, No. 2, Summer 1997.

24. For a discussion of Iran's policy toward the Islamic factor in Central Asia, see Mohiaddin Mesbahi, "Tajikistan, Iran, and the International Politics of Islam." *Central Asian Survey*, Fall 1997.

25. Opening book fairs, art exhibitions, artistic displays, and so on, are characteristic. Obviously these efforts are "Islamic" in nature, yet they are carefully scanned for their nonpoliticized content and emphasis on Islamic cultural and scholarly dimensions. For an early manifestation of these efforts see the details of cultural ties established between Iran and Central

Asian states including Kyrgyzstan covered in *FBIS-SOV,* 21 October 1993, pp. 70–72, *FBIS-SOV,* 25 October 1993, pp. 65–66. It is worth noting that on purely Islamic aspects, Saudi Arabia, Pakistan, and Afghanistan are more active than Iran.

26. For example, see comments by Iranian diplomats at the gathering of Muslim dignitaries of the Commonwealth of Independent States on February 21, 1998, on the need for the spiritual message of Islam among the Muslims of the newly independent states and the need for unity of all "divine religions in the region" neutralizing "the propaganda of opposing cultural and political currents," *FBIS-NES-98–052 Daily Report,* February 21, 1998, p. 20.
27. Although Uzbek officials denied the reports of Karimov's comments, Iran's decision to cancel the scheduled trip of Uzbek Foreign Minister, Abdulaziz Kmalov, to Tehran, indicated Iran's dissatisfaction with the Uzbek official explanation. See, for reports on Uzbekistan's official denial of support for the U.S. embargo, *Ettela'at,* May 8, 1995, p. 8. On cancellation of the visit, see *Ettela'at,* May 15, 1995. The two countries, however, have engaged in damage limitations and have tried since 1996 to lessen the tension of diplomatic overtures and economic agreements. The visit of Iran's Foreign Minister to Uzbekistan in February of 1996 should be considered in this context. For the coverage of the visit and the meetings with Karimov, see *Ettela'at,* March 1, 1996, p. 10.
28. The visit of U.S. Defense Secretary William Perry, in April 9, 1995, to Tashkent marked a considerable step toward improvement in U.S.–Uzbek relations.
29. *New York Times,* March, 27, 1999, p A17.
30. The views of the American oil companies have been best illustrated by Mobil Corporation's prominently placed essay advertisements in the *New York Times* editorial pages throughout 1998–99, which strongly advocated the Iranian alternative for the Caspian. For a sample, see "Iran: Food for Thought," *New York Times,* April 6, 1999, p. A 27. The editorial argued, "U.S.-Iran rapprochement would go a long way to bolster regional harmony. . . . When U.S. policy—like unilateral sanctions—prohibits us from doing business in a country, we will abide. But that doesn't prevent us from speaking out against the use of unilateral sanctions." Sanctions "cost American companies sales and jobs. . . . Maintaining sanctions on Iran, while foreign companies can invest there with no restrictions, not only puts U.S. companies on the sidelines, but more importantly weakens America's foreign policy in the region."
31. "In their hearts, many American oil executives believe the best export route for Caspian oil is through Iran." For this and a discussion of the contra-

diction between the U.S. Caspian policy and the American oil companies, see Stephen Kinzer, "Caspian Competitors Embrace Foreign Powers on Sea of Oil," *New York Times*, January 24, 1999, p. A18.

32. For reports on U.S.-NATO politicomilitary activities and interests in the Caucasus and Central Asia, see Stephen Kinzer, "Caspian Competitors in Embrace Foreign Powers Race for Power on Sea of Oil"; James Kitfield, "Stars and Stripes on the Silk Route," *National Journal*, March 13, 1999, and; David Stern, "East-West Fault-lines Deepen in Caucasus as NATO Meets," *Agence France Press*, cited in *Turkistan's Newsletter*, vol. 3, no. 93, April 26, 1999, pp. 9–11.

33. "A Farewell to Flashman: American Policy in the Caucasus and Central Asia," *Deputy Secretary Talbot's Address at the Johns Hopkins School of Advanced International Studies in Baltimore, Maryland, July 21, 1997*. Available at http://www.state.gov/regions/nis/970721talbot.html.

34. The relative thaw in U.S.-Iranian relations since Khatami has consistently been accompanied by tough U.S. measures, thus, a group of mixed signals: Khatami's remarkable acknowledgement of the values of Western civilization, Clinton's intriguing acknowledgement of Western guilt in Iran, the lifting of agricultural sanctions, replacing "dual-containment" with "engagement and containment," all positive signals, have been qualified, by simultaneous reinforcements of the sanctions opposing the Mobil bid for the oil swap in Iran, and even an Israeli-inspired congressional measure to punish the International Atomic Energy Agency (IAEA) for working with Iran! See Gary Sick's discussions of the "Mixed Signals" in *gulf2000–list@colombia.edu*, on May 1, 1999, 18:42:32—0400 (EDT).

35. In the words of Kamal Kharazi, Iran's Foreign Minister, "Iran is naturally a part of or partner in any political development in regions such as Central Asia, Caspian Sea, Caucasus, East of the Arab World, Persian Gulf, and Southwest Asia." See Kharazi's statement on "Iran's Caspian Policy."

36. For an Azeri discussion of these issues, see *Zerkalo*, 15 March 1997, which warns that the two countries are losing historical opportunities for cooperation in view of the continuous tensions in the relationship.

37. For the implications of the radicalization of the Armenian position after Ter-Petrossian's downfall, see *New York Times*, February 9, 1998, p. A8.

38. Iran will, for example, oppose Turkmenistan's attempts to construct a pipeline through the Caspian Sea, thus bypassing Iran; a project heavily lobbied and supported by the United States. For a report on Iran's opposition expressed in the gathering of several hundred oil executives in Ashkabad in early March 1999, see *Turkistan Economic Bulletin*, vol. 99, no. 25, March 12, 1999, pp. 1–3, 5.

39. For a recent and rather comprehensive review of Tajikistan from an Iranian point of view, see the special issue on Tajikistan of *Envoy: West and Central Asian Business Magazine*, October 1997, especially S. Farrokhyar, "Conservatism and Moderation: Will Peace and Tranquility Return to Tajikistan," M. Aliev, "Gas and Oil Industries in Tajikistan," S. Farrokhyar, "We Seek Democracy to Propagate Islam: An Interview with Abdullah Nouri, Leader of the Tajikistan Islamic Movement." N. Bruker and I. Guseinova, "Prostitution: The Profession of Poverty and War," O. Panfilov, "To Whom Will the Child of the Uranium Industry Belong?"
40. In an attempt to further consolidate its hold on Tajikistan in view of developments in Afghanistan, and an implied response to Uzbek distance from the CIS, and gravitation toward the West, Russia has reached an agreement with Dushanbe to establish a permanent military base in Tajikistan, a measure severely criticized by Uzbekistan. Iran's response has been muted. Bruce Pannier, "Tajikistan: Uzbek President Criticizes Proposed Russian Base," in *Radio Free Europe Radio Liberty Report*, April 9, 1999, printed in *Turkistan Newsletter,* vol. 3, no. 79, April 13, 1999, pp. 9–11.
41. See Mohiaddin Mesbahi, "Tajikistan and Iran," in A. Rubinstein and O. Smolensky, *Regional Rivalry in the New States of Eurasia* (Sharpe, 1995), pp. 113-143.
42. For the details of the Tajik-Iranian relations, see Mohiaddin Mesbahi, "Iran, Tajikistan, and the International Politics of the Islamic Factor," *Central Asian Survey,* Fall 1997, and "Iran and Tajikistan," in A. Rubinstein and O. Smolensky, *Regional Rivalries in the New Eurasia: Russia, Turkey, and Iran* (NewYork: M.E. Sharpe, 1995), pp. 113-143.
43. The improved relationship with Kyrgyzstan was underscored by the fact that the seizure of Iranian weapons destined for pro-Iranian factions in the Afghan civil war by the Kyrgyz authorities at Osh did not create any controversy. The weapons were part of a larger package of humanitarian aid, and were returned to Iran, while the humanitarian aid was allowed to pass. See *Turkistan Newsletter,* vol. 98, no. 2, November 18, 1998, p 1.
44. The Kazakh-Iranian oil swapping project discontinued in 1997 under U.S. pressure, will resume in 1999 based on a new agreement between the two countries. *IRNA,* April 11, 1999, and *Iran-TASS,* April 12, 1999, reprinted in *Turkistan Economic Bulletin,* vol. 99, no. 40, April 21, 1999, p. 2.
45. For an early official elaboration of Iran's views on Central Asia and on the issue of regionalism, see Abbas Maleki, "Cooperation: Iran's New Foreign Policy Objectives," in *Majalleh Motaleate Asia-ye Markazi va Qafqaz [The Journal of Central Asian and Caucasian Review]* (Tehran), vol. 1, no. 2 (Fall 1992): pp. 336–37.

46. For an early report on the pipeline project, see "Central Asia Turning South," *The Economist,* October 29, 1994, p. 40.
47. This rivalry has diminished Turkey's and Iran's leverage vis-à-vis the United States and Russia, respectively. Fearing this, and in spite of pressure from their great power clients, Ankara and Tehran have engaged in some significant economic cooperation, including the very ambitious $20 billion gas treaty signed in 1996. For details on this and related projects between Turkey and Iran, see "Iran-Turkey Natural Gas Export," *IRNA,* April 2, 1999, cited in *Turkistan Economy Bulletin,* vol. 99, no. 35, April 5, 1999, p. 4.
48. Some of these functionalist views are expressed in the newly established journal called *Envoy.* See for example, *Envoy,* September 1997, in the issue devoted to the Caspian Sea. Also see *The Iranian Journal of International Affairs, Amu Darya, Majalleh Motaleate Asia-ye Markazi va Oafqaz,* and *Journal of Central Asia and the Caucasus,* especially issues published from September 1995 to the present.
49. The early enthusiasm over the "Gold Rush" in the Caspian Sea has gradually been replaced by more realistic and modest assessment of its potentials, especially in view of the decline of oil prices. Judith Matloff, "Letting Caspian 'Black Gold Lie,'" *Christian Science Monitor,* March 1999, p. 10–11, and M. Culler, "The Rise and Fall of the Caspian Sea," *National Geographic Magazine,* May 1999, pp. 46-49.
50. This culturalization of the Iranian view of the region is best reflected in a lecture delivered by Ataollah Mohajerani, Iran's Minister of Culture and Guidance, in the gathering of students, faculty, and officials of Makhtoumqoli University in Ashkhabad, Turkmenistan. "Every human being has the obligation to know his own history, and today, the Persian language is the key to know the history of this region." Referring to Makhtoumqoli, Hafez, and Rumi, he said that "The Persian language belongs to all the nations of the region, for we all have lived in different periods in one common civilizational and cultural milieu. The great personalities of literature and thought belong to everybody in this region and we should not separate them based on new geographical boundaries." Cited in *Iranian,* no. 48, April 1999, p. 2.

8

The Iranian Revolution and International Politics: Some European Perspectives

Fred Halliday

Introduction: A Revolutionary State in International Politics

The two decades following the triumph of the Iranian revolution underscored the difficulties involved, for both sides, in stabilizing relations between revolutionary states and their status quo interlocutors. If it is relations with the United States that were most difficult, those with the neighboring Arab states, and with Western Europe, were little easier. The course of relations with the former U.S.S.R. was also turbulent. In the region, Iran was able to construct a durable alliance only with Syria. Of the permanent members of the Security Council, it is only with China—sympathetic, but distant—that Iran sustained normal diplomatic relations.

The reasons for this recalcitrance are several. They apply to relations with Western Europe as well as to those with the United States. They involve analysis of Iran's domestic politics as much as of its international relations. They also highlight the degree to which Iran's revolution and foreign policy shared common features with other revolutionary states of the twentieth century.[1]

In analyzing this record from the Iranian side, four factors are of particular relevance. First, Iran's primary external focus was not on the West as such, on the United States or Europe, but on how these states interacted with regional issues in the Middle East and West Asia. Its policy was regional, not global. From its own perspective, Iran found itself beleaguered and threatened by external powers in this regional context. Within a year of the revolution, Soviet forces had occupied Iran's neighbour to the East, Afghanistan, and were to conduct a nine-year war there against an Islamist opposition: that opposition, for its part, was largely controlled by Pakistan and the United States and, hence, seen by Iran as part of a U.S. encirclement on the East. Khomeini spoke disparagingly of *islam-i imrikai*, "American Islam," to denote this dimension of the Afghan war. The Afghan war also brought two million refugees to Iran. On the West, Iran soon became embroiled, partly through its own adventurism, in a conflict with Iraq that was to last for eight years and cost the lives of up to one million Iranians: it was this "imposed" war, *jang-i mahmul*, more than the revolution itself, which forged the institutions and tempered the personnel of the Islamic Republic. From the start, Iraq was also seen in Iran as acting at the behest of the West; from 1982 this became to a considerable degree a reality, as Iraq became the recipient of weapons from France, the U.S.S.R and Britain, and of substantial financial and other support from Saudi Arabia, Kuwait and the United States. Iraq was in the end held to a draw, but the price of that war was to bring the U.S. navy into the Gulf under the "reflagging" policy. Two years later, Saddam was to strengthen that U.S. presence by his invasion of Kuwait, occasioning the subsequent deployments of Western forces before, during, and after, the war of 1991. It was therefore the regional that refracted the international.

Second, Iran, like all revolutionary states, pursued what E. H. Carr writing of the Bolshevik revolution termed a "dual policy."[2] This meant that Iran conducted diplomatic relations with other states and at the same time provided assistance—political, financial, military—to opposition forces in other countries. The Iranian revolution, no less than its predecessors, sought to export the revolution through a variety of means: With regard to three countries in particular—Afghanistan, Iraq, Lebanon—this involved a sustained, if only partially successful, commitment.[3] Like other revolutionaries, the Iranians at times concealed, and at times exaggerated, this commitment: it was, however, a central feature of Tehran's foreign policy. With regard to Lebanon, at least, it remains so.

Third, foreign policy in Iran was subject to the vagaries of domestic politics. Although this is true of all states, it is particularly so for revolutionary states: The insecurities of revolutionary leaderships on the one hand, the factionalism to which they are prey on the other, combine to render the conduct of foreign policy particularly difficult. In Iran's case, this factionalism persisted long after the initial revolutionary years: Iran did not become a totalitarian state, ruled by a monolithic party. Rather, the very diversity of centers of power, and of political currents, made consistent and coherent diplomacy less possible: This was evident in the events of November 1979, when the "liberal" government of Mehdi Bazargan was overwhelmed in the crisis over the U.S. hostages; and in the Rushdie affair of 1989, itself an outcome of domestic uncertainty following the end of the war with Iraq. It remains true today as internal debates over a range of issues—not only relations with the West, and Israel, but also those with the Taliban in Afghanistan—demonstrate.

Finally, Iranian foreign policy has been prey, in several respects, to a set of illusions about the outside world. This was the case with Iranian leaderships prior to 1979: the history of Iran in the twentieth century has been punctuated by miscalculations by its leaders—be they Reza Shah in 1941 or Mossadeq in 1953. After 1979, revolutionary rhetoric and anticipation, however, compounded this. Thus, on the one hand, Iranian leaders believed that their revolution would spread to other countries, that their confrontation with the status quo powers would, in the end, be rewarded. If this was so for the Muslim and Middle Eastern worlds in general, it was especially, and tragically, so for the country with which Iran was most embroiled: Iraq. Just as hope of a German revolution sustained the Bolsheviks, so the chimera of an uprising against Saddam Hussein, producing a sister Islamic Republic of Iraq, sustained Iran for several years.

On the other hand, and again in common with other revolutionary powers, Iran believed that in dealing with status quo powers it was possible to shift between different blocs and form tactical alliances: thus, in a style that echoed Chinese manoeuvrings in the 1960s and 1970s between the "first" and "second" worlds (the latter including Western Europe), Iranian leaders seem repeatedly to have sought to offset their confrontation with the United States by developing relations with Europe. This was a double illusion: No normalization with the international economic and financial systems, let alone any resolution of the security problems in the Middle East, was possible without a minimal dialogue with Washington; for their part, the European states, and European firms, although not adhering completely to U.S. policies, were nevertheless careful to limit relations with Iran and avoid undue conflict with Washington.

European Approaches

The history of European relations with the Islamic Republic illustrates the difficulties of these tensions in dealings between revolutionary and status quo powers.[4] European states sought to continue trading with Iran and maintained some degree of diplomatic contact. European-Iranian relations may be said to have fallen into three phases. Relations with Iran were particularly difficult in the first phase, which lasted from the revolution until 1989, a result not only of Iranian rejection of Western *istikbar*, arrogance, or imperialism, but of such issues as the U.S. hostages crisis, the arming of Iraq, the seizure of Western hostages in Lebanon, and the killings of Iranian opposition figures abroad. The end of the war with Iraq was followed by the Rushdie affair, in February 1989. Attempts were made in the second phase, coinciding with the presidency of Rafsanjani, to engage in "critical dialogue," but this was broken off in 1997 after the Berlin court verdict on the Mykonos killings. The election of Khatami has opened a third phase in European-Iranian relations: a new dialogue, not qualified as "critical," has begun, and a number of high-ranking EU visitors have been to Tehran. President Khatami visited Italy in February. Even with Britain there has been improvement: An agreed statement on Rushdie, in September 1998, issued by the two foreign ministers, removed this as an official obstacle. In July 1999, relations were raised to the ambassadorial level, and there was talk of cooperation on Afghanistan and narcotics.

Three aspects of the European record merit particular attention here. First, whereas European states were able to sustain relations with Iran at some diplomatic level after 1979, they found no stable solution to the problems of relations with revolutionary Iran. Those states who appeared best positioned in 1979 to have good relations soon found their hopes confounded: France, which had given shelter to Khomeini in 1978, was embroiled in several conflicts during the 1980s; Britain, the historic enemy, had several disputes, culminating in the Rushdie affair in 1989; Germany, Iran's historic European ally, and its main trading partner, sought to continue a dialogue through the 1980s and 1990s, but antagonized Iran over sales of chemical warfare equipment to Iraq and was forced to suspend further discussion in 1997 over Mykonos. Iran was not able to sustain consistent and different relations with any, let alone all, of these. Indeed at times the more radical voices in Iran appeared to see little difference between the United States and its European allies. All were part of the enemy camp.

Second, European attempts to influence Iranian diplomacy or domestic politics were ineffectual. European states themselves pursued their policies toward Tehran in two registers: bilateral relations with Iran, multilateral relations via the E.U. On this, as on all other issues, the former prevailed over the latter. That said, there were no major, sustained, differences between European states over Iran. Rather, whether in bilateral or multilateral form, European pressure appeared to produce few results. To say this is not to say that an alternative, more combative, policy would have succeeded: Iran's policy on human rights was a response to domestic considerations, of power and political change; its policy on the Arab-Israeli question was, equally, a response to regional developments. In particular, it would be mistaken to say that the Mykonos affair showed the errors of the "critical dialogue" policy: The Mykonos shootings occurred in June 1992, and were presumably ordered earlier; the "critical dialogue" did not commence until the latter part of 1992. Just as Europe's policy on the Arab-Israeli question was largely rhetorical, and so ineffectual, so it was on Iran. The failure of European initiatives, like those made by the United States in 1979 and 1985–86, was not that there was a better policy available. Rather, given the character of Iran's revolutionary regime and politics, it was not possible for any outside power, or policy, seriously to inflect it.

The third relevant aspect of European policy on Iran is its implications for relations with the United States. There is an argument for saying that after 1979 a certain division of labor, generally welcomed by both sides, operated: The Europeans maintained a dialogue with Iran while Washington exerted strategic, military, and economic pressure. Moreover, whatever the strains in European–U.S. relations over Iran they were, in a broader perspective, secondary: compared to those over Suez, in 1956, over the Soviet pipeline in 1980–1981, or over Central America in the mid-1980s, disagreements on Iran were not the cause of a major U.S.-European conflict. Perhaps the moment of sharpest conflict came in 1995–96 with the imposition of controls on foreign investment in the Iranian energy sector: yet, even here, Washington itself spoke with two voices—Congressional and Presidential. In sum, from 1979 onward, Iran was a significant and enduring, but secondary, source of discord between the United States and its European allies.

International Relations: A Two-Sided Historical Legacy

Against this background, it is possible to assess the obstacles that any normalization of Iran's relations with the outside world will encounter. Let us begin with perceptions outside Iran, not only in the West, and specifically the United States, but also in something that affects U.S. and European policy, views of Iran in the Middle East, in the Arab world and Israel. Prior to the revolution of 1979, Iran was a close ally of the West, and had, to a considerable degree, reasonable relations with the Middle East: The least reasonable relations were in the Persian Gulf—Iran fought an undeclared war against Iraq from 1969 to 1975, a conflict that, in my view, was the first Gulf War and was the root of the two later conflicts bearing that name; it imposed its will on the region, and in particular occupied three Arab islands, Tumbs, and Abu Musa in November 1971. With the revolution, Iran entered into a revolutionary confrontation with the region: It committed itself to the destruction of Israel, it encouraged Islamist insurrection in a range of Arab states, saluting, inter alia, the assassins of Sadat in Egypt in 1981 and Boudiaf in Algeria in 1993, and it fought an eight-year war with Iraq, from 1980 to 1988. As we have seen, relations with the West soon entered crisis.

This has all added up to a negative record. It is one that will have to be addressed, at least in the sense that any improvement will involve clear, and sustained, evidence that Iran has altered its policies. It would not take much for elements in the Iranian state opposed to President Khatami, by word or deed, to sabotage any such improvement, replicating abroad the kinds of violent provocation to which they have resorted at home. This is a history that weighs over any normalization. It has led some, especially in the United States, to qualify Iran as a "rogue," or "outlaw," state. But there is another side to this issue, one that must qualify any view that the onus of historical rectification lies with Iran. It may be argued here that for all the crimes that Iran has committed, in regard to U.S. hostages or terrorist acts, and the irresponsible policies it has pursued, the onus of history and of rectification does not lie with Iran, but with those opposed to it.

Let us take the three major conflicts of this century: in World War I, foreign troops, from Britain, Russia, and Turkey all occupied parts of the country; in World War II, Russia and Britain, in violation of international law, occupied the whole of Iran—a neutral country—in August 1941; in the Cold War, the U.S. and British governments, or more specifically the CIA and MI6, organized riots and a military coup that overthrew the democratically elected government of Iran and its premier Dr. Mossadiq—an action that, its criminality aside, was, by removing the nationalist and secular opposition movement, to pave the way for the rise of Khomeini a decade later. Nor is this all: for perhaps the greatest act of irresponsibility toward Iran was to come in the context of the Iraqi invasion of Iran in September 1980. Whatever provocation Iran had offered prior to September 1980, Iraq's invasion was a clear violation of international law and the U. N. charter, an undisputed case of aggression. What such an act necessitates is an immediate resolution by the U. N. Security Council not only condemning the aggressor, but insisting that it return to the frontiers prior to hostility. As has been well documented, this did not occur: Iraqi obstruction and Western collusion delayed the Security Council until SCR 479 of September 28, 1980 and even then it called only for a cease-fire in place, not a return to the status quo ante: only in July 1982 did SCR 514 call for a return to international recognized borders. Only in 1991 was Iraq formally declared to be the aggressor by the U.N. Secretary General.

Iraq received a green light, and large-scale military and financial help, from the West in its war with Iran, and was later joined by the U.S. navy that, under the reflagging operation, sank an estimated third of the Iranian navy in the Gulf, before going on to shoot down an Iranian civilian airliner with 269 people on board. Iran's repeated insistence on the naming of the aggressor, and on compensation, was finally incorporated into resolution 598 of July 20, 1987, but it remained a dead letter until the declaration of 1991. Iraq was, lamely, named as the aggressor after it invaded Kuwait in 1990: but no money has been paid, and Iranians remain prisoners of war in Iraq to this day. This whole story is a disgraceful one. There will be those who say that Iran deserved what it got because of the U.S. hostages affair. But this, itself illegal, act has no bearing, and should have had no bearing, on the Security Council determination of aggression.

The historical legacy does, therefore, matter, but some element of recognition that Iran is far being the only transgressor is in order. A sanctimonious, one-sided, pressure on Iran to apologize will be a waste of time. Until and unless this is recognized any resolution of the historical balance sheet will be incomplete.

One further historical point needs to be made. Much is made in current critical commentary on Iran of its aggressive character, and there are Arab states that talk of Iranian expansionism *al-tawassu' al-irani*. Iraqi propaganda has even compared Iran to Israel, a "Zionism" of the East, compared to that already installed in the West. It was also common, in the 1970s at least, to regard Iranians living in the Arab states of the Gulf as settlers, part of some sinister expansionist conspiracy, like that in Palestine. Anti-Persian racism was a stock in trade of Bathism at least, as was anti-Shiism part of the officially promoted orthodoxy in Saudi Arabia. Saddam's uncle and father-in-law, Khairullah Tulfah, published a book entitled *Three Whom God Should Not Have Created–Persians, Jews and Flies*—and note the order. We should be wary of how far such stereotypes remain latent in Arab criticism of Iran. As for the record on matters of aggression the picture is rather different. Compared to any of its near neighbors—Russia, Turkey, Iraq, all of whom have repeatedly invaded other countries—Iran has, over the past two centuries, a record more pacific than any. The last time that Iran occupied any other country was when Aga Mohammad took, or rather retook, the Transcaucasian states of Armenia and Georgia in the 1790s. These had long been part of the Iranian political and cultural world. In the 1820s, Iran lost these areas to Russia, a loss it has remained remarkably reconciled to: Almost no one in twentieth-century Iran, a century noted for its obsessive and self-pitying nationalist claims to territory far and near, has challenged that loss of territory. Iran did occupy the three islands in 1971, but this was after it had conceded on the much larger and more sensitive claim to Bahrain, and had sought a peaceful resolution of the islands issue. We may accept, or not accept, the legality of the treaty concluded with the Amir of Sharjah on Abu Musa and deny the right of Iran to take the two Tumbs from the Sheikh of Ras al-Khaima by force: But the occupation of these islands is no indication of a broader, expansionist drive. To sum up, Iran has, throughout modern history, been one of the most pacific, and restrained, of states in the Middle East.

Iran and Regional Conflict

Turning from the past to the contemporary, we can now consider Iran's current place in the region, and its relation to regional conflicts on or near its frontiers. It may be that the first such conflict that will occur to people is the Arab-Israeli, but this would be mistaken. The Arab-Israeli is far from being the sole, or most costly in human lives, of the conflicts besetting the region; any policy toward Iran driven by Iran's views on this conflict would be distorted. The Arab-Israeli dispute is one of several, indeed close on a dozen, regional conflicts in which Iran has been, and remains, involved. The record is not always one that does credit to Iran, but nor is one that sets Iran in an especially, or uniquely, negative light.

Let us take the Gulf itself. Few can doubt that, over the past two decades, the main source of aggression and instability in the Gulf has been Iraq. One need not labor the history of the eight-year war with Iran or the occupation of Kuwait. Iran, it must be emphasized again, paid the heaviest price for this: hundreds of thousands dead, cities destroyed, economy disrupted. Much is made of the Scuds that Iraq launched against Saudi Arabia and Israel in 1991, and rightly so: but Iraq has, in all launched around 390 Scuds in its recent wars, 308 of them, that is, around 80 percent, against Tehran and other Iranian cities, with the loss of over 2,226 lives and 10, 705 injured.[5]

The Iranian Revolution and International Politics 183

There is no reason, despite recent diplomatic developments, to presume that this pattern of Iraqi behavior is over. Far from it: Whatever its immediate outcome, the current crisis promises more danger for the whole region. Iraq will, on current expectations, become a major oil exporter, it will, whatever the U.N. inspectors and special groups may have wished, become a significant military power, and in all likelihood it will turn on that state that has been its historic enemy, Iran. That is why for the foreseeable future Iran's major security concern, and the issue that gives meaning to its foreign and security policy, will remain Iraq.

Elsewhere in the Gulf, in the early 1980s Iran was supporting opposition groups in Kuwait, Bahrain, Saudi Arabia, even Oman, but this has now ceased, in large measure, to be the case. The causes of opposition in those countries are not made in Iran but in the denial of democratic and legal guarantees to the populations of those countries. In the case of Bahrain in particular, we see a stubborn ruling family, the al-Khalifa, refusing to meet the demands of the mass of the people for a return to the constitution abolished in 1975, and still unwarrantedly indulged, to their discredit, by Britain and the United States in this refusal. On the islands, there remains room for compromise, but it is not one that will be helped by Arab nationalist exaggeration of Iran's overall plan, nor by moves, such as support for and recognition by Gulf states of the Afghan Taliban, that are seen as part of an Arab attempt to encircle Iran on the East.

Turning to Afghanistan, we have here one of the sorriest, most criminal, chapters in the history of West Asia, one in which three countries in particular—Pakistan, Saudi Arabia, and the United States—have over two decades sought to destabilize that country and impose on it a collection of ultraconservative gangsters. The PDPA regime that came to power in April 1978 in Kabul was, in its first 20 months in power, responsible for terrible crimes: But I was, and remain, of the view that the stabilization of that regime, accompanied by an opening to opposition groups, was the best hope for the future of Afghanistan. Nowhere is the myth of Western hostility to political Islam turned on its head more than here, where in the largest covert operation in its history, the CIA backed the likes of Gulbuddin Hekmatyar, who first rose to prominence throwing acid in the faces of women students at Kabul University, in this fight against the PDPA regime.[6]

With the predictable civil war between supposed allies that followed the collapse of the PDPA regime in 1992, Pakistan, with Saudi money, has now created an even greater monster, the Taliban, an organization whose contempt for human rights, for women, and, now, for the rights of ethnic minorities is known to all. That Pakistan is now reaping the fruits of this irresponsibility, through the proliferation of arms, drugs and interethnic strife should bring no comfort. It does, however, set in some perspective any claim that it is Iran, a country that has hosted over two million Afghan refugees largely at its own expense, but that played a secondary role in the Afghan conflict, which is the major source of instability in the region. Indeed, it is a strange irony that the one area in which Washington and Tehran are now, prior to any general normalization, engaged in direct negotiation, through what is termed the "Six plus 2 talks," with a view to conflict resolution, is Afghanistan.

With regard to the former Soviet Union, Iran has not pursued particular advantage in the former Muslim republics of the U.S.S.R.; it has pursued what has been termed *siasat-i dast-i gol*, the policy of the bouquet of flowers, that is, greeting whoever turns up at Tehran Airport from those countries irrespective of ideology. In Tajikistan Iran has, in conjunction with other Central Asian states, sought to mediate. In the Nagorno-Karabagh dispute Iran has, contrary to any supposition of Islamic solidarity, formed an alliance with Armenia against Shii but pro-Turkish and pro-American Azerbaijan. It may indeed be that Iran has, if anything, encouraged Armenia, or rather the more hardline elements now in power in Erevan, president Robert Kocharian and defense Minister Vazgen Sarkissian, to resist compromise with Azerbaijan, an unwise move that ignores the realities of the strategic situation in which Armenia finds itself.

Iran's policy in another bit of the former communist world, namely Bosnia, is also worth mentioning: From the imprecise information available, it would seem that Iran supplied arms and security personnel to Bosnia in the period 1993–95 in violation of the embargo on supplies to both sides. A mistaken policy, it might be said, and evidence of Iran's interference in countries far from its frontier—the first time, indeed, that Iran had played a militarily significant role on European soil since the time of the battle of Thermopylae, in 480 B.C., a while ago. But on closer examination it turns out that this Iranian involvement, for which it has subsequently been condemned in the West, was carried out with the knowledge of, and tacit acceptance by, the U.S. government and the CIA in particular. Just as Washington was doing what it could to circumvent the embargo, and aid both the Croatians and the Bosnians, it allowed Iranian men and materiel to reach Sarajevo. This was, therefore, hardly an index of Iran's rogue or outlaw behaviour.

We can now revert to the most contentious issue of all, the Arab-Israeli dispute. Here the record is one that certainly merits criticism. Since the revolution of 1979, Iran has not only had no relations with Israel but has, implicitly and on some occasions explicitly, denied the right of an Israeli state to exist. In this, its policy is rather similar to that which China, forever denouncing Soviet "revisionist" indulgence of Israel, pursued from the mid-1950s until the late 1970s. Iran has in addition provided some material aid to one of the Palestinian groups most opposed to the state of Israel, Islamic Jihad, and has also, through Syria and its Islamic Guards units in Lebanon, backed Hizbullah. The central point, that Iran has not only criticized Israeli policy, but has also promoted a policy aimed against a two-state solution, was until recently valid. It represented a throwback to the intransigent, rejectionist, Arab attitudes of the 1950s and 1960s and in no way accorded with Iran's national interest. Nor does it accord with the interests of those, in Palestine and Israel, who support the kind of two-state compromise that is made possible by the 1993 Oslo accords.

The idea of a binational state, involving Palestinians and Israelis, has long ceased to be relevant, if it ever was: but the peace process *is* a binational one, as it involves support, what in Northern Ireland would be termed "sufficient consensus," in both communities. The last thing the Palestinians need is Iran, or any other state, engaging in self-indulgent rhetorical excess. They, and the large number of people in Israel who are willing to envisage a two-state compromise, including on East Jerusalem, need a firm, critical, and responsible engagement by Iran in the process, the better to secure a just and lasting settlement. This is something the Syrians could also do more to engage in. But this is not a one-way process either. Iran is criticized for having refused to recognize the right of the Israelis to a state, but the obverse also applies: An Iranian engagement in negotiations on a two-state solution will make little difference if those in Israel and the United States who, in a mirror image of anti-Israeli rejectionism, have persisted in their refusal to accept the right of the Palestinians to their state, on the territory occupied by Israel in 1967, continue to do so. Denial of Palestine's right to exist is, morally and legally, equivalent to the denial of Israel's right.

The support for Islamic Jihad and, indirectly, for HAMAS may be less significant than is claimed: No one argues that these groups get their main support from Iran. In the late 1990s, the main recruiting agent for Palestinian rejectionism was, by its provocative obstructionism, the Israeli government of Benjamin Netanyahu. As for the Lebanese Hizbullah, we are dealing here with an organization that is both political and military: Like Sinn Fein/IRA, it is not a purely military organization, in Hizbullah's case it has representatives in the Lebanese parliament. The hope must be that the issue of the illegally occupied security zone in southern Lebanon can be resolved, by an Israeli withdrawal, something many Israelis support. Iran would be best advised to assist this process, supporting the incorporation of Hizbullah into Lebanese political life, and encouraging an Israeli withdrawal in return for security guarantees.

Disputed Issues: Weapons of Mass Destruction, Terrorism

The picture painted here of Iran's regional involvements is designed to underline two points: first, that Iran's regional policies cannot be seen in relation to one specific conflict, and certainly not the Arab-Israeli, but as part of a broader attempt to manage, and in some cases take advantage of, a broader mosaic of conflicts; second, while some of Iran's policies—its official position on Israel most of all—have contributed to exacerbating regional problems, Iran is far from being the only, or even main, source of instability in the region.

There are, however, two more specific questions that stand in the way of an improvement of Western relations with Iran, issues that, in addition to the Arab-Israeli question, recur in U.S. and E.U. statements and that have to be addressed in their own right. Involving both the Gulf and Arab-Israeli contexts is the issue of weapons of mass destruction, specifically nuclear weapons. The charge is twofold: one, that Iran is, at its Bushehr nuclear plant, engaged in a program that will give it nuclear weapons material, probably in a few years; two, that at the Shahid Himmat Industrial Group research facility south of Tehran it is, with Russian help, assembling the materials for a missile based on the Russian SS-4 with a range of 1,250 miles. Both are being carried out, it is claimed, with Russian help, and Israel and the United States, not to mention British Prime Minister Tony Blair and Foreign Minister Robin Cook, have been trying to get the Russians to stop this flow of material and expertise to Iran, just as they have with the two other states believed to be helping Iran, China and North Korea. The Iranians, of course, deny both charges, but given the region they are in, and given the to date quite unreliable character of Russian export controls, one would be prudent in suspecting that such a program is afoot. It is not necessarily a crash program and much will depend on what happens in Iraq, but as Gary Sick has written, the probability is of such an intention.[7]

No one suggests that Iran would use this material in the short run: It is in all likelihood designed as a deterrent against Iraq. But in Israel in particular there is alarm. The Israeli position is that Iran and Iraq now constitute its two main enemies, and they believe that Iran will within a short time have a missile capability capable of hitting Tel Aviv. In these circumstances, and given the precedent of the 1981 Israeli attack on the Osirak nuclear plant in Iraq, there is a danger of an Israeli strike against Iran within a year or so.

Iran has, of course, denied any such intention or capability. It has signed the Non-Proliferation Treaty and the International Atomic Energy Act, both of which permit international inspection. In the current climate of the region, however, this will not be sufficient. The long-term solution has to be to find a way of creating a security framework for the region, through arms control agreements and confidence building measures, that will, if not remove all nuclear weapons, reduce fears of their irresponsible, or first, use. Here it is essential to remember why Iran faces a threat: It is not from Israel, nor from the West, but from states nearer home, notably Iraq. The precedent for such a security framework exists in the European case—in the negotiations and building of confidence that began in the 1960s and have continued to this day in the context of the OSCE. Of little relevance to the Middle East, it may be said, given the even lower levels of trust, the disproportion between Israeli and other states' capacities, and the multiplicity of conflict lines, in contrast to the single, East-West, division in Europe.

All this is true, but there are countervailing arguments. First, Israeli predominance is, as the Israelis are the first to say, a dubious one, given the very small geographical space their country occupies: Other states in the region could survive a nuclear hit, Israel might not. Second, we have elements of confidence building over the past 20 years: The frontiers between Egypt and Israel, and Syria and Israel, have been stable. In the Gulf, Iran has engaged in some limited confidence building measures, such as prior notification of naval and air manoeuvres. In the case of the arms race of the Cold War, I was one of those who argued that the core issues were not the race, or weapons, themselves. Politics had not been overtaken by some determinist, technological, let alone exterminist logic. The choices, and issues, remained political. Looking back, I would argue that history has vindicated this position. Political change, in international and domestic spheres, occurred and led to a widespread reduction of tension.

In the case of the Middle East the same applies, and the time to think about it is now. It is a pity that, when, on the initiative of Prince Hassan of Jordan, suggestions on this were floated in 1997, Iran rejected them. It would seem to be wiser to look again at this, something that involves the interests of all in the region. Linked as it could be to a significant shift on the Arab-Israeli question, this could provide a way of lessening concern about the purposes of Iran's military programs.

The issue of terrorism, the other issue of dispute on the list, also has been given prominence by Iran's critics. It is one that President Khatami has sought to address, distinguishing as the OIC final statement did between terrorism, which was condemned, and acts of violence in pursuit of national liberation, which were legitimate. This is a distinction that everyone, in any religious or ethical system, can accept. If we look at the Iranian practice, we see that for much of the revolutionary period Iran has pursued its political enemies with ferocity and has violated human rights in the process, to a degree far greater than did the Shah. Iran's enemies have certainly made much of this, especially in the United States. Sometimes this has been based on facts, but sometimes not: The passage of the Iran-Libya Sanctions Act in 1996 took place at a time when both the Oklahoma bombing, and the TWA 800 disaster, were blamed on Islamic groups linked to Iran.

There needs to be more precision here, too. First of all, by far the greatest number of human rights violations by the Islamic Republic occurred inside, not outside, Iran, and against Iranians themselves. Everyone in Iran knows this, and it is the end of such abuses that is, in part, the promise of Khatami's support for the rule of law. How it works out in the future is a matter for Iranians, not least the question of how to resolve, and settle, the deaths and disappearances of the early part of the 1980s. Perhaps Iran needs a truth commission, perhaps a center of documentation. Iran is not the only country in the region where this has occurred: In at least three of Iran's neighbors, the human rights record over the past two decades is worse.

Terrorism abroad involves two forms of activity: support for armed groups, and assassination of enemies of the Iranian regime. Support for armed oppositions has certainly occurred, although not always, as the cases of Afghanistan, Iraq, and Bosnia show, in ways that Western states disapprove. The case of Lebanon allows for a political solution, linked to rationalization of Iran's position on Israel. As for the Arabian Peninsula, it would seem that Iran has abandoned support for armed opposition groups in these Arab states. This leaves unanswered the question of the Khobar bombing in Saudi Arabia in 1996: But as there is no published evidence on this, and as Saudi Arabia has itself sought to improve its relations with Iran and denied Tehran's involvement, this should not constitute an obstacle to improved relations between Iran and the West.

Assassination of enemies abroad was a pattern of state activity up to the early 1990s: It claimed the life of, among others, two people I knew, Abdel-Rahman Qassemlu, the KDPI leader, enticed by regime agents into supposed negotiations in Vienna in 1989 and then murdered at the third meeting, and Shahpur Bakhtiar, a longtime opponent of the Shah and transition prime minister in 1979, who entered in the 1980s into an unwise alliance with Iraq, and the CIA, against Tehran. More recently, there was the murder of more KDPI leaders in the Mykonos Restaurant in Berlin, in 1992. But incidence of that kind of action has virtually ceased thereafter: There are two as yet unclarified incidents, in Paris and Rome, but it would appear, on the available record, that since 1992 Iran has ceased this kind of activity.

The situation in the countries immediately around Iran is, of course, less clear, but here one has to distinguish between those such as the PMOI who are themselves involved in military opposition to the Iranian regime and those which are not: For the Iranian regime to attack those who are themselves seeking to overthrow it by force is hardly, by any international standards, a form of terrorism.

Prospects

In the longer run, and arising out of the analysis I have offered above, I would suggest four areas to which attention might be drawn. First, if there is talk of history, and of historical wrongs, this must be two-sided. It is no good the West criticizing Iran for what it has done in this century, if the West does not in proper measure acknowledge what it has done. Second, the solution to the regional problems, not least those of nuclear weapons and missiles, cannot come through military means alone. The source, and the solution, lies in the overlapping of interstate tensions in the region: These have to be addressed, not by trading one insecurity for another, but in a spirit of confidence building in order to create a regional security system. If Iran's particular sensibility vis-à-vis Iraq has to be recognized, Iran has, for its part, to address the consequences of its policy toward the Arab-Israeli question. Third, in Iran's relations with the Arabs, we should get away from the presentation of the conflict, beloved by nationalists, as being something timeless and inevitable: The two peoples have rubbed along reasonably well over the centuries, it is modern nationalism, shaped by the antagonisms and lies of states, that has given the Arab-Iranian relationship its critical character. I did not say they can, or will, love each other, but they do not need to go to war, or sustain strategic rivalries. Finally, everyone in this process will need to have strong nerves, and some patience and understanding. President Khatami has, in the substance and tone of what he has said, given lead in this regard. It is now up to the outside world, and other centers of power in Iran, to follow his example. Everyone will need a bit of skill in conducting the *bandbazi,* the balancing act, that is now required of them.

Notes

1. I have discussed this comparative study of revolutionary foreign policy in my *Rethinking International Relations* (London, Macmillan, 1994), chapter 6, and in my forthcoming *Revolution and World Politics: The Rise and Fall of the Sixth Great Power* (London: Macmillan and Durham, NC: Duke University Press, 1999).
2. *The Bolshevik Revolution,* Vol. 3 (Harmondsworth: Pelican, 1973).
3. R. K. Ramazani, *Revolutionary Iran: Challenge and Response in the Middle East.* Second Edition (London: Johns Hopkins University Press, 1988); Wilfried Buchta, *Die iranische Shia und die islamische Einheit 1979–1996* (Hamburg: Orient Institut, 1996).
4. Fred Halliday, "Western Europe and the Iranian Revolution, 1979–97: An elusive normalization, in Barbara Roberson, ed., *The Middle East and Europe: The Power Deficit* (London, Routledge, 1998)—an earlier version was published in *Middle East Journal,* vol. 48, no. 2, spring 1994; Anthony Parsons, "Iran and Western Europe," *Middle East Journal,* vol. 43, no. 2, 1989; Anoushiravan Ehteshami and Manshour Varasteh, eds., *Iran and the International Community* (London: Routledge 1991); V. Matthias Struwe, "The Policy of Critical Dialogue: An Analysis of European Human Rights Policy towards Iran from 1992 to 1997" (MSc essay, Hamburg University, 1998); Andreas Riech, 'Iran: die Mullahs als Dialogspartner?' in Kai Hafez, ed., *Islam und der Westen* (Frankfurt: Fischer, 1997).
5. S. Taheri Shemirani, "The War of the Cities," in Farhang Rajaee, *The Iran-Iraq War* (Gainesville: University of Florida Press, 1993).
6. Fred Halliday and Zahir Tanin, "The Communist Regime in Afghanistan: Institutions and Conflicts," *Europe-Asia Studies,* vol. 50, no. 8, 1998.
7. Gary Sick, "Rethinking Dual Containment," *Survival,* vol. 40, no. 1, Spring 1998.

9

The Clouded Mirror: The United States and Iran, 1979–1999

Gary Sick

For the first two decades after the Iranian revolution, the United States and Iran had no authoritative contacts. With a few important and generally lamentable exceptions, these two major states, each with deep and enduring political, economic, social, and strategic interests in the Persian Gulf, relied on the media, on intelligence reporting, on third-hand observations, and on the work of a handful of scholars to sculpt policies that would have the most profound influence on the future of the region and on the wellbeing of their own people.

It is not unheard of for two countries to shun each other, even for prolonged periods of time. Given the marvels of modern communications, such estranged states may continue to be remarkably well informed about each other. Moreover, there are hosts of multilateral institutions—both governmental and private—that can provide opportunities to observe each other without necessarily rubbing elbows.

There are, however, real costs associated with such alienation. Arm's-length communication is often miscommunication. Distance breeds stereotypes. Grievances fester. Wrongful intentions are imputed, and a mythology emerges on either side that becomes comfortably embedded in the national psyche. Most important, the cadre of individuals on either side of the divide who have personal knowledge and experience of the other society gradually dwindles away, and is replaced by those whose knowledge too often is derived from the prevalent demonology of detachment and indifference.

This paper will examine some key turning points in the 20 years of U.S.–Iran relations after the revolution. These incidents are characterized by missed communications, mistaken signals, policy gaffes, and opportunities that were overlooked or mistakenly discarded. The objective of this sorry catalogue, in which blame is shared by both sides, is to draw some conclusions about the fundamental nature of the relationship, to assess the costs of past policy actions, to identify some long-term trends, and, finally, to consider the prospects for the future.

America, the Shah, and the Revolution

The overthrow of the Iranian monarchy in 1979 and its replacement some months later with an Islamic Republic was a stunning blow to the United States, whose political and military strategy in the Persian Gulf was firmly anchored to the person and rule of Mohammad Reza Shah Pahlavi. Especially after 1972, when President Richard Nixon and his national security adviser, Henry Kissinger, met with the Shah in Tehran, U.S. policy relied on Iran to protect its major interests in the region: first, to ensure access by the industrialized world to the vast oil resources of the region; and second, to prevent the Soviet Union from acquiring political or military control over those resources.

In return, the United States permitted Iran to purchase, at its own discretion, any military system in the U.S. arsenal short of nuclear weapons. The United States provided military advisers and trainers, shared intelligence information on regional and Soviet activities, collaborated on the most sensitive regional issues (including a covert operation in conjunction with Israel to support a Kurdish uprising in Iraq), and conducted joint military exercises.[1]

Although the so-called Twin Pillar policy of the United States was based on cooperation with both Iran and Saudi Arabia, Iran was unquestionably the more important of the two. In February 1979, when Iran renounced cooperation and dependence on both the United States and the Soviet Union, under the slogan of "Neither East nor West," the United States was left with no strategic safety net and had to reinvent its entire regional strategy.

Initially, the United States attempted to establish working relations with the provisional government of Prime Minister Mehdi Bazargan and Foreign Minister Ibrahim Yazdi. That experiment terminated abruptly on November 4, 1979, when a group of Iranian students, "followers of the line of Imam Khomeini," invaded the U.S. Embassy in Tehran and took

The Clouded Mirror: The United States and Iran   193

hostage 66 U.S. diplomats and other Americans who happened to be present on that fateful day.[2]

Bazargan and Yazdi opposed the takeover as a serious breach of international law and submitted their resignations in protest. Their resignations were accepted by Ayatollah Khomeini and the Revolutionary Command Council, setting the stage for a prolonged and bitter confrontation between the revolutionary authorities and the United States, which eventually resulted in the U.S. imposition of trade sanctions, a formal rupture of diplomatic relations, and an ill-fated U.S. military rescue mission.

The hostage crisis was an international confrontation that permanently altered Iran's relations not only with the United States but also with the United Nations and the entire international community. It was, however, above all a domestic issue for both Iran and the United States.

In Iran, the hostage taking was perceived as a declaration of independence from Western influence and was hailed as the "second revolution." It silenced domestic critics of Islamic rule, facilitated the overwhelming passage of a referendum on a controversial Islamic constitution, and helped to institutionalize clerical rule over the objections of those who had fought in the revolution in favor of greater democracy, human rights, and a secular government with Islamic oversight. It was a rallying point for radical Islamic elements, who successfully stifled dissenting voices and placed Iran on a new course of militant subversion in the name of exporting the revolution.

As a talisman of Islamic extremism, this action indelibly stigmatized Iran as a dangerous and unpredictable state with no regard for its undertakings in international law. The hostage crisis created an image of the Islamic Republic that would endure for decades and would greatly complicate Iran's efforts to establish itself as a reliable member of the international community.

Nowhere was this more true than in the United States, where the wrenching experience of the prolonged hostage episode was seared into the American mentality by media saturation, compounded by Washington's obsessive focus on the issue. The hostage crisis assumed major importance in U.S. domestic politics, initially bolstering President Carter's standing in the polls, but eventually wounding him and contributing to his massive electoral defeat in November 1980. In effect, the hostage crisis helped to install a clerical government in Iran and to eject a Democratic president in the United States.

The Iran–Iraq War

On September 22, 1980, the government of Iraq launched simultaneous strikes against all Iranian airfields within reach of its bombers, while its massed armies advanced along a 450–mile front into Iran's Khuzestan Province. The United States supported the Arab position at the United Nations, where the Security Council declared the invasion to be a "situation" rather than a war, thereby evading the requirement to determine if aggression had occurred, and called for a cease-fire in place, which permitted Iraqi forces to remain on Iranian territory. Both Iran and Iraq ignored this half-hearted attempt at peacemaking, and the United Nations simply shelved the entire issue for the next two years.

Iran immediately concluded that the United States was behind Saddam Hussein's attack, in an effort to punish Iran for the hostage-taking and to bring maximum pressure on Iran to settle the crisis. This has remained the accepted wisdom in Iran and is accepted as an obvious truth by Iranians of all political persuasion.

The reality was much more complicated. There were, indeed, Americans in senior positions who saw the Iraqi invasion as a potential blessing that would force an end to the hostage crisis after nearly a year. Among other things, it was assumed, Iran would need U.S. military equipment and spare parts. Other policy makers, also in senior positions, feared that the United States would be blamed for the Iraqi invasion and this would eventually result in physical harm to the hostages.

Although there had been evidence of an Iraqi military buildup over the previous five months, the timing and scale of the invasion took Washington completely by surprise. There had been no advance contacts between Iraq and the United States, nor were there any consultations with Baghdad until much later in the war, but those facts would never persuade Iran to change its collective mind.

Iran also confounded U.S. assumptions. After some veiled inquiries about regaining its military assets from the United States, and after initiating negotiations to resolve the hostage crisis before the U.S. presidential election of November, Iran suddenly lost interest in both arms and negotiations. Contacts between Tehran and Washington dried up in the month before the election, and a last-second Iranian offer that was unacceptable to the United States only exacerbated the situation.[3]

After Carter's defeat, Iran proposed using Algeria as an intermediary, and talks proceeded in a roller coaster fashion. The hostages were released, apparently quite deliberately, a few minutes after Ronald Reagan took the oath of office. The U.S. negotiator in this melodrama was Deputy Secretary of State Warren Christopher. Years later, he would have another opportunity to deal with Iran.

The Iran-Contra Affair

By mid-1982, Iran had pushed Iraqi forces back almost to the original border and faced a crucial decision whether to stop the war or to launch a campaign across the border into Iraq. After considerable internal debate, Iran unwisely chose the latter course. There was widespread concern, especially among the Arab states of the Gulf, that Iran's military momentum might defeat the Iraqi army and bring down the government in Baghdad. The war had begun because of Saddam Hussein's desire to bring down the Khomeini regime and establish Iraq as the major regional power in the Gulf. There now appeared to be a possibility that the results might be reversed entirely, leaving the revolutionary Iranian regime as the dominant power.

In a major shift of U.S. policy, William Casey, the director of Central Intelligence in the Reagan administration, opened an intelligence channel to Iraq, providing intelligence on Iranian military activities and other benefits to strengthen the Baghdad regime, while launching a major effort to stop Iranian arms purchases. The U.S. "tilt" to Iraq was quite apparent and was consistent with a classic U.S. balancing strategy in the Gulf, strengthening one power to prevent hegemony by a rival. It was also supported by America's Arab allies in the Gulf and elsewhere.

Consequently, there was consternation when it was discovered in 1986 that the United States had secretly been providing intelligence information and arms to Iran. The U.S. opening to Iran was based on a classic Cold War analysis. In the absence of a U.S. presence, Iran, it was feared, would turn to the Soviet Union. This assessment owed more to prevalent Cold War anxieties than to any careful reading of the facts. There was, in fact, very little evidence that Iran was drifting toward the Soviet Union. Nevertheless, the impulse for a reopening of relations with Iran was not unreasonable, and it was strongly reinforced by an Israeli desire to regain some contact with this non-Arab state that had played such an important role in Israel's strategy and commerce prior to the revolution. The initiative was also intended to help free American hostages in Lebanon.[4]

The execution of this strategic opening, however, could hardly have been conducted more clumsily. The White House relied on an activist lieutenant colonel on the National Security Council staff to organize the operation, maintaining coordination with his counterpart in Israel and several arms dealers who acted as intermediaries with the Iranians. The proceeds from the sale of arms to Iran were to be used to provide covert support to the contra forces in Central America. The entire operation was concealed from other agencies in the government—including the Departments of State and Defense, which were pursuing conflicting policies to isolate Iran and cut off its arms supply—and the Congress, which by law had oversight responsibility over covert actions.[5]

There is much less information available about the handling of this operation within Iran, but apparently it was relegated to a handful of senior officials who also failed to consult with their colleagues. There was sufficient interest within Iran to accept the arrival in May 1986 of a high-level U.S.–Israeli delegation headed by former U.S. national security advisor Robert McFarlane and to conduct talks over a period of several days before the project collapsed in confusion and acrimony.

Months later, as word of these extraordinary contacts seeped out within Iran, a radical group under the direction of Mehdi Hashemi[6] leaked the story, first in the form of leaflets that were posted at the University of Tehran and elsewhere, then to a series of publications in Lebanon. The story was eventually published in November 1986 by an obscure Lebanese magazine and was quickly confirmed by the international media, setting off a scandal of monumental proportions.

In the United States, the revelations that the Reagan administration had sold military equipment to Iran as part of an effort to release American hostages and to divert the proceeds to the Nicaraguan contras, was taken up in sensational congressional hearings and subsequent trials of many of the participants. The scandal severely wounded the Reagan administration and led to calls for the president's resignation.

In Iran, Speaker of the Majles Ali Akbar Hashemi Rafsanjani gave a partial and tendentious public account of Iran's secret dealings with the United States. Several Majles members demanded an inquiry, and it required the personal intervention of Ayatollah Khomeini to keep the situation from spinning out of control. Mehdi Hashemi and a number of his associates were arrested and Hashemi was later executed, despite the intervention of Ayatollah Montazeri. This incident appeared to be the galvanizing event that eventually led Ayatollah Khomeini to renounce Montazeri as his successor, thereby altering the course of the Iranian revolution.[7]

The Internationalization of the Iran–Iraq War

At the beginning of 1987, U.S. Persian Gulf policy was in a state of absolute disarray. After the Iran-Contra debacle, U.S. credibility with the Arab Gulf states plummeted to its lowest level since the Arab–Israel War of 1973. The United States responded with a damage limitation strategy that tried to reassure Arab states that the Iran-Contra incident was an isolated occurrence and by aligning U.S. policy much more closely and more openly with Iraq. The door to possible improved relations with Iran was not shut entirely, however.[8]

As Iranian attacks on shipping to and from Kuwait began to mount in the fall of 1986, Kuwait asked the United States to register a number of its tankers under the U.S. flag for protection. In April 1987, when it appeared that the Soviet Union would accept Kuwait's invitation, the United States agreed to reflag 11 Kuwaiti tankers. Although the reflagging decision was seen at the time as a temporary U.S. response to a specific problem, in retrospect it was a historic shift. Not only did the United States indirectly enter a regional war, but the military infrastructure required to assure cover for transiting tankers led the United States to gradually develop and sustain a much higher level of military presence than at any time since World War II. It also brought the United States into direct military confrontation with Iran in a series of incidents over the following 15 months.

Shortly after the reflagging decision was taken, Assistant Secretary of State for Near East Affairs Richard Murphy visited Iraq and met with Saddam Hussein. As a diplomatic counterpart to the reflagging, Murphy reportedly promised Saddam that the United States would lead an effort in the United Nations Security Council for a resolution calling for mandatory halt of arms shipments to Iran. The U. N. resolution would not name Iran directly. Rather, it would first call on Iran and Iraq to cease fire and withdraw their forces to the international boundaries. Then "enforcement measures," such as a worldwide arms embargo, would be imposed on the party that rejected the demand. Since Iran was holding Iraqi territory, it was expected to reject, while Iraq, which had now been driven out of most Iranian territory, would accept.[9] That is exactly what happened.

Resolution 598 was passed unanimously by the Security Council on July 20, 1987. The first paragraph called for both parties to "withdraw all forces to the internationally recognized boundaries without delay." Paragraph six proposed creating an impartial body to inquire into responsibility for the conflict. Paragraph 10 implicitly threatened sanctions for noncompliance. For a full year, Iran and Iraq wrangled over the primacy of paragraphs one and six, while the United States made a concerted effort to impose stringent international sanctions on Iran. The one-sided U.S. role was unhelpful at best and may have delayed acceptance of a cease-fire.

Starting in April 1988, the military tide again turned in favor of Iraq, which reoccupied most of the territory captured by Iran and then drove back into Iran. Iran desperately attempted to stem the tide, but its efforts were futile and were further shattered on July 3 by the tragic shootdown of a commercial Iranian aircraft by the *USS Vincennes,* killing all 290 passengers and crew. On July 18, Iran formally accepted Resolution 598, a decision that Khomeini said was "more deadly than taking poison."

"Good Will Begets Good Will"

After eight years of conflict, the forces of these two bitterly hostile foes ended the fighting very close to where they had begun. Neither side achieved its war aims. As the cease-fire took effect and as the Iran–Iraq War ground to a halt, attention in the United States once again shifted to the fate of the American hostages that were being held in Lebanon by groups known to be associated with Iran.

In his Inaugural Address in January 1989, President Bush held out the prospect of a change in U.S. policy. In a clear reference to Iran, he said "Good will begets good will. Good faith can be a spiral that endlessly moves on."[10]

Iran welcomed this remark and responded by working with the U.N. Secretary General to free the U.S. hostages in Lebanon.[11] That process, however, was very slow. The last American hostage, journalist Terry Anderson, was not released until December 1991, almost a year after the ejection of Iraqi forces from Kuwait by a U.S.–led coalition; and by that time another U.S. presidential election campaign was already getting underway. There was no reciprocal gesture to Iran on the part of the United States, which was seen in Iran as evidence of U.S. unwillingness or inability to keep its commitments.

When President Clinton took office in January 1993, there was no talk of good will. On the contrary, shortly after taking office the new administration announced a policy that it called "dual containment." This policy explicitly rejected the classic U.S. strategy of balancing Iran and Iraq against each other, arguing instead that "we don't need to rely on one to balance the other," as the United States, as the predominant power in the Persian Gulf, had the "means to counter both the Iraqi and Iranian regimes."[12]

The dual containment policy called for Iran to: (a) cease its support of international terrorism and subversion; (b) end its violent opposition to the Arab-Israeli peace talks; and (c) halt efforts to acquire weapons of mass destruction.[13] In pursuit of this policy, the United States would attempt to tighten international restrictions on military sales to Iran. The United States would also oppose development loans to Iran by the World Bank and the IMF, and would seek to persuade its allies to maintain pressure on Iran so it could not "pursue normal commercial relations."

American officials developed a special vocabulary in which Iran was routinely branded as a "rogue," "terrorist," "outlaw," or "backlash" state. This relentless drumfire of attacks—the mirror image of Iranian depictions of the United States as the "Great Satan"—had its effects in the media, in the Congress, in the public, and in the attitudes of lower-level bureaucrats. With a Democrat in the White House and the Republicans in control of the Congress, a domestic political contest developed over which party could be most vigorous in promoting U.S. policies to deal with Iran.

The debate was galvanized in 1995 when the U.S. oil company Conoco Inc. announced that it had signed a $1 billion contract with Iran to develop the Sirri gas field in the Persian Gulf. Privately, Iran let it be known that the choice of a U.S. company for this important investment was deliberate and was intended to demonstrate that, despite their political differences, Iran and the United States could do business with each other.

Although this contract was perfectly legal under U.S. law at the time, the prospect that this deal would breach the wall of containment around Iran generated such a wave of outrage that the company was forced to renounce it. The Congress and the American-Israel Public Affairs Committee (AIPAC) began preparing legislation that would end all trade with Iran and punish any corporations that engaged in investments there. President Clinton, who was preparing for his reelection campaign, quickly preempted it by issuing two executive orders that made it illegal for American oil companies to operate in Iran and established penalties for any U.S. person or corporation doing business with Iran.[14] Both decisions were announced by senior administration officials before major Jewish organizations. The U.S. business community, apparently intimidated by the public outcry, remained totally silent.[15]

This process was replayed in the presidential election year of 1996. The Congress prepared a bill that would impose sanctions on any foreign corporation that invested $40 million or more in the Iranian oil and gas sector.[16] Libya was later added on the floor of the Senate, and the bill became known as the Iran-Libya Sanctions Act (ILSA). Although the bill was certain to create serious problems with America's allies, the Congress saw ILSA as an opportunity to take a public stand against terrorism. The bill passed the House of Representatives 415–0 and was signed into law by President Clinton on August 5.

The Khatami Election and the U.S. Response

In May 1997, Seyyed Mohammad Khatami was elected to a four-year term as President of Iran in a stunning electoral surprise. He conducted a grassroots campaign on the issues of rule of law, civil society, and dialogue among competing ideologies. His campaign struck a resonant chord with the Iranian population, particularly among women and the burgeoning population of young people, many of whom had no memory of the ancien régime. Paired against the well-known speaker of the Majles (parliament), who represented revolutionary orthodoxy, Khatami attracted the largest number of voters in Iranian history and won a decisive victory with 69 percent of the vote. He carried all of the urban centers in Iran and virtually every province. When he formally took office in August 1997, his reformist cabinet was accepted without exception by the Majles.[17]

Although Khatami was widely regarded as a candidate of domestic reform, it was his foreign policy that attracted the most attention during his first 18 months in office. In December 1997, Iran hosted the Organization of the Islamic Conference and won plaudits for its conciliatory positions and moderation. Iran began a concerted effort to improve its relations with Saudi Arabia and its other Arab neighbors in the Persian Gulf region, with some substantial initial success. Iran also courted closer cooperation with the United Nations, an institution it had shunned as a Western tool after the revolution. The United Nations General Assembly designated the year 2001 as the "Year of Dialogue Among Civilizations" after Khatami introduced the idea in his address to the General Assembly in September 1998.

In January 1998, Khatami made an unprecedented "Address to the American People" in the form of an interview on CNN.[18] He praised the achievements of American civilization, went as far as an Iranian politician could go in expressing regret for the hostage crisis, and spelled out very clearly Iran's positions on all of the major issues of concern to the United States:

- On terrorism: "Any form of killing of innocent men and women who are not involved in confrontations is terrorism. It must be

condemned, and we, in our turn, condemn every form of it in the world."
- On the peace process: "We have declared our opposition to the Middle East peace process, because we believe it will not succeed. At the same time, we have clearly said that we don't intend to impose our views on others or to stand in their way."
- On weapons of mass destruction: "We are not a nuclear power and do not intend to become one."

Washington responded to the Khatami initiative cautiously but generally positively, and the speech inspired a burst of exchange activities in sports, the arts, and the academe.[19] The United States toned down its rhetoric and took some small steps to improve relations. But problems remained.

Less than 60 days after Khatami took office, the French oil major Total, together with state-owned partners Gazprom of Russia and Petronas of Malaysia, concluded a $2 billion deal to develop an Iranian gas field. These negotiations, which had been underway since Conoco withdrew in 1995, placed Total and its partners in apparent violation of ILSA.

In May 1998, the United States announced that it would waive the provisions of ILSA on grounds of national security. That decision was due almost entirely to pressure from America's European allies, but it was nevertheless received positively in Tehran.[20] The United States also announced a major redeployment of its Persian Gulf forces, sharply reducing the number of ships and aircraft permanently stationed in the region.[21] This was due primarily to cost factors and personnel pressures, but again it was received positively by Tehran. The United States also officially designated the Iranian opposition group *Mojahedin-e Khalq* as a terrorist organization, removed Iran from the list of major drug-producing states, and met with Iranian representatives in the Afghanistan "Contact Group" at the United Nations, among other things.

On June 17, 1998, Secretary of State Madeleine Albright delivered a major speech that responded almost point-by-point to the issues that Khatami had addressed in his interview six months earlier. The speech was notable for its conciliatory tone and for the absence of the rhetoric that had characterized U.S. statements about Iran over the previous five years. The speech offered no specific new policies or initiatives, but it held out the prospect for a new beginning:

"We are ready to explore further ways to build mutual confidence and avoid misunderstandings. The Islamic Republic should consider parallel steps. . . .

As the wall of mistrust comes down, we can develop with the Islamic Republic, when it is ready, a road map leading to normal relations."[22]

These remarks reflected the political climate in Iran, where the issue of an opening to the United States had become a major point of contention in the contest between conservative forces and the reformist elements around Khatami. Most significantly, Iran's supreme leader, Ayatollah Ali Khamenei, asserted that, "Even though the American officials' tone appears to have changed, the truth is they will not be satisfied with anything less than domination of Iran's resources and a return to the situation before the Islamic revolution.... Some people ... are trying to make our people stop saying 'no' [to America]. But, by God's grace, they will fail."[24]

On the 20th anniversary of the Iranian revolution, Iran and the United States were addressing each other more politely than at any time over the previous two decades. There was, however, very little evidence of genuine progress toward a resumption of direct contacts.[25]

The Primacy of Domestic Politics

Even this rudimentary sketch of 20 years of interaction between the United States and Iran provides the basis for some general conclusions about the relationship. Hostility has been deep since the Iranian revolution, yet both parties periodically attempted to break through the hostility to seek some measure of contact. The Iran-Contra initiative was grounded in an effort to fashion a strategic opening, and President Bush's offer of good will suggested that, even after the earlier policy disaster, the door to improved relations remained ajar. Iran's investment of political capital to free American hostages in Lebanon, and its controversial decision to select an American company to develop an offshore gas field suggested that Iran also retained some degree of interest in expanding contacts.

These efforts were mostly clumsy and lacked the kind of careful preparation and execution that would have been necessary to overcome the suspicions of the past. They demonstrated, however, that at least some officials on each side were prepared to take risks, presumably in the conviction that a breach in the wall of hostility would serve their own national interests. The reality is that Iran is the largest and most populous nation in the Persian Gulf, while the United States is the dominant military and political power in the region. A policy of mutual hostility was certain to complicate life for both parties and to make a dangerous neighborhood even more dangerous.

Nevertheless, mutual hostility prevailed. Sporadic efforts at accommodation backfired and often made things worse. The reasons for this were the poisonous combination of history and domestic politics.

Sources of Hostility

One of the major objectives of the Iranian revolution was to free Iran from what was perceived as its crippling dependency on external powers. The United States in particular had become synonymous with the ancien régime after the U.S.-engineered coup of 1953 that deposed the nationalist Prime Minister Mohammad Mossadeq and restored the Shah to the throne.[26] The prolonged confrontation with the United States over the kidnapping of U.S. diplomats, with its denunciations of the "Great Satan" and ritual chants of "Death to America," seared this into the political consciousness of Iran.

As the revolution matured and as the earlier unity of forces dissolved into factionalism, opposition to the United States became a useful—if not indispensable—rallying point. President Khatami's attempt to open a dialogue with the American people was sharply constrained by Ayatollah Khamenei, and public expressions in favor of direct contacts with the U.S. government were subject to severe retribution. Opposition to relations with the United States eventually became synonymous with support for Ayatollah Khamenei, especially after his pronouncements on the subject were directly contradicted by his most influential rival, Ayatollah Montazeri. Discussion became taboo.[27]

In the United States, the humiliation of the hostage crisis, the calamity of the Iran-Contra affair, fear of Islamic fundamentalism and deep-seated paranoia about terrorism combined to make Iran politically untouchable. The gradual evolution of Iran away from the excesses of the early 1980s went largely unnoticed by the U.S. public and even government officials. Perversely, it was just at the moment when genuine reform was beginning to make some headway in Iran that the Clinton administration chose to begin its systematic demonization of Iran as part of the dual containment policy. The timing of this policy shift had more to do with the U.S. focus on the Arab-Israel dispute, and especially Israel's attitudes toward Iran, than it did with developments in Iran itself.

The Israeli Factor

For decades, Israel had pursued close relations with Iran in the context of its "Doctrine of the Periphery." This strategy tried to cultivate non-Arab states just outside the ring of hostile Arab states surrounding Israel. Utterly nonideological, it extended the adage that "the enemy of my enemy is my friend" to the level of high strategy.[28] Even after the revolution, Israel continued to explore the possibility of continued contacts with Iran at the covert level, as evidenced by Israeli support of the Iran-Contra affair. That policy changed after the collapse of communism, the end of the Cold War, and progress in peace talks with the Palestinians.

The new anti-Iran policy was inaugurated by Prime Minister Yitzhak Rabin and Foreign Minister Shimon Peres in January 1993, just as the new Clinton administration took office.[29] The Clinton administration required little persuasion on this subject, particularly Secretary of State Warren Christopher, who had had his own experiences with Iran. Moreover, with the Soviet Union gone and both Israel and the United States engaged in intensive peace efforts with the Palestinians, having an all-purpose enemy in the shape of Iran was politically convenient.

The drumbeat of attacks by the administration and by Israel found a ready audience in the U.S. population and especially in the Congress, where the powerful pro-Israeli lobby AIPAC weighed in vigorously. As an anti-Iran competition developed between the administration and the Hill, one result was the missed opportunity of the Conoco affair; another was ILSA.[30]

The Clouded Mirror

In a curious sense, Iran and the United States are mirror images of each other. Both countries are prone to a moralistic air of self-righteousness, especially in foreign policy matters; and both are inclined to ideological rigidity and a sense of moral superiority. Each perceives itself as the indispensable state. Above all, these are two interpenetrated societies whose mutual sense of grievance, humiliation, and betrayal has infiltrated their respective internal politics until the line between foreign and domestic policies is often indistinguishable.

In any traditional foreign policy calculus, the shared interests between Iran and the United States would be at least as numerous and important as those that divide them. In Afghanistan and South Asia, U.S. and Iranian objectives are quite similar. The U.S. military containment of Iraq has been of great strategic value to Iran and was facilitated in turn by Iran's tacit acquiescence. Iran's policy of cultivating more amicable relations with the Arab states of the Gulf is consistent with U.S. interests in regional stability, and Iran's deliberate silence about U.S. military rela-

The Clouded Mirror: The United States and Iran 205

tions with its Arab neighbors has removed a potentially important obstacle to U.S. prepositioning and military operations from Arab territory. Iran and the United States share an interest in the stability and development of the new states of Central Asia and the Caucasus, symbolized by Iran's promotion of a new "Silk Route" from the Persian Gulf; but they disagree about the routing of oil and gas pipelines from these land-locked states to world markets. Iran and the United States have similar interests in halting the narcotics trade from Afghanistan and South Asia, in environmental issues in the Persian Gulf, and in a number of global issues such as population control, where they have often found themselves on the same side in international conferences.

These areas of congruence have emerged, not as artificial concessions but rather as independent and entirely pragmatic interpretations of their own national interests. Iran and the United States, after all, were close allies for decades before the revolution, and the relationship was grounded in a set of mutual concerns that have gradually reasserted themselves as Iran has relinquished the millennarian ambitions of the early 1980s in favor of a more nationalist approach. As the Islamic revolution confronted the practical problems of managing the affairs of a strategically located nation of more than 60 million people, its early exuberance was slowly replaced by a set of policies that began to reflect increasingly the strategic objectives of the monarchy that had preceded it. That is typically the fate of revolutions as they mature, and Iran's transition was rather quicker and more orderly than the French or the Chinese or the Soviets before them.[31]

This slow convergence of U.S. and Iranian interests cannot disguise the many real problems that remain. Revolutionary Iran believes (as did the Shah) that it is destined to be the dominant power in the Persian Gulf. That inevitably generates friction with the United States, which emerged as the regional military and political hegemon after the second Gulf War. In this uneven rivalry, Iran has elected patience and is wisely playing the long game, while the United States has avoided reckless effrontery. If that remains true, the conflict is manageable.

Iran and the United States have both identified a series of instrumental or mid-term changes that would contribute to more amicable relations. Iran has called on the United States to lift direct and indirect economic sanctions; to permit decisions on pipelines from Central Asia to be made on purely economic grounds; to settle the outstanding claims for Iran's assets that were taken at the time of the revolution; to cease opposing Iran in international financial, monetary, and trade organizations; and to permit the transfer of advanced technology for peaceful purposes to Iran. More generally, Iran objects to past U.S. interference in its internal affairs, from the Mossadeq "counter-coup" in 1953 and support for the shah during the revolution, to the more recent appropriations by the U.S. Congress targeting the Islamic Republic and the establishment of an Iran Service as part of Radio Liberty/Radio Free Europe. In turn, the United States identifies three major areas of concern with Iranian policy: (a) opposition to Israel and the Arab-Israel peace process; (b) support for terrorism; and (c) pursuit of weapons of mass destruction (WMD) and development of long-range missiles. More generally, the United States is critical of Iran's human rights record and deplores its past support for the taking of hostages in Iran and Lebanon.

This is the agenda that must be addressed by both the United States and Iran if two decades of hostility is to be replaced by a more businesslike relationship. Of the three major areas of dispute identified by the United States, the first is clearly related to Israel. Charges of terrorism focus almost entirely on Iran's support for Hizbullah and HAMAS and also are therefore most directly associated with Israel, while the threat of Iranian missile and WMD development are normally measured in terms of their proximity to Israel. It is evident that Israel's concerns will feature prominently in any U.S.-Iranian rapprochement. That is likely to complicate the process on the U.S. side, not only because of Israel's considerable influence in Washington but also because Israel's nuclear status will be a factor in any serious discussion of Iran's prospective WMD development.[32]

Prospects for Change

By the time of the 20th anniversary of the Iranian revolution, there was a perceptible momentum building in the United States to question the merits of continued U.S. hostility to Iran, particularly the sanctions that arbitrarily closed off a potentially lucrative market to American businesses. There was growing admiration for Khatami's political and social reforms and a sense that the United States was fortunate—as were the people of Iran—to have a leader devoted to tolerance and peaceful accommodation, rather than the repressive ideologue who might have been expected to emerge at that stage of the revolution.

There also was understandable caution, since Iran's politics remained in flux. Socially conservative forces continued to dominate many of the key power centers and were prepared to resort to violence when their interests were threatened. As the United States had virtually no influence over the internal political dynamics in Iran, it was inclined to watch from

The Clouded Mirror: The United States and Iran 207

a comfortable distance and to reap the benefits of any positive changes without responding or reciprocating. Although the rhetoric of the old dual containment policy was abandoned, no new strategy was devised to take its place, and all of the accoutrements of hostility remained in place. The situation in Iran was much the same. Mutual acrimony had been replaced by mutual complacency, and neither side was yet willing to take any significant risks in its domestic politics to move the relationship to a new level.

In early 1999, Iran and the United States were leaning toward each other but neither was prepared to move. Would it take a new set of unpleasant shocks to persuade these two adversaries to break the impasse?

Notes

1. There is a vast literature on the Iranian revolution and U.S. Iran policy. This account is drawn primarily from Gary G. Sick, *All Fall Down: America's Tragic Encounter With Iran* (New York: Random House, 1985).
2. Thirteen Americans were released in the first weeks of the crisis. Another was released in July 1980 after he developed a serious medical condition. The remaining 52 hostages were held in various locations until January 20, 1981, when their release was negotiated with the assistance of the Algerian government. An additional group of six eluded capture in the original takeover and managed to escape the country in January 1980 with the assistance of the Canadian government.
3. Many observers claimed that the suspicious timing of these events was due to Republican efforts to delay the resolution of the hostage crisis until after the November 1980 election. These allegations were detailed in Gary G. Sick, *October Surprise: America's Hostages in Iran and the Election of Ronald Reagan*, (New York: Random House/Times Books, 1991, 1992). Investigations by committees of the U.S. Senate and House of Representatives found no convincing evidence to confirm these allegations, and the intelligence agencies of Iran and other countries have remained silent on the subject.
4. In fact, several U.S. hostages were released, apparently as a result of Iranian pressure, after Iran received covert U.S. arms deliveries from Israel. In each case, however, new hostages were taken to replace those released.
5. For an authoritative account of this episode, see Theodore Draper, *A Very Thin Line: The Iran-Contra Affairs* (New York: Hill and Wang, 1991).
6. Mehdi Hashemi was closely associated with the son of Ayatollah Montazeri, the designated heir of Khomeini, and operated from the protection of

Montazeri's office. He and his "gang" (as it is referred to in Iran) were actively involved in the creation and activities of Hizbullah in Lebanon, effectively pursuing an independent, ultraradical foreign policy that proved to be an embarrassment to the government in Tehran and largely outside its control.
7. The text of Khomeini's letter to Montazeri of March 1989 was subsequently published in the newspaper *Abrar* on November 22, 1997, p. 2. It refers repeatedly to Montazeri's association with Mehdi Hashemi and his "clique" as justification for the dismissal. At the time of the Iran-Contra affair, Montazeri had called publicly for improvement of relations with the United States, which may have been in Khomeini's mind when he asked rhetorically, "Can you see what valuable services you have offered to arrogance [United States]?" Although in disgrace and under house arrest, Montazeri continued to hold that Khomeini's original ban against ties with the United States was "temporary and can change according to political and economic conditions" (Associated Press from Tehran, February 6, 1999).
8. Secretary of State George Shultz went out of his way to reassure Iran that the United States recognized the Iranian revolution and that there were some issues, for example, the Soviet Union and Afghanistan where some cooperation might be possible (see his statement on January 6, 1987, in *The New York Times,* January 7, 1987). Rafsanjani said that "[W]e do not believe that our relations with [the United States] have to be cut forever. . . . But I think it will be very hard." (Press conference with foreign and local correspondents April 20, 1987 [FBIS May 4, 1987])
9. *Washington Post,* May 30 and 31, 1987. These reports were based on a background briefing at the State Department, apparently with Murphy.
10. *The New York Times,* January 21, 1989, p. 10.
11. Throughout the Iran–Iraq War, as the U.N. Security Council evaded its peace-keeping responsibilities, Secretary General Javier Pérez de Cuéllar quietly maintained contact with the parties in the search for a settlement. This won him the respect of Iran and facilitated the hostage negotiations, which were conducted by his special representative, Assistant Secretary General Giandomenico Picco.
12. Martin Indyk, "The Clinton Administration's Approach to the Middle East," Keynote Address to the Soref Symposium on "Challenges to U.S. Interests in the Middle East: Obstacles and Opportunities," *Proceedings of the Washington Institute for Near East Policy,* May 18–19, 1993, pp. 1–8. Martin Indyk at the time of this speech had just joined the National Security Council staff. He later became the U.S. ambassador to Israel, and still later the Assistant Secretary of State for Near East Affairs.

13. *Ibid.* In Indyk's original formulation, he called for changes in Iran's behavior in five areas: (a) support of international terrorism; (b) support for Hamas and attempted sabotage of the Arab-Israel peace talks; (c) subversion through support of Islamic movements in Sudan and elsewhere; (d) acquisition of conventional weapons that would permit Iran to dominate the Persian Gulf region; and (e) prospective acquisition of weapons of mass destruction. He also referred briefly to human rights.
14. See Executive Order 12957 of March 15, 1995, and Executive Order 12959 of May 6, 1995
15. For a detailed analysis of the politics associated with the development of Iranian sanctions, see Laurie Lande, "Second Thoughts," *The International Economy,* May/June 1997, pp. 44–49.
16. The trigger level was reduced automatically from $40 million to $20 million on the first anniversary of the legislation in August 1997.
17. Khatami's minister of the interior, Hojjatolislam Abdollah Nouri, was forced by the conservative forces in the Majles to resign in June 1998. Khatami immediately appointed Nouri as vice president in charge of development and social affairs and replaced him with another reform-minded candidate. The minister of information (intelligence), Hojjatolislam Qorban Ali Dorri Najafabadi, resigned in February 1999 after it was discovered that officials in his department were directly implicated in a series of murders of opposition leaders and intellectuals.
18. The transcript of this interview was posted on the CNN Web site immediately after it was aired on January 7, 1998. Large portions of the text were published in a number of newspapers the following day.
19. For a summary of exchange activities between the two countries, see the Web site established by Search for Common Ground and the Gulf/2000 project: www.sfcg.org/IRAN/iran.htm
20. The European Union threatened to take the case to the World Trade Organization if the United States imposed sanctions on the French company, on grounds that the U.S. policy was in violation of international trade agreements.
21. See Dana Priest, "US Cuts Forces in Persian Gulf," *The Washington Post,* May 27, 1998, p. 1. This decision effectively reduced the U.S. standing force in the Persian Gulf by about half, while greatly increasing the number of cruise missiles.
22. Secretary of State Madeleine K. Albright, Remarks at 1998 Asia Society Dinner, Waldorf-Astoria Hotel, New York, New York, June 17, 1998, as released by the Office of the Spokesman, June 18, 1998, U.S. Department of State.

23. Remarks by H. E. Dr. Kamal Kharrazi Foreign Minister of the Islamic Republic of Iran at the Asia Society, New York, September 28, 1998 (http://www.asiasociety.com/kharrazi.htm).
24. As reported in Reuters, November 3, 1998.
25. A call by former Secretary of State Cyrus Vance for a resumption of U.S. diplomatic relations with Iran went unheeded. See "US-Iran Relations: has the time come?" *Speech Delivered by the Honorable Cyrus R. Vance,* The Asia Society, New York City, January 13, 1999.
26. For a detailed account of this event, see Mark J. Gasiorowski, "The 1953 Coup D'Etat in Iran." *International Journal of Middle East Studies* vol.19, no. 3(August 1987), pp. 266–79.
27. See above for Montazeri's intervention on this issue. The antipathy became so intense that a clerical court in 1999 ruled that it was impermissible for the press even to mention Montazeri (Agence France Press, March 4, 1999).
28. For a more detailed examination of the Doctrine of the Periphery and its implications for Israel-Iran relations, see Gary G. Sick, *October Surprise,* op. cit., pp. 58–72.
29. Peres compared the new threat to communism, noting "Since the collapse of communism in the Soviet Union, we consider Khomeinism the greatest danger the Middle East is facing—not only us but the Arabs as well, . . . It has many of the characteristics of communism. It is fanatic, it is ideological, it is religious and it claims, like communism, that the goal justifies the means." Reportedly, the whole Israeli political and intellectual establishment was galvanized to put across this message. See Michael Parks, "Israel Sees Self Defending West Against Militants: Tel Aviv Calls Itself The 'First Target' Of Islamic Fundamentalists With Aims Beyond The Region," *Los Angeles Times,* January 2, 1993, p. 22.
30. For a detailed analysis of these developments, see Gary G. Sick, "Rethinking Dual Containment," *Survival: The IISS Quarterly,* vol. 40, no. 1 (Spring 1998), pp. 5–32.
31. For an elegant elaboration of this point, see Richard Bulliet, "Twenty Years of Islamic Politics," *Keynote Address to the Middle East Institute Annual Conference,* Washington, D.C., October 16, 1998.
32. The gradual improvement of U.S.-Iran relations after the election of Khatami was not reflected in AIPAC's positions. In fact, by early 1999 only AIPAC, the Iranian monarchists in exile and the terrorist *Mojahedin-e Khalq* persisted in their relentless insistence that little or nothing had changed in Iran.

10

Reflections on Iran's Foreign Policy: Defining the "National Interests"

R. K. Ramazani

One of the most crucial intellectual challenges facing Iran as it enters the third decade of its revolution, I would argue, is how it will define its "national interests" (*manafa-e melli*). Five years before the eruption of the Iranian revolution, I asked a similar question at the conclusion of a two-volume study of Iran's foreign policy from 1500–1973, when Iran had been ruled by monarchical dynasties from the Safavids to the Pahlavis in modern history.[1] Since the revolution destroyed the ancient monarchical polity, one might inquire why I am still asking such a question. My study of the foreign policy of revolutionary Iran reveals that this question still requires an answer.[2] More important, the need to seek an answer has become more acute since the revolution for reasons that will become clear as I proceed.

This essay is not intended to answer the question I continue to ask. In fact, I do not believe an answer is in sight in the near future. Profound cultural, social, political, and psychological challenges that beset Iran as a Third World society in transition all have bearing on how Iran will ultimately settle on a coherent conception and definition of its national interest. And such a goal will come within the reach of Iran only when its triple-hybrid civilization (Iranian, Islamic, and modern) is able to cope more effectively with the drama of its century-plus encounter with the realities of the modern world on its own terms.[3]

Instead, through this essay, I propose to explore this conundrum. Doing so requires that I set forth, up front, the following basic assumptions that lie behind my exploration of the subject:

1. In order to pour meaning into the abstract concept of *national interest*, it is necessary to identify the character of *polity;*

2. More than two decades of discourse about the Islamic Revolution have obscured the deeper reality: that the Iranian state and society are both in a state of *transition* as are so many Third World nations;
3. Definition of national interest is affected by the nature of the polity's interaction with the domestic situation, including politics, but not limited to it, and with the external situation, including international politics, but not limited to it. In other words, the concept of "situation" as used here extends beyond the political realm to cultural, social, economic, intellectual, psychological, and philosophical arenas, whether internal or external.[4]
4. Definition of the national interest requires taking into account world views of leaders as well as their foreign policy in action.

Various combinations of the above assumptions constitute the underpinnings of my approach, on the basis of which I shall proceed to explore the meaning of Iran's national interests in terms of four ideal types of interest as guides to foreign policy in Iran's modern history. These are *Sultanic, Ideological-Islamic, Pragmatic-Islamic,* and *Democratic-Islamic.* The inclusion of the prerevolutionary Sultanic type in the discussion is necessary. The revolution destroyed the ancient political *institution* of monarchy, but I submit it has not done away with Sultanic sociocultural tendencies that shape the behavior of individuals and groups even during the revolutionary period.[5] It is also necessary to note that the revolutionary types are not mirror images of historical reality. They are analytical devices. As such, they overlap in historical reality. For example, the Ideological-Islamic type of interest corresponds generally with the first decade of revolutionary developments, but it by no means implies that Pragmatic-National considerations did not figure in the definition of interest during the Khomeini era. In other words, the ideal types are constructed on the basis of *the relative balance* between any two components in each type.

Sultanic Interest

In Weberian terms "sultanism" arises whenever traditional society develops "an administration and military force which are purely personal instruments of the master."[6] Within sultanism, the master makes decisions and chooses courses of action on the basis of "nonrational discretion." The Iranian historical experience includes two types of sultanism: traditional and modernizing or transitional. The ruler's mastery of the bureaucracy and the military obtains in both types. But the bureaucracy and the military in the traditional type are more informal than formal and the opposite holds true in the transitional type.

The best example of the traditional Sultanic type of interest prevailed during the Safavid dynasty. Shah Abbas I (1587–1629) represents sultanism in the extreme. There was perhaps not in the whole world, says a keen observer, "a king that is more Master of the life and fortunes of his subjects, than is Shah Abbas and his successors."[7] The interest that guided Iran's foreign policy was his self-interest. He and other Safavid shahs modeled their rule after the ancient traditions of Sassanian kings. The Safavid wars with the Ottoman Empire were primarily irredentist and imperial in nature, although they were cast in terms of conflict between the Twelver Shii and Sunni state creeds.[8]

Shah Abbas I's ties with European powers aimed primarily at using them as a counterweight against the Ottoman Empire. Neither he nor other Safavid kings had any genuine interest in understanding the underpinnings of European civilization and power. The great age of European religious revolution passed by Islamic Iran. The extant religious writings (*shariat-namehs*) and secular writings (*siyasat-namehs*) reflected and endorsed both the kings's mastery over the people at home and imperial belligerency abroad. The influential *siyasat-nameh* of Khajeh Nezam al-Mulk, for example, advised rulers on the basis of the traditions of pre-Islamic kings that "people are chattel" (*rameh*) and the king is a "shepherd" (*shaban*). To the shah belonged "all the country and the people."[9] Religious writings, by contrast, viewed the Christian West in terms of Islam's conflict with *dar al-harb,* the un-Islamic abode of war. Recent research concludes that the "Safavid society did little to explore the underlying dynamics of European society and culture."[10]

The rule of Mohammad Reza Shah represents modernizing sultanism. Iran's interest was defined largely in terms of his self-interest. He and his father as Safavid kings modeled their rule after the Sassanians. Social scientists rightly list Muhammad Reza Shah side by side with, for example, Duvaliers in Haiti, Trujillo in the Dominican Republic, Marcos in the Philippines, Ceausescu in Romania, and others as examples of sultanism.[11] His absolutism matched Shah Abbas I's, especially after his return to the throne as a result of the CIA-engineered coup. According to a 1965 State Department intelligence report, the Shah personally made all important military, political, economic, educational, social, and other decisions, because "He is convinced that his personal rule is the only way Iran can be governed at the present time."[12] Foreign policy decisions were his special preserve. He wooed the United States as early as 1941 and won the policemanship of the Persian Gulf by 1968. His foreign-policy blunders over a quarter century contributed to losing America in the end.[13] The revolutionary epithet "American king" reflected the people's alienation from him and from America for supporting him. My own research as early as 1979 led me to characterize this phenomenon as the "twin revolution."[14] In his last will and testament Ayatollah Ruhollah Khomeini labeled the Shah's Sultanic polity as satanic (*shaitanic*) rule.[15]

Ideological-Islamic Interest

The interest that guided Iran's foreign policy during the Khomeini era reflected on balance more the influence of his interpretation of Twelver Shii Islam than the interest of Iran as a *nation-state*. As a historical member of the League of Nations and as one of the original 50 founding members of the United Nations, Iran had defined its interest ever since the late nineteenth century and particularly after the Constitutional Revolution (1905–11) in terms of its "political independence and territorial integrity." Modern ideas entered Iranian diplomatic thought—including the very concept of "foreign policy"—side by side with the concept of "national interest." Khomeini rejected this idea, as it derived from his dislike of the idea of "nationalism" (*melli-garai*), and instead interjected a historically unprecedented notion of Islamic governance, derived from his novel interpretation of Twelver Shii jurisprudence, into Iran's political and diplomatic discourse. His favorite motto was "independence, freedom, and the Islamic Republic." The Islamic Republic idea stemmed from his conception of *velayat-i faqih*, the rule of the jurisprudent.[16] This rule emanated from the belief that sovereignty belonged to God, to the Prophet, and to the "infallible imams" (*masumin*), and by extension to the *Faqih*. In the absence of the Twelfth Imam and until his appearance at the end of time to create a just and equitable world order, the *Faqih* will rule the Islamic Republic of Iran supremely.

In anticipation of this millennarian world order, Khomeini believed that the existing world order should emulate his version of the Islamic state paradigm. Since Man's weak mind created the modern international system of nation-states subsequent to the Treaty of Westphalia, Khomeini believed, an "Islamic world order" (my appellation) capable of engulfing all humanity should take its place. "Islam is not peculiar to a country," he said, "to several countries, a group [of people or countries] or even the Muslims. Islam has come for humanity.... Islam wishes to bring all of humanity under *the umbrella of its justice"* (my emphasis).[17] The most vivid example of the interjection of this worldview into Iranian foreign policy concerned the Soviet Union. In Khomeini's letter of January 1, 1989, to the Soviet leader Mikhail Gorbachev, he castigated the bankrupt materialist ideologies of both the East and the West and offered to fill this "ideological vacuum" with Islamic values that alone, he wrote, "can be a means for the well-being and salvation of all nations," including, of course, the Soviet Union.[18]

The interest that guided Iran's foreign policy on the basis of this tenet of Khomeinist ideology was twofold: negation of both superpowers' domination of the international system as evidenced by his well-known slogan "Neither East, nor West, but the Islamic Republic," and the export of the Islamic Revolution across the world. No wonder then that Iran's interest defined in terms of these doctrines put it at odds with much of the rest of the world in practice.[19]

Consider these examples:

The revolutionary government headquartered numerous foreign "liberation movements" in Tehran and was suspected of acts of international subversion and terrorism, especially in the Persian Gulf region. Khomeini wished to see Gulf Arab monarchies adopt governments similar, not identical, to that of the Islamic Republic of Iran, cut their "subservient ties" with the superpowers, and all find safety under the Iranian security umbrella (*chattr-e amniyat*).

The reasons for Iran's prolongation of the war against Iraq in pursuit of a "final victory" are still controversial, but the ideological factor cannot be entirely ruled out.[20] To understand this problem it is necessary to remember that U.N. Secretary General Javier Perez de Cuellar, in his report to the Security Council, characterized Iraq's invasion of Iran on September 22, 1980, as "aggression against Iran."[21] But the question has persisted to date about the Iranian prolongation of forays into Iraqi territory on and after July 13, 1982, by which time Iran had liberated most of its territory from the Iraqi occupation forces.[22] Why then did it carry the war into Iraqi lands? In 1989 Khomeini himself said, "We exported our revolution to the world through the war...."[23] The explanation of former president Hashemi Rafsanjani in 1999 still did not seem to rule out the possible influence of ideology. He said that Khomeini "decreed that our forces should not enter [Iraqi] populated regions and the armed forces carried out the decree."[24] That directive seems to have left the un-inhabited areas of Iraq as open targets.

Two even clearer examples of the influence of ideology on the definition of interest as a guide to Iran's foreign policy should also be mentioned. Khomeini's life-threatening *fatwa* (religious opinion) on Salman Rushdie for "blasphemy," which marred Iran's relations with the West for years, was heavily marked by ideological preoccupation. It is likely though that he used the *fatwa* as a means of balancing domestic political factions so as to keep order.[25] Perhaps the most clear indication of Iran's national interest defined primarily in terms of ideology is the annual dispute between Iran and Saudi Arabia over political demonstrations of the Iranian pilgrims in Mecca.[26] The worst happened in the 1987 *hajj* season when some four hundred pilgrims, including 275 Iranians, died in the clash between the pilgrims and the Saudi police force.

Yet, the definition of Iran's interest even during the Khomeini decade was not completely devoid of practical and national considerations. As a nation-state, Iran had to live in the real world of the international system. In fact, no one changed the Khomeini Line in light of world realities more than Khomeini himself, both in terms of declaratory and practical policies. Just one landmark example of each should suffice. After the hostage crisis, when Western powers in general and the United States in particular imposed sanctions on Iran in order to isolate it, Khomeini declared, " We must become isolated in order to become independent."[27] Yet, after the consolidation of power by his supporters, the settlement of the hostage dispute, and the liberation of Khorramshahr from Iraqi occupation forces, he blamed his zealous followers for Iran's "hermit" status in world affairs, cited the example of the Prophet Muhammad in sending ambassadors to all parts of the world to establish proper relations, criticized his hardline supporters for demanding that Iran should have no relations with the outside world, and declared that such a demand would make no sense because for Iran "it would mean defeat, annihilation and being buried right to the end."[28]

The best example of the consideration of pragmatic interests in Iran's foreign policy during the Khomeini era is the secret purchase of arms from the United States and Israel.[29] Iran's defensive war against Iraq required such a bold move. A deal was struck through intermediaries—American and Israeli arms in return for Iran's help with the release of Western hostages in Lebanon. Six shipments of arms went to Iran, several American hostages were released, each after Iran received a shipment of arms. Embarrassed by the disclosure of the secret deal by Mehdi Hashemi, a militant Islamist, all Iranian leaders in chorus tried to cover up the transactions by denouncing the Great Satan and ridiculing the American mission arriving in Tehran with a bible and a cake![30] In the end, Khomeini himself intervened to quash a demand for parliamentary investigation of the scandal, known in the United States as the Iran-Contra Affair.

Pragmatic-Islamic Interest

The end of the Khomeini era witnessed the beginning of a significant shift in the balance between the influence of ideological and pragmatic aims in Iran's foreign policy in favor of the latter. The shift was subtle and gradual and lasted a good eight years. The notion of an Islamic world order began to wane. The idea of Islam in one country began to gain momentum. Iran was still viewed as the "Islamic citadel" (*umm-al qora*), but it was viewed so as a model to emulate not as one to export through incitement of political opposition in other Muslim states. The doctrine of "Neither East, nor West, but the Islamic Republic" was also turned on its head when the Soviet Union disintegrated.[31]

More specifically, the confluence of three sets of events, domestic, regional, and global, underpinned the shift of emphasis in definition of Iran's interests and its foreign policy orientation. Domestically, two factors figured prominently. First, the chaos of the early years of the Khomeini era had been checked for years before Khomeini's death in 1989. In the three years after the outbreak of the revolution, for example, Iran had changed three presidents, four prime ministers, and seven foreign ministers. Both the hostage crisis and the Iraqi invasion of Iran played into the hands of militant forces following "The Khomeini Line" (*Khat-e Imam*). They suppressed both secular and religious opposition forces, tightened the clerical grip on the social and political organs of the nation and consolidated and monopolized power.

Second, the problem of succession to Khomeini was resolved speedily. A new president was also elected. Even before Khomeini's death the expected successor, Ayatollah Hossein Ali Montazeri had been passed over. Khomeini's choice of Sayyed Ali Khamenei as successor was facilitated by amending the Constitution. The requirement that the *Faqih* should be a "source of emulation" (*marja-i taqlid*) was dropped and Khamenei was elevated politically to the rank of Ayatollah. Also, Hashemi Rafsanjani, the influential speaker of the Majles, was elected president. The American media persistently viewed the two leaders simply as rivals. That was true only in part. Despite stylistic differences, the two leaders' larger interest in the survival of the revolution prevailed. Their dual leadership structure resembled a political-tandem bicycle (*daw charkheh-ye daw nafareh*).[32]

Both leaders had shown pragmatic Islamic tendencies. For example, in 1987, when militant Islamists objected to Iran's ties with Soviet-bloc or Western countries, and even Turkey on ideological grounds, Rafsanjani said, "I believe our principles are obeyed, but in some cases we may be limited and we may have to forego some of these principles."[33] Rafsanjani also constructed the foundations of close military, economic, and political relations with the Soviet Union, which endured after its disintegration. To cite an example about Khamenei's pragmatic tendencies, as president he initiated the idea of Iran's "open-door foreign policy" after a visit to China. He said that "Iran seeks to have rational, sound, and healthy relations with all countries" so as to serve both its national interest and Islam.[34]

Regionally, the most important factor underlying the shift of balance of influence between ideology and pragmatic considerations in favor of the latter was the end of the eight-year Iran–Iraq War. The bitter consequences of the war helped Iran to focus attention on its interests as a nation-state in two ways, rather than to behave as a redeemer of the Muslim states and the world beyond. First, Iranian leaders accorded priority to Iran's political independence and territorial integrity as a nation-state. Second, they decided to reconstruct Iran's military capability and increase its economic productivity, which had been devastated by the Iraqi invasion and occupation. The blatant United States intervention in the war on the side of Saddam Hussein against Iran deepened the latter's military and economic plight. While the Iraqi forces rained missiles on Iranian people and used chemical weapons on Iranian soldiers, the United States attacked the Iranian navy, dismantled a couple of Iranian offshore oilfields in the Persian Gulf, and created and supported Iraq's tanker war against Iran.[35] This in part explains the dogged determination of the new Iranian leaders to reconstruct the Iranian military and economy, despite all domestic and international difficulties. In a candid admission, Rafsanjani said that although Iran had great potential for economic growth, "since we came to power, we have not done so much to [achieve it]."[36] In his inaugural address to the Majles, he was equally candid about Iran's failure to clarify its national interest when he said, "We have not come forward with clear theses (definition of the national interest) in our foreign policy."[37]

Globally, the end of the Cold War and the disintegration of the Soviet Union had far-reaching effects on Iranian thinking about national interest. For the first time in 70 years, Iran's stable international frontiers with the Soviet Union seemed threatened as a consequence of the emergence of a congeries of weak and unstable new republics in Transcaucasia and Central Asia on both sides of the Caspian Sea ("North West Asia," my appellation).[38] As we shall see below, Iran's political independence and territorial integrity in the north became a major source of concern just shortly after it seemed that the end of the Iran–Iraq War had put to rest, at least momentarily, the threat from Saddam Hussein's Iraq.

This rise in Iranian consciousness about the critical importance of national interest in the making and execution of foreign policy found many practical expressions in Iran's relations with other nations across the world. But priority was accorded to the protection and promotion of the country's security interest in the south, the Persian Gulf region, and the country's stability in Northwest Asia.

Historically, Iran has viewed the security of the Persian Gulf region to be indispensable to maintaining its political independence and territorial integrity. But in the Khomeini era, as seen, the ideological crusade and the provocative behavior of Iranian rogue elements in and out of government caused animosity with the Gulf Arab monarchies, who established the Gulf Cooperation Council (GCC) as an antidote to the contagion of the Iranian Revolution. Iranian support of anti-Iraqi forces also contributed to the outbreak of the Iran–Iraq War. By contrast, the Rafsanjani administration pursued a national policy of reconciliation with the Arab monarchies. He said categorically that "we do not want to become the policeman [of the Persian Gulf and] humiliate or intimidate our neighbors or make them feel insecure." He pursued consistently a conciliatory policy toward the GCC member states, contained the annual conflict with Saudi Arabia over the *hajj* issue, and sought earnestly to improve Iran's relations with the GCC as a whole, despite the old dispute with the United Arab Emirates (UAE) over three Persian Gulf islands. In recognition of this conciliatory stance, the GCC, for example, expressed eagerness in its 12th summit meeting (December 25, 1991) to "lend momentum to bilateral relations with" Iran "in the service of common interests."[39]

Two examples in particular indicate that the Rafsanjani administration's courses of action were in keeping with his rhetoric. First was Iran's stance in the Persian Gulf War. To the chagrin of Islamic extremists at home, the Rafsanjani government condemned the Iraqi invasion of Kuwait; maintained amicable relations with the Kuwaiti government-in-exile; made common diplomatic cause with Algeria, France, the Soviet Union, and others to find a peaceful solution before Desert Storm; observed U.N. resolutions imposed on Iraq; and made no real attempt to exploit the Shii and Kurdish rebellions in Iraq against all expectations of the rebels to the contrary. In recognition of Iran's realistic stance, Secretary of State James Baker III believed after the war that "Iran as a major power in the Gulf"[40] should not be excluded from postwar security arrangements in the region, although Washington did exactly the opposite. To the great dismay of Iranian leaders, President George Bush increased unprecedentedly the US military presence in the Persian Gulf.[41] It also concluded bilateral strategic agreements with most individual GCC states without the slightest understanding of Iran's ancient self-perception about its important role in the security of the Persian Gulf.

Second, despite President George Bush's exclusionary policy, Rafsanjani displayed unusual understanding of the U.S. military presence in the Persian Gulf by saying that Iran was "not afraid of them [foreign military forces]" and that "they do not constitute a threat."[42] He also said that the United States "always had bases in Bahrain and Qatar. We have never liked that and always criticized it, and will continue to do so in the future." And Foreign Minister Ali Akbar Velayati said, "It is not reasonable to say that the foreigners must not be present in the region in circumstances in which there is no solution for ensuring the security of the region."[43] This shrewd observation meant if Saddam Hussein were to try to unleash another invasion against Iran or Kuwait, or for that matter against any other state in the region, the U.S. military presence could act as an effective deterrent after all.

In the north as in the south, Iran's national interest was accorded a higher priority than ideology. While in the south, the security of the Persian Gulf was its main concern, in Northwest Asia the region's stability was at stake. Four sets of factors underpinned Iran's interest in the stability of Northwest Asia.

First, given its bitter historical experiences with imperial Russia dating back to the eighteenth century, Iran did not wish to see a new Russian empire rise on its border lands on the ashes of the disintegrated U.S.S.R. At the same time, Rafsanjani wanted to make sure that the multifaceted agreements he had made with the Soviets prior to his presidency would be honored by Moscow subsequently. This required tightrope walking between the divergent and convergent interests of Tehran with Moscow.

Second, Iran needed to contain the contagion of the ethnic revivalist movement in former Soviet Azerbaijan, across the border from its own eastern and western provinces of Azerbaijan. As early as 1990, illegal border crossing had concerned Iran, and the call for the creation of "Greater Azerbaijan" by non-Iranian Azeri nationalists could pose a potential threat to Iran's northern borders.[44]

Third, Iran was deeply concerned that the bloody armed conflict between Armenia and Azerbaijan might spill over into the Iranian northern border areas.

Fourth and finally, Iran's increased geostrategic significance as a result of the disintegration of the Soviet Union required a stable Northwest Asia for the promotion of Iran's interests in the region. The newly independent states could provide a vast market for Iranian exports. Iran could become the cheapest and shortest transit trade route for the transport of oil and gas supplies of the Caspian Sea basin across Iran to world markets through the Persian Gulf. Such opportunities could benefit not only Iran, but also Western oil companies and Western democracies, as well as, of course, the Northwest Asian republics.

Given these interests, Iran pursued an active and pragmatic policy toward Northwest Asia. To cite a few examples, it forged ties with every single new republic; it took the initiative to include them in an expanded Economic Cooperation Organization (ECO); it created a five-member Caspian Sea organization for better handling of the geopolitical situation and serving the interests of all the littoral states in shipping, fisheries, and the desperately needed protection of the environment; and above all, it mediated effectively between the warring republics of Armenia and Azerbaijan, brokering a ceasefire agreement that facilitated the fact-finding mission of U.N. special envoy Cyrus Vance, an accomplishment that earned Iran the praise of the U.N. Secretary General Boutros Boutros-Ghali. Eight years later, on March 17, 2000, Secretary of State Madeleine K. Albright acknowledged that it is in the common interest of Iran and the United States to encourage "stable relations between Armenia and Azerbaijan."[45]

Enough has been said to show how ideological influences of the first decade of the revolution in the conduct of Iran's foreign policy had begun to be replaced by pragmatic considerations by the end of Rafsanjani's presidency. Embedded in this important shift of emphasis was the resurgence of the concept of Iran as a nation-state in the international community. Despite all the American media propaganda about the threat of Islamic fundamentalism to Northwest Asia through Iran, objective research has made such a claim empirically indefensible. The Islamic component of Iran's national interest became a cultural basis for friendly ties with neighbors rather than a militant ideology for export.

The new pragmatic "Islamic-Iranian" (my appellation) paradigm had a special appeal to Northwest Asian republics for various reasons. The Azerbaijanis share Imami Shii Islam with the majority of the Iranian population and ethnic and linguistic ties with the minority Iranian Azerbaijanis. The Tajiks, by contrast, share ethnic and linguistic bonds with Iranian culture and society, and they, as well as Uzbeks, celebrate the Iranian New Year, Nowruz.

Democratic-Islamic Interest

The balance between the Ideological-Islamic and Pragmatic-Islamic influences in the thinking and the conduct of Iran's foreign policy, as seen above, had begun to tilt in favor of the latter during the Rafsanjani era. This tilt reflected a degree of domestication of the Islamic Revolution, or in Kenneth N. Waltz's comment on revolutions in general, it reflected the process of "socialization" of revolution to the international system.[46] This process in the redefinition of Iran's national interest occurred despite the fact that both constitutionally and institutionally the concept of *velayat-i faqih* continued to dominate Iran's thinking in its domestic and foreign policies. Lucian W. Pye noted decades ago that it is a characteristic of transitional societies for leaders to have a greater freedom of action in the international arena as opposed to the domestic situation.[47]

Yet, the Iranian Constitution provided the foundation for not only socializing the Islamic Revolution to the international system, but also for democratizing the Iranian polity as well as foreign policy. Not until the resounding presidential victory of Seyyed Mohammad Khatami on May 23, 1997 (*dovom-e khordad*), was any serious discussion of this democratic aspect of the Constitution in vogue. And ever since his accession to the presidency, he has invoked the Constitution repeatedly as the framework within which both Iran's domestic and foreign policies can and should be democratized.

The legal basis for this view rests on Constitutional provisions that amount to something like the principle of popular sovereignty.[48] Articles 56 and 6 acknowledge the "sovereign right of the nation," and command that "no one shall take away this God-given right." Numerous other provisions provide for a whole variety of individual and other freedoms including, for example, freedom and equality of individuals before the law; security and protection of reputation, life, property, dwelling, and vocation; immunity from search and seizure; presumption of innocence; prohibition of torture; and inviolability of dignity and honor of any person who has been apprehended, detained, arrested, or exiled under any circumstances. They also include freedom of the press and publications; freedom of forming parties, groups and associations; freedom of thought and prohibition of interrogation of people's beliefs; judicial security and the government's obligation to secure "the rights of the people on an all-out basis, men and women alike. . . ."

Yet, paradoxically, the Constitution also embodies the sovereign right of the *Faqih* based on the incorporation in Article 110 of Khomeini's interpretation of governance in Twelver Shii Islam. At the very inception of the Constitution, religious as well as secular individuals and groups objected to this dual sovereignty.[49] For example, Grand Ayatollah Shariatmadari believed that Article 110 contravened Articles 56 and 6 mentioned above, but such critical voices were suppressed and were not revived until after the presidency of Khatami.

The significance of this fundamental constitutional argument for the definition of Iran's national interest should not be overlooked for the all-important reason that Article 9 of the Constitution makes Iran's independence "inseparable" from freedom. And Article 152 provides in part, "The foreign policy of the Islamic Republic of Iran is founded on the basis of . . . safeguarding the complete independence and integrity of the territory" of Iran. In other words, democratization of the Iranian society and state is indispensable to the protection of Iran's complete political independence and territorial integrity as a modern nation-state.

The profound demographic, social, economic, intellectual, and global changes of nearly two decades that underpin the democratic movement led by President Khatami; the unprecedentedly popular elections held for the first time since the revolution of village, town, and city councils; and the domestic struggle and sometimes violent clashes between the "conservatives" (*muhafezeh-karan*) and the "reformers" (*eslah-talaban*) are beyond the scope of this study. Shortly after President Khatami's election, I suggested elsewhere that the synergy between his agenda for reforms at home and peace abroad had been overlooked.[50] I also suggested that President Khatami's worldview resembles the concept of "democratic peace" in the theory of international relations.[51] The analogy, however, is not intended to be complete. The sovereign right of the *Faqih* in the case of Iran transforms that essentially secular democratic theory into a peculiar hybrid concept of "*Faqih*-guided democratic peace." Despite this fundamental limitation of the concept of democratic peace in the case of Iran, it is nevertheless useful to point out briefly the intellectual underpinnings of Khatami's worldview, its practical effects on Iran's foreign policy in action, and its potential for redefinition of Iran's national interest in terms of Democratic-Islamic interest.

Some of the more basic tenets of Khatami's worldview may be listed as follows:

1. Religion and liberty are compatible and so are Islam and freedom;
2. Freedom requires the creation of a civil society based on the paradigm of "The City of the Prophet" (*madinat al-Nabi*), as opposed to the Western concept of civil society that is founded on the model of the Greek city-state.[52] The reason for this distinction is to emphasize the spiritual and moral dimensions of his concept of civil society. At the international level the concept of civil society becomes "global civil society," in the words of Foreign Minister Kamal Kharrazi.
3. The rule of law at home is projected to the international system by emphasizing the role of international law, at least in declaratory policies.
4. Since liberalism is associated, in his view, with secularism, it is regarded as incompatible with Islam, although he insists that Iranians must learn the positive achievements of liberal democracy, such as freedom, limiting and supervising raw power, and "constitutionalizing governance on the basis of the people's will and demands."[53]
5. Although he acknowledges that Western civilization is the preeminent civilization in today's world, Khatami believes that neither it nor its political offspring, secular liberalism, will be triumphant for all time. Yet, this conviction should not be a stumbling block in the way of dialogue among civilizations. Khatami's interpretation of the Renaissance, it seems to me, aims, at least in part, at providing a basis for dialogue between the Islamic and Western civilizations. "Renaissance's real aim was not to revive classical Greek Culture,"[54] he argues; rather its aim was "to revitalize religion by giving it a new language and fresh ideas." This meant that Man would not negate, but embrace, religion by "reforming and propagating" it instead of opposing it. Yet, he thinks that over time modernity lost touch with this spiritual origin of the Renaissance and, hence, led to the sociopolitical phenomenon of Western colonization that failed to adopt "a humanitarian and ethical approach" to Man and the Universe. At President Khatami's initiative, the United Nations designated the year 2001 as the year of dialogue among civilizations.[55] He hopes that through such dialogue the East can teach the West the vital importance of spirituality in human life and the East can learn the positive achievements of Western civilization.

6. Despite these and other ideas, Khatami does not claim to have an answer for the future of his fellow Iranians. He believes that a future different from secular liberalism is awaiting humanity. But the important question, he asks, will be whether "we will be able to play a role in human destiny or at least in our own destiny. If the answer is positive, then with what light should we illuminate our path and what should be our journey's provisions?"[56]

The path of dialogue and détente that President Khatami has pursued in international relations within a few short years clearly has led to an unprecedented degree of reconciliation with the rest of the world. This is an unambiguous departure from the first decade of the revolution. Iran's proactive and peaceful foreign policy since 1997 has encompassed the globe. At the most general level it consists of three general components; "decontainment," deterrence and detente. Decontainment aims at circumventing the American policy of isolating Iran economically, diplomatically, and militarily across the world. Deterrence aims at sufficient military capability to deter any other act of aggression such as Iraq's against Iran, especially in its now even more "dangerous neighborhood," to use Secretary of State Madeleine K. Albright's words. India, Israel, and Pakistan are three nuclear powers in the vicinity of Iran. And detente aims at not only assisting the other two goals of Iranian foreign policy, but also at overcoming the deepening pains of what President Khatami calls Iran's "sick economy." With these general outlines in mind, a few concrete examples of Iran's foreign policy since the presidency of Khatami should suffice.

First and foremost, Iran and Saudi Arabia have achieved a degree of rapprochement that had not existed since the outbreak of the Iranian revolution.[57] The worldviews of President Khatami and Crown Prince Abdullah happen to converge significantly as both oppose hegemony of the great powers in world politics, both urge their own and other Muslim societies to engage in self-criticism, and Khatami's concept of dialogue and Abdullah's notion of "call" (*dawah*) aim at providing the world with the paradigm of ethical Islamic behavior. The interests of the two countries also converge considerably, though not completely. Both sympathize with the sufferings of the Iraqi people under the United Nations sanction established in 1991, both consider the Iraqi regime as a potential source of threat to their security, both wish to prevent oil prices from hitting rock bottom in the world market, and both share an interest in the development of the Organization of Islamic Conference (OIC), which has been bankrolled for decades by Saudi Arabia and is currently chaired by Khatami, so that the Muslim states might play a larger role on the world scene. From the Iranian perspective, rapprochement with Saudi Arabia is a key to improving relations with other GCC states as well, despite the dispute with the UAE and that country's unspoken discomfort over the Irano-Saudi rapprochement and as a means of convincing the Arab monarchies of the need for the littoral states of the region to maintain the security of the Persian Gulf themselves.

Second, Iran has taken giant steps toward transforming the European past policy of "critical engagement" into a policy of positive engagement with it. The key object of the Iranian policy of friendship within the European Union states has been Britain. Iran took the bold initiative to remove the single greatest stumbling block in its relations with London by distancing itself publicly from the Khomeini *fatwa* on Salman Rushdie. In a news conference on September 22, 1998, in New York, President Khatami suggested that the *fatwa* was the expression of Khomeini's own view as an Islamic jurist, reportedly adding that, "We should consider the Salman Rushdie issue as completely finished."[58] Two days later, the seasoned Foreign Minister Kamal Kharrazi reportedly told British Foreign Secretary Robin Cook: "The government of the Islamic Republic of Iran has no intention, nor is it going to take any action whatsoever to threaten the life of the author of *The Satanic Verses* or anybody associated with his work, nor will it encourage or assist anybody to do so."[59] Britain announced immediately afterward that it would upgrade its diplomatic relations with Iran by an exchange of ambassadors.

By January 2000, improved relations had entered a level such that for the first time since the revolution an Iranian minister visited London. Foreign Ministers Cook and Kharrazi committed their nations to resolve common difficulties regarding the Iraqi regime, Iraqi refugees in Iran, terrorism, and weapons of mass destruction.[60] In tandem with improving relations with Britain, Iran also has developed ever-closer relations with Italy, France, Germany, Greece, Austria, and others, especially in the economic field, the single most important incentive for better relations with the European Union. From a strategic perspective, of course, Iranian-European rapprochement fits Iran's policy of decontainment vis-à-vis the United States.

Third, and finally, against the backdrop of mutual satanization between Tehran and Washington since the seizure of American diplomats as hostages on November 4, 1979, until the election of President Khatami on

May 23, 1997, there seemed to be no real hope for normalization of Iran–U.S. relations. Yet, President Khatami surprised the world on December 14, 1997 when he said that "I, first of all, pay my respect to the great people and nation of America," and that he hoped that in the near future he would have "a dialogue and talk with the American people...."[61] True to his words, on January 7, 1998, he pointed out the philosophical similarity, if not commonality, between the origins of the American and Iranian republics in combining religion and liberty. He then proposed to Americans the idea of an "exchange of professors, writers, scholars, artists, journalists, and tourists," which have been underway ever since.[62]

Apart from people-to-people exchanges between the United States and Iran and a relative thaw in the hostile rhetoric and symbols that has occurred ever since these two Iranian initiatives, the Clinton administration has taken a few tentative steps toward improving the atmosphere of U.S. relations with Iran. For example, it waived the threat of sanctions against the French Total firm and its Russian and Malaysian partners when, in defiance of the Iran-Libya Sanctions Act (ILSA), Total signed a $2 billion investment contract with Iran for its gas field in the Persian Gulf. It allowed U.S. firms to sell food and medicine to Iran; allowed the Boeing Company to provide Iran's national airline with parts to ensure the safety of its 747 passenger aircraft contract; lifted the U.S. embargo on Iranian export of carpets, caviar, and dried fruits; and promised a "global settlement" of legal claims and counter claims of Iran and the United States at the Hague Tribunal.

Perhaps Iran was more impressed by certain statements on the part of the United States than by these small symbolic steps. Long after President Khatami had expressed regrets in January 1998 for the sufferings of the American people during the hostage crisis, President Clinton surprised even the officials of his own administration in April 1999 by saying that Iran "has been the subject of quite a lot of abuse from various Western nations,"[63] and that sometimes "it's quite important to tell people, look, you have a right to be angry at something my country or my culture or others that are generally allied with us today did to you 50 or 60 or 100 or 150 years ago." It was even more music to Iranian ears when Secretary of State Madeleine K. Albright publicly admitted on March 17, 2000, the American role in the overthrow of the popular government of Dr. Mossadeq and expressed regret for the United States' having sided with Iraq in its war against Iran.[64]

All these small steps and the improved tone by the Clinton administration, the positive Arab response to Iranian efforts for rapprochement, and the ever-increasing ties between Iran and European nations show that Iran's definition of its national interest has begun to move away from the ideological emphasis of the first decade of the revolution, although in fairness it must be admitted that Rafsanjani's foreign policy initiatives over eight years paved the way for further conciliatory moves on the part of the Khatami leadership. Overall, ever since the accession of Rafsanjani to power and the presidency of Khatami, the foreign policy of Iran has played a significant role in the painful process of the as-yet-incomplete reintegration of Iran into the international system.

The Enduring Question

To return to the beginning of this essay, when I asked a quarter century ago what is the meaning of Iran's national interest, I also tried to illustrate the question for American readers by pointing out the enduring debate between realists and idealists about the American national interest. In the 1950s and 1960s, the dominant thinking in the American academy was what is today called "traditional realism" (Kenneth N. Waltz's appellation),[65] as expounded especially by Hans J. Morgenthau. This influential international relations thinker defined national interest in terms of power for its own sake.[66] Today, the neorealists led by Kenneth N. Waltz, define national interest in terms of power as an instrument of security. Conversely, Reinhold Niebuhr, the eminent "theologian realist" (my appellation), said that, to be sure, preservation of self-interest is "tentatively necessary," and the balancing of power can serve self-interest, but it is not sufficient. In other words, that the United States should embrace a scheme of higher values than national interest defined merely in terms of power or security.[67]

The founding fathers of the United States are said to have sought to use foreign policy as a means to such higher ends and purposes as individual right to life, liberty, and the pursuit of happiness as embodied in the American Declaration of Independence. In 1974, when the Shah was still in power, I asked, What about Iran? What are those higher ends that Iran's foreign policy is trying to serve? And now when the Islamic Republic of Iran has entered its third decade of existence, I ask the same question again. What are those higher ends beyond self-interest that the Islamic Republic of Iran will try to serve?

This essay has shown that, since the revolution, Iran has tried to experiment with various kinds of definitions of national interest. In the first decade of the revolution, the Khomeinist ideological crusade, aimed at an Islamic world order, outweighed practical-national considerations in Iranian foreign policy thinking and action. During the following eight years, practical-national considerations outweighed the ideological ones. And since the presidency of Mohammad Khatami, democratic-national thinking has been introduced into Iranian foreign policy discourse and practice. The pro-Khatami reformers call Iran's new thinking the "democratic-Islamic paradigm" (*olgo-ye mardom salari-e Eslami*).

As seen, in trying to point out the similarity between the American and Iranian peoples' revolutionary experiences, President Khatami spoke of the combination of religion and liberty in the founding of the American republic and mentioned de Tocqueville as well. Assuming that his American audience had read de Tocqueville, President Khatami did not elaborate, but my guess is that he had this passage in mind: "I do not know whether all the Americans have sincere faith in their religion; for who can search the human heart? But I am certain that they hold it to be indispensable to the maintenance of republican institutions. This opinion is not peculiar to a class of citizens or to a party, but it belongs to the whole nation, and to every rank of society."[68]

I shall return to this parallelism, but it is worth mentioning here that there is a more fitting parallel in the experience of American and Iranian revolutionaries. Religion played a significant role in mobilizing support for resistance of both revolutionary peoples to foreign domination, Britain in the American and, ironically, the United States in the Iranian experiences. Regarding the American case, James H. Hutson says: "The plain fact is that, had American clergymen of all denominations not assured their pious countrymen, from the beginning of the conflict with Britain, that the resistance movement was right in God's sight and had His blessing, it could not have been sustained and independence could not have been achieved. Here is the fundamental, the indispensable, contribution of religion and its spokesmen to the coming of the American Revolution."[69]

There is, however, a fundamental difference between the Iranian and American revolutionary experiences in so far as combining religion and liberty is concerned. The American founding fathers did not institutionalize such a combination in the American Constitution; in fact, they separated them in the First Amendment's Establishment Clause. This separation was never intended to be an antireligious or anticlerical move, a reality that is little understood in Iran. As a matter of fact, it has been argued that the Jeffersonian metaphor of the "Wall of Separation" has never been as absolute as it has been commonly assumed.[70] To date, in fact, American courts are trying to draw boundaries, case by case, between church and state in American society to protect both religion and state.

The Iranian Revolution, however, created the world's only quasi-theocratic state which, as seen, was debated at the very inception of the republic. The Constitution in effect embodies, it seems to me, two God-given rights, one that belongs to the *Faqih* and the other to the people, but the former enjoys superior powers relative to that of the latter. President Khatami, who embraces the Constitution and acknowledges, necessarily, the supreme leadership of the *Faqih,* seems to be trying to upgrade people's rights within the existing constitutional framework by reforming the Islamic polity. This is fully in keeping with his rejection of "secular liberalism" as seen above. In American political science jargon, he is a "transformational" president. But fierce, and often violent, opposition to his reform efforts seems to be forcing him toward some kind of an "incremental" presidency. A more apt characterization, I believe, is that he is transformational in vision and incremental in strategy.

The deceptive nature of the main opposition, it seems to me, lies in the fact that it is expressed all in the name of Islam. For example, the 20 year old gunman who shot Saeed Hajjarian, a close advisor to President Khatami, told the court with a smile that he believed his victim was "un-Islamic" and that he attacked Hajjarian because he believed he was performing his "religious duties." In the case of Iran, as opposed to most other Muslim states, the problem is deeper than religious fanaticism. I believe it is compounded by what may be called "sociocultural sultanism," a phenomenon that is observable at every level of society in the behavior of the individual, group, and polity.[71] President Khatami seemed to be putting his finger on this very problem when he said, "Autocracy has become our second nature. We Iranians are all dictators, in a sense."[72]

But the quest for individual freedom and democracy in Iranian society is more than a century old. Twice in the twentieth century, the glimmer of hope for democratic polity was dashed, once by Britain and Russia and once by the United States. The revolution first revived that hope and then scotched it, despite the fact that the Constitution couples inseparably, as seen, political independence with freedom. President Khatami believes that the Khomeini motto "independence, freedom, and the Islamic Republic" constitutes three "enduring" (*javidan*) slogans of the revolution. The first two principles are the products of Iran's painful encounter with the modern world since the late nineteenth century. They have survived all the turmoil and tragedy of Iranian history because they are compatible with modern standards of international relations and law. The real question is whether the principle of the Islamic Republic, in its present constitutional and institutional configurations, will become increasingly compatible with the realities of the modern world, including Iran's own disrupted, but enduring, democratic movement.

As long as this question remains largely unanswered, definition of the national interest in Iran's foreign policy in the future will remain problematic. It will largely reflect the effects of muddling through the pressures and counter pressures of domestic and international circumstances, without achieving a coherent core of values as the clearly articulated higher ends and purposes of foreign policy. This is the crucial challenge that faces the Iranian foreign policy community, including thinkers and practitioners of all stripes.

Yet, as an Iranian American thinker who has watched from the United States for over half a century the painful process of Iran's civilizational maturation and the beginnings of the process of democratic transition, I am more hopeful than fearful that the quest of the Iranian people for freedom will not be extinguished in the twenty-first century as it was twice in the twentieth. If my hopes are realized, perhaps liberty can become the highest end and purpose of Iran's foreign policy at the turn of the new millennium, for I firmly believe that without justice, there can be no durable order, and without liberty, there can be no justice.

Notes

1. My interest in the foreign policy of Iran dates back to 1952 when I was doing research and writing on the legal and political aspects of the Iranian nationalization of the oil industry for my doctoral dissertation. I then discovered that there were no systematic studies of Iran's foreign policy in any language. That set me on the path of working on the subject over the past half a century. See my *The Foreign Policy of Iran, 1500–1941: A Developing Nation in World Affairs* (Charlottesville: University Press of Virginia, 1966). The influential *Foreign Affairs Quarterly* recognized that "R. K. Ramazani's book is the only work in any language which gives an objective and detailed account of Iran's international role during this entire period." The book won the first prize of the American Association for Middle East Studies, subsequently renamed MESA. See also my *Iran's Foreign Policy, 1941–1973: A Study of Foreign Policy in Modernizing Nations* (Charlottesville: University Press of Virginia, 1975). This book was recognized by *Guide to American Foreign Relations Since 1700* as "the best single volume on Iran's foreign policy in the postwar period."

2. See my *Revolutionary Iran: Challenge and Response in the Middle East* (Baltimore and London: Johns Hopkins University Press, first printing 1986 and second printing, with a new epilogue on American-Iranian Arms Deal, 1988).
3. I first used this concept of "triple hybridity" in a paper on "Secularism and Islam" delivered at the 50th Anniversary Meeting of the Middle East Institute, Washington, D.C., September 28, 1996.
4. I developed the concept of interactions between foreign and domestic situations and vice versa, between foreign policy and the external situation and vice versa, and between external and internal situations in 1966 and have used it ever since in all subsequent studies. It is characterized as "dynamic triangular interaction."
5. Weber uses the concept of "sultanism," as will be seen, with reference to a type of polity. For reasons given in note 71 *infra* I have extended it to apply to individuals and groups as well.
6. See Max Weber, *Economy and Society: An Outline of Interpretive Sociology*, ed. Guenther Roth and Claus Wittich (Berkeley: University of California Press, 1978), vol. 1, 231–32. Historically speaking, I find it suggestive to compare the sultanism of ancient China and Iran. See *From Max Weber: Essay in Sociology*, trans. and ed. H. H. Gerth and C. Wright Mills (New York: Oxford University Press, 1958), especially pp. 442–44.
7. For details, see my first volume cited in note 1 above pp. 13–32.
8. Ibid.
9. See Seyyed Javad Tabatabai, *Tarikh-e Andishe-ye Siyasi dar Iran* [A History of Political Thought in Iran] (Tehran: The Institute for Political & International Study, 1988), pp. 61–62.
10. See the thoughtful article of Rudi Matthee, "Between Aloofness and Fascination: Safavid Views of the West," *Iranian Studies*, vol. 31, no. 2, Spring 1998, pp. 219–46.
11. See Juan J. Linz and Alfred Stepan, *Problems of Democratic Transition and Consolidation: Southern Europe, South America, and Post-Communist Europe* (Baltimore and London: The Johns Hopkins University Press, 1996), p. 51. It should be noted that the author's typology of polities does not include theocratic or quasi-theocratic such as that of Iran, which is now facing the problems of transition to democracy. This theoretical gap requires research by social scientists. Also, the success or failure of the democratic experiment in the Islamic Republic of Iran could have a far-reaching impact on the Muslim world.
12. I am indebted to Professor Abbas Milani for bringing this report to my attention. See Bureau of Intelligence and Research, Department of State,

Reflections on Iran's Foreign Policy 233

Studies in Political Dynamics in Iran, Secret Report No. 13, NSA., no. 603.

13. See my *The United States and Iran: The Patterns of Influence* (New York: Praeger Publishers, 1982). See also my "Who Lost America? The Case of Iran," *The Middle East Journal,* vol. 36, no. 1, Winter 1982, pp. 5–21.
14. See my "Iran's Revolution in Perspective," in American Foreign Policy Institute, *The Impact of the Iranian Events upon Persian Gulf and United States Security,* Washington, DC, 1979, pp. 19–37; "Iran's Foreign Policy: Perspectives and Projections," Joint Economic Committee of the United States Congress, *Economic Consequences of the Revolution in Iran* (Washington, D.C.: U.S. Printing Office, 1980), pp. 65–97; and " Iran's Revolution: Patterns, Problems and Prospects," *International Affairs* (London), Summer 1980, pp. 443–57.
15. See *Imam Khomeini's Last Will and Testament,* Embassy of the Democratic and Popular Republic of Algeria, Interests Section of the Islamic Republic of Iran (Washington, D.C., n.d.), p. 23.
16. See Ayatollah Ruhollah Khomeini's work in Persian, *Hokomat-e Islami Va Velayat-i Faqih* (Tehran: Amir Kabir Publishers, 1977).
17. See FBIS-MEA, December 18, 1979.
18. See FBIS, *Near East and South Asia,* January 9, 1989.
19. See my "Iran's Export of the Revolution: Politics, Ends, and Means," in John L. Esposito, ed., *The Iranian Revolution: Its Global Impact* (Miami: Florida International University Press, 1990), pp. 40–62.
20. See my *Revolutionary Iran,* op. cit. pp. 750–85, especially pp. 74–76.
21. See his report, "Further Report of The Secretary-General on The Implementation of Security Council Resolution 598 (1987)," U.N. SCOR, 46th Sess., Doc. S/23273 (1991). See my commentary on the report, "Who Started the Iraq-Iran War?" *Virginia Journal of International Law,* vol. 33, no. l, Fall 1992, pp. 69–89.
22. I pondered critically the issue of the prolongation of the war as early as 1986. See my *Revolutionary Iran,* op. cit.
23. See FBIS-NES, February 24, 1989.
24. See Hashemi Rafsanjani's interview in *Hamshahri,* December 22, 1999.
25. Although Khomeini considered his *fatwa* a means of punishing Rushdie for "blasphemy and apostasy," the edict also had a factional balancing dimension to it. See my "Iran's Export of the Revolution," op. cit. and my piece in note 35 *infra.*
26. For details see my *Revolutionary Iran,* op. cit. See also my "Iran's Islamic Revolution and the Persian Gulf," *Current History,* January, 1985, pp. 5–8 and 40–41, and the note *infra.*

27. See Institute for Political and International Studies, *Gozaresh-e Seminar,* Tehran, no. 2, 1983/1984, p. 36.
28. See FBIS-SA, October 30, 1984.
29. See my *Revolutionary Iran,* op. cit. (1988 edition).
30. See my "Iran and the United States; Islamic Realism?," in Robert O. Freedman, ed., *The Middle East from the Iran-Contra Affair to the Intifada* (Syracuse, N.Y.: Syracuse University Press, 1991), pp.167–182.
31. See my "Iran's Foreign Policy: Both North and South," *The Middle East Journal,* vol. 46, no. 3, Summer 1992, pp. 393–412.
32. The American media in general depicted Khamenei and Rafsanjani as rival leaders without comprehending that despite their differences in style they both upheld the same basic goals of the revolution. The same habit surfaced with respect to Khamenei and Khatami after the latter's presidential election. Again, on the fundamentals of the revolution, they ride a political tandem bicycle as well.
33. See FBIS-SA, April 17, 1987.
34. This landmark call for an open-door foreign policy was first made on July 20 and again on August 6, 1984. See FBIS-SA, July 31, 1984 and August 7, 1984.
35. For details, see my "Iran's Resistance to U.S. Intervention in the Persian Gulf," in eds. Nikki R. Keddie and Mark J. Gasioroswski, eds., *Neither East Nor West : Iran, The Soviet Union, and the United States* (New Haven and London: Yale University Press, 1990), pp. 36–60.
36. See Ramazani, R.K. ed., *Iran's Revolution: The Search for Consensus* (Bloomington and Indianapolis: Indiana University Press, 1990), pp. vii-xi.
37. Ibid.
38. See my article in note 31 above.
39. *Ibid.*
40. Ibid.
41. See my *Future Security in the Persian Gulf: America's Role* (Washington, D.C.: Middle East Insight's Policy Review, No. 2, 1991).
42. See FBIS-NES, September 23, 1991.
43. Ibid., January 2, 1991.
44. As a matter of fact, in January 1990 thousands of Soviet Azeris rioted near the Iranian border, harassed Soviet and Iranian border guards, and illegally crossed into Iran. The Rafsanjani administration wished to see no repetition of the same, especially after Azerbaijan became the first among the former Soviet republics to declare its independence on August 30, 1991.
45. See U.S. Department of State, Office of the Spokesman, "Secretary of

State Madeleine K. Albright: Remarks At Conference On American-Iranian Relations," Washington, D.C., March 17, 2000.
46. See Kenneth N. Waltz, *Theory of International Politics* (New York: McGraw-Hill, 1979).
47. See Lucian W. Pye, *Politics, Personality, and Nation Building: Burma's Search for Identity* (New Haven and London: Yale University Press, 1962), especially at p. 28.
48. For a comprehensive legal analysis of the Iranian Constitution, see the two-volume study by Dr. Seyyed Mohammad Hashemi, *Hoqouq-e Assasi-e Jomhouri-e Islami-ye Iran* (Tehran: University of Shahid Beheshti in cooperation with the Yalda Publication Institute, 1995 and 1998).
49. See my earliest commentary on the Constitution, "Document: The Constitution of the Islamic Republic of Iran," *The Middle East Journal*, vol. 34, no. 2, Spring 1980, pp. 181–204, especially pp. 181–83.
50. See my "The Shifting Premise of Iran's Foreign Policy: Towards A Democratic Peace?" *The Middle East Journal*, vol. 52, no. 2, Spring 1998, pp. 177–87.
51. The "democratic peace" thesis holds that democracies are intrinsically peaceful. Most scholars agree that democracies are at peace with each other (dyadic version), while many proponents of the theory suggest that democratic states are less prone to use force even if the regime type of their enemies is nondemocratic (the monadic variant). Recently, Edward D. Mansfield and Jack Snyder have argued that democratization can cause war. See their minority view in the anthology edited by Michael E. Brown, Sean M. Lynn-Jones, and Steven E. Miller, *Debating the Democratic Peace* (Cambridge, MA: MIT Press, second printing 1997).
52. See Permanent Mission of the Islamic Republic of Iran to the United Nations, "Statement by H. E. Seyyed Mohammad Khatami, President of the Islamic Republic of Iran and Chairman of the Eighth Session of the Islamic Conference," December 1997, p. 2.
53. See Seyyed Mohammad Khatami, *Az Donia-ye Shahr Ta Shahr-e Donia: Sayri dar Andisheh-ye Siyasi-e Gharb* ["From the World of the City State to the City of the World"] (Tehran: Nashr-e Nay, 1994), p. 285.
54. See Seyyed Mohammad Khatami, Statement at the European University in Florence, Italy, entitled "A Message for Europe," March 10, 1999. Courtesy of the Permanent Mission of the Islamic Republic of Iran to the United Nations.
55. This proclamation, which is entitled "The United Nations Year of Dialogue among Civilizations," was embodied in the U.N. Resolution 53/22. See U.N. General Assembly, 54th session, Agenda item 34, November 12, 1999.

56. See Seyyed Mohammad Khatami, op. cit., p. 293. (My translation).
57. See my "The Emerging Arab-Iranian Rapprochement," *Middle East Policy,* vol. VI, no. 1, June 1998, pp. 45–62.
58. As quoted in *The New York Times,* September 23, 1998.
59. As quoted in *The Washington Post,* September 25, 1998.
60. See *Hamshahri,* January 12, 2000.
61. Quoted at Khatami's news conference in Tehran, reported in FBIS-NES *Daily Report,* December 14, 1997.
62. President Khatami's televised statement was broadcast on Cable News Network (CNN) International.
63. Despite this statement by President Clinton, 10 days later Assistant Secretary of State Martin Indyk repeated the usual litany of "dual containment." See *The Washington Post,* May 1, 1999.
64. See note 45 above.
65. See Kenneth N. Waltz, "Realist Thought and Neorealist Theory," *Journal of International Affairs,* vol. 44, no.1, Spring 1990, pp. 21–37.
66. See Hans J. Morgenthau, *Politics Among Nations,* (New York: Alfred A. Knopf, 5th ed., 1972).
67. I am basing my characterization of Reinhold Niebuhr not only on the basis of his own works, but also on Michael Joseph Smith, *Realist Thought: From Weber to Kissinger* (Baton Rouge and London: Louisiana University Press, 1986).
68. Alexis de Tocqueville, *Democracy in America,* vol. II. trans. by Henry Reeve (London, 1835), pp. 232–33.
69. See James H. Hutson, *Religion and the Founding of the American Republic* (Washington, D.C., Library of Congress, 1998), p. 40.
70. Ibid.
71. My extension of Max Weber's concept of "sultanism" from polity to society, including individuals and factions, is based not only on Iran's own historical experience with both rampant factionalism and authoritarianism, but also on the basis of demonstrated intolerance and violence of extremist conservatives against moderate reformers in the name of Islam. In this context, they are practicing "religious sultanism." This characterization fits perfectly what the Iranian writers are saying about their fate at the hands of diehard conservatives within and outside the regime. I suggest only a number of new sources in Persian in order to illustrate the depth of the problem of religious sultanism that Iranian reformers face today. On the serial political murders, see, for example, Hamid Kaviany, *Dar Jostojouy-e Mahfel-e Jenayatkaran* [In Search of the Criminal Circle] (Tehran: Nashr-e Negah-e Emruz, 1999) and Emad ed-Din Baqi, *Trajedy-e Domokracy Dar*

Iran [The Tragedy of Democracy in Iran] (Tehran: Nashr-e Nay, 2nd ed., 2000). Regarding the special clerical court's trials of Abdullah Nouri and Mohsen Kadivar respectively, see *Defa'iyat-e Abdullah Nouri* [The Defense by Abdullah Nouri] (Tehran: Farhang-e Umomi, 1999) and Zahra Rudi Kadivar ed., *Baha-ye Azadi: Defa'iyat-e Mohsen Kadivar dar Dadgah-e Vizheh-ye Ruhaniyat* [The Price of Freedom: The Defense of Mohsen Kadivar in the Special Clerical Court] (Tehran: Nashr-e Nay, 1999). For an informed analysis of the Iranian sociopolitical predicaments, see Ali Akbar Mahdi, *Farhang-e Irani, Jama'-ye Madani va Daghdagheh-ye Domokracy* [Iranian Culture, Civil Society and Concern for Democracy] (Tehran: Nashr-e Javan, 1998).
72. Mohammad Khatami, "On the Virtues of the West," *Time* (electronic version), World/Essay, January 19, 1998, vol. 151, no. 2.

Contributors

MEHRZAD BOROUJERDI is Associate Professor of Political Science at the Maxwell School of Citizenship and Public Affairs, Syracuse University. In addition to numerous articles in English and Persian-language journals, Dr. Boroujerdi is the author of *Iranian Intellectuals and The West: The Tormented Triumph of Nativism* and General Editor of the book series Modern Intellectual and Political History of the Middle East. He has been a postdoctoral Fellow at the Center for Middle Eastern Studies, Harvard University, and a Rockefeller Foundation Fellow at the University of Texas, Austin.

HALEH ESFANDIARI is Consulting Director for the Middle East Project at the Woodrow Wilson International Center. Formerly, she was an Instructor and Lecturer in Persian Language and Literature at Princeton University's Department of Near Eastern Studies, Deputy Director of the Shabbanou Farah Foundation in Tehran, and Director of the Bagh-e Ferdows Cultural Center, also located in Tehran. She is the Editor of *Iranian Women: Past, Present and Future* and the co-Editor of *Economic Dimensions of Middle Eastern History*. She specializes in the Iranian Women's Movement and modern Iranian literature.

JOHN L. ESPOSITO is University Professor, Professor of Religion and International Affairs, and Director of the Center for Muslim-Christian Understanding at Georgetown University. He is Editor-in-Chief of *The Oxford Encyclopedia of the Modern Islamic World* and *The Oxford History of Islam*, and General Editor of Oxford University Press' Religion and

Global Politics Series. Esposito's other publications include: *The Islamic Threat: Myth or Reality?; Islam and Democracy* and *Makers of Contemporary Islam* (with John O. Voll); *Islam and Politics; Political Islam: Revolution, Radicalism, or Reform?; The Iranian Revolution: Its Global Impact; Islam and Secularism in the Middle East* (with Azzam Tamimi); *Islam: The Straight Path; Islam, Gender and Social Change* (with Yvonne Haddad); *Islam in Asia: Religion, Politics, and Society;* and *Women in Muslim Family Law.*

FARIDEH FARHI has been a writer and researcher in Iran for the past five years. Formerly, she was an Associate Professor of Political Science at the University of Hawaii in Manoa and an Instructor and Researcher at the University of Colorado in Boulder. Her publications include *States and Urban-Based Revolutions in Iran and Nicaragua,* "Motale'at-e Zanan va Engelab" (Women's Studies and Revolution), "Considerations and Iranian Foreign Policy," and "Toward a New Sociology of Revolutions." She focuses on theories of revolution and Iranian Politics and Foreign Policy.

FRED HALLIDAY is Professor of International Relations at the London School of Economics and Senior Fellow of the Institute for Policy Studies in Washington, D.C. Additionally, he is a member of the Management Committee at the Center for Near and Middle Eastern Studies at the School of Oriental and African Politics Project, the Council on Foreign Relations in New York, and a regular contributor to the BBC. Formerly, Dr. Halliday served as the Chairman of the Research Committee of the Royal Institute of International Affairs and was elected to its Governing Council. His publications include *Iran: Dictatorship and Development* and *The Myth of Confrontation.* Five of his books have been published in Persian.

BIJAN KHAJEHPOUR is the Managing Director and Owner of Atieh Bahar Consulting, Tehran. Additionally, he is the Editor of *Iran Focus* and *Iran Quarterly Report.* He is also a member of the Editorial Board of the Iranian Political Review, *Goftogu.* His articles include: "The 1996 Majlis Elections in Iran," "Iran: A Waking Regional Giant?," and "Where is Iran Heading?"

MOHIADDIN MESBAHI is Associate Professor of International Relations at Florida International University in Miami, Florida and co-Chair of the Asian Studies Program at FIU. He teaches in the areas of International

Relations Theory, Central Asia and Post-Soviet Studies, Strategic Studies, and National Security. He has received numerous fellowships, including Senior Iranian Fellow at Oxford University and the Albert Pick Fellowship, University of Miami. His publications include: *Russia and the Third World in the Post-Soviet Era* and *Central Asia and the Caucausus after the Soviet Union: Domestic and International Dynamics.*

MOHSEN M. MILANI is Professor and Chair of the Department of Government and International Affairs at the University of South Florida in Tampa. Dr. Milani served as a Fellow at Harvard University, Oxford University, and the Foscari University in Venice. His publications include: *The Making of Iran's Islamic Revolution* (Second Edition) and "Iran's Islamic Revolution," recently published in *The Encyclopedia of Political Revolutions.* He is currently working on ideological implications of President Khatami's victory in Iran and is coediting a book on the New World Order and the Middle East.

R. K. RAMAZANI is the Edward R. Stettinius Professor Emeritus of Government and Foreign Affairs at the University of Virginia, where he has specialized in the Middle East since 1952. Widely acknowledged as "the Dean of Iranian Foreign Policy Studies in the United States," his many books include: *The Foreign Policy of Iran: 1500–1941, Iran's Foreign Policy: 1941–1973, Revolutionary Iran,* and *The Gulf Cooperation Council,* as well as over 100 articles and book chapters. A former Vice President of the American Institute of Iranian Studies, Dr. Ramazani served on numerous governing boards, including those of the Middle East Institute and the American-Iranian Council. He has been consulted by the White House, the Congress, the State Department, the Department of Defense, and the Department of Treasury, as well as the United Nations' Secretariat General.

ABDULAZIZ SACHEDINA is Professor of Religious Studies at the University of Virginia. Formerly, Dr. Sachedina taught as a Visiting Professor at McGill University, Haverford College, Kulliyat al-Shari'a in Jordan, and the University of Waterloo in Canada. His publications include: *Islamic Messianism: The Idea of the Mahdi in Twelver Shi'ism, The Just Ruler in Twelver Shi'ism: The Comprehensive Authority of the Jurist in Imamite Jurisprudence, Human Rights and the Conflict of Cultures: Western and Islamic Perspectives on Religious Freedom,* and *The Prolegomena to the Qur'an.*

GARY SICK is Senior Research Scholar and Adjunct Professor of International Affairs at Columbia University, where he earned his Ph.D. He previously served on the National Security Council staff under Presidents Ford, Carter, and Reagan, and was the principal White House aide for Iran during the Iranian Revolution and hostage crisis. Dr. Sick is the executive director of Gulf/2000, an international research project on political, economic, and security developments in the Persian Gulf.

Index

Abbas I, Shah, 213
al-'adl (justice), 128, 131
Afghanistan, 8, 149, 151, 160, 162, 164–165, 176, 178, 183–184, 188, 201, 205
Albright, Madeleine, 10, 201–202, 225, 227
Algar, Hamid, 133
Algeria, 180, 219
Alviri, Morteza, 33
American-Israel Public Affairs Committee (AIPAC), 199, 204, 210 n.32
Amoli, Ayatollah Javadi, 124
Anderson, Terry, 198
Ansar-e Hezbollah, 40, 49
Arab-Israeli dispute, 8, 182, 184–186, 199, 201, 203, 204, 206
Araki, Ayatollah, 27 n. 21, 125, 126, 141
Armenia, 161–162, 165, 184, 221
Asadi, Bani, 133
Asre-Ma, 43
assassinations, 43, 178, 188–189
Association of the Combatant Clergy of Tehran, 32
Azad University, 90–91
Azerbaijan, 157–158, 160, 161, 184, 220–222, 234 n.44

Badamchian, Assadollah, 46
Bahrain, 183, 220
Baker, James, III, 220
Bakhtiar, Shahpur, 189

Balkans, 154, 155
Bani Sadr, Abolhasan, 1, 47, 53
bayat (allegiance), 15
Bazargan, Mehdi, 1, 44, 81, 133, 177, 192–193
Bonyad Mostazafin va Janbazan (Foundation for the Deprived and the War Veterans), 111, 120
Bosnia, 7, 154, 155, 184, 188
Bush, George, 198, 202, 220
Bushehr nuclear power plant, 152, 186

Carter, Jimmy, 193, 194
Casey, William, 195
Caspian Sea, 152, 153, 155, 159–160, 163, 166, 167, 219
Caucasus, 7, 149–167, 205, 218–219
Center for Women's Participation, 87
Central Asia, 7, 8, 11, 149–167, 205, 218–219
Chechnya, 8, 154
China, 153, 175, 177, 185, 186, 218
Christopher, Warren, 195, 204
civil society, 3, 4, 11, 30, 42, 45, 200
clerical leadership: ayatollahs, 31; guardianship by, 4, 14, 17–18, 61–65; influence of, 6; resistance to, 18; role of, 13, 46–47
Clinton administration, 9–10, 199–200, 204; and "dual containment" policy, 198–199, 203, 227–228

Conoco oil deal, 199, 201, 204
Conservatives, 3, 31–32, 34, 35, 36–37, 40, 41–42, 44–45, 46, 48–49, 52, 100, 202
Constitutional Movement of 1906, 30, 40, 214
constitutionalism, 30
Council of Experts, 27 n. 21, 32, 44, 49, 66, 89
Council of Guardians, 11, 27 n. 21, 31, 33–34, 35, 40, 46–47, 49, 51, 52, 61, 67–68, 83, 88, 115, 119, 123, 135, 139, 141, 142
cult of martyrdom, 61, 68–69, 76
cultural imperialism of West, 39
Cultural and Social Council for Women, 83
Cultural Revolution, 25–26 n. 10, 36

Dagestan, 8, 154
Damad, Mostafa Mohaqeq, 84
Daoodi, Mahindokht, 89
democracy, 15, 29–30, 50, 51, 193
"Democratic-Islamic interest," 222–228
democratization, 3, 4, 11, 30, 41
dialogue between civilizations, 11, 86, 124, 154, 157, 163, 165, 172 n.34, 178, 179, 200, 203, 224–225, 227

Ebtekar, Massoumeh, 87
Economic Recovery Plan, 114–115
economic reform, 3
Egypt, 180, 187
Ettelaat-e Banovan, 77
Europe, 8, 11, 41, 120, 153, 164, 175–190, 226, 228

Family Courts, 5, 76, 78, 80, 83
family planning, 78, 80, 85–86, 96, 99
Family Protection Act, 5, 76, 78, 80, 83
faqih, role of, 4, 30, 32–33, 34, 35, 39, 40, 43, 45, 46–48, 49, 51, 52, 214, 217, 223, 230
Farabi, Abu Nasr, 37
Farzaneh, 87
Fear of the Waves, 37
Five Year Plan, First, 97–99, 118
Five Year Plan, Second, 5, 99–101
Five Year Plan, Third, 115–119

Fourohar, Daryoush, 43
freedom, 30, 34
From the World of the City to the City of the World, 37

Geramizadegan, Ashraf, 90
Ghaffari, Hadi, 34
globalization, 60, 72 n.5, 157
Gol Agha, 63, 74 n.15
Golpaygani, Ayatollah, 125, 126
Gorgi, Monireh, 81
Great Britain, 50, 150, 178, 226
Greece, 164, 165

Habibi, Shahla, 83
Hajjarian, Saeed, 230
HAMAS, 185, 206
Hashemi, Faezeh, 77, 83, 85, 90, 91
Hashemi, Fatemeh, 77
Hashemi, Mehdi, 196, 207–208 n.6, 216
Hekmatyar, Gulbuddin, 183
Heyatha-ye Motalefe-e Islami, 44, 46
Hidden Imam, 6, 128, 129, 130, 139
High Council of Non-Oil Exports, 114
Hizbullah (Iran), 49
Hizbullah (Lebanon), 1, 9, 185–186, 206
Hoquq-e Zanan, 90
hostage crisis, 9, 31, 76, 87, 95, 177, 178, 180, 192–193, 194–195, 203, 207 n.2, 3 and 4, 226–227
hostage-taking, 1, 178, 195, 198, 202
hukumat (authority to administer justice), 131, 132
al-Hukumat al-Islamiyyah (Islamic Government), 132
human rights, 22, 188, 193
Hussein, Saddam, 176, 177, 194, 197, 218, 219, 220

'ibadat (God-human relationship), 137
identity, pre-Islamic Iranian, 18–19; Shii, 7
"Ideological-Islamic interest," 212, 214–217
ideology, Islam and, 15
ijma (consensus), 15
al-imma (leadership), 128
Independents, 45

India, 150, 153, 164, 165
intellectuals, 3, 14, 23–24
Iran Contra Affair, 9, 10, 195–197, 202, 203, 204, 216–217
Iran-Iraq War (1980–1988), 2, 3, 5, 9, 10, 19, 38, 60, 76, 80, 93, 95, 176, 180–181, 194–198, 215, 218, 219, 227
Iran-Libya Sanctions Act, 9, 188, 199–200, 201, 204, 227
Iran's Liberation Movement, 44
Iran's Plan and Budget Organization, 97, 108
Iraq, 8, 149, 151, 153, 160, 176, 177, 178, 180–181, 182–183, 186–187, 188, 189, 192, 194–195, 204, 219, 225, 226
Islami, Saeed, 43
Islamic Conference, 91
Islamic fundamentalism, 9, 22, 203
Islamic Games for Women, 85
Islamic Guards, 185
Islamic Jihad, 1, 185
Islamic Law of Retribution, 80
Islamic Leftists, 31–32, 33, 35, 36, 37, 42, 100
Islamic political philosophy, 37
Islamic Republic of Iran: and regional dynamics, 160–167, 181–186; and the United States, 9, 191–207; as host to refugees, 160, 184, 226; as theocracy, 14; attitude toward opposition, 17, 32; banking sector in, 100, 102–103, 110, 119; black market in, 96, 108, 113; constitution of, 14, 17, 22, 31, 35, 37, 39, 44, 46, 47, 48, 50, 80, 81, 83, 94–95, 116, 118–119, 126, 134, 139, 140, 193, 222–223, 230; culture in, 17, 18–19, 25 n.7, 36, 40, 57, 59–61, 116, 121, 163, 166, 170–171 n.25, 174 n.50; debt, 5, 98, 106; development of, 6, 96–121; economy of, 3, 5–6, 11, 22, 31, 32, 33, 38, 46, 51, 76, 93–121, 163–164; education, liberalization of, 18; elections in, 3, 23, 29–30, 32–34, 35–36, 40–41, 44–45, 46, 62–64, 70, 73 n.8 and 9, 119, 121 n.4; exchange rate in, 96, 98–99, 100, 106–108, 118, 121 n.3; factionalism in, 11, 31–34, 35, 99–100, 112; financial sector in, 100, 101–103; fiscal sector in, 100–101; foreign investment in, 95, 102, 114, 115, 119, 120; foreign policy of, 10–11, 33, 115, 116, 149–167, 175–190, 211–231; foreign trade of, 104–108, 110; global integration of, 59; ideology of, 8, 110; industrialization of, 103–104; inflation, 95, 98–99, 100, 101, 102, 106, 111, 118; liberalization of economy, 97–98, 118; middle class of, 112–113; national interest of, 211–231; nationalization of industries, 5, 94; nature of, 2, 3; nuclear armament of, 7, 9, 152–153, 167 n.3 and 6, 168 n.8, 186–187, 189, 192, 199, 201, 206, 218; oil production and exports of, 104–106, 113–114, 118; political changes in, 57–59; population of, 25 n.6, 38, 96, 99, 113; press in, 11, 19–20, 25–26 n. 9, 10, 26 n. 14 and 15, 36, 43–44, 49–50, 66–67, 88, 90–91; prisons in, 64–5, 73 n.11; private sector in, 94, 97, 109–110, 115, 118, 119–120; public sphere in, 57–72, 119–120; reforms in, 30, 33, 47–48, 51–52, 115, 116–117, 121; social engineering in, 112; socioeconomic changes in, 57–58, 59, 61, 109–110; support for terrorism, 9–10, 180, 188–189, 200–201, 206, 215
Islamic Republican Party, 1, 31, 32
Islamic Revolution, 1978–79: changes due to, 59; export of, 1, 7, 8, 10, 156; opposition to, 1
Islamic Women's Association, 88
Israel, 7, 9, 10, 152, 153, 159, 161, 177, 179, 180, 181, 184–187, 192, 195, 203–204, 206, 216

Jalaiepour, Hamid Reza, 69
Jameeh, 69, 74 n.15 and 16, 90
Jameyate Motalefe-ye Islami, 35
Janati, Ayatollah, 46, 142

Jordan, 187
Joumhuri-e Islame, 43

Kadivar, Hojjatolislam Mohsen, 48
Kadivar, Jamileh, 87, 89
Kani, Ayatollah Mahdavi, 40
Karbaschi, Gholamhossein, arrest and trial of 49, 64–65
Karubi, Fatemeh, 76–77, 88
Karubi, Mehdi, 32, 33–34, 77
Kashf-i asrar (Unveiling the Secrets), 131–132, 133, 134
Kayhan, 36, 43
Kazakhstan, 163
Khalkhalli, Ayatollah, 34
Khamenei, Ayatollah Ali, 2, 4, 6, 27 n. 21, 32, 33, 34, 35, 36, 40, 46, 47, 48–49, 50, 52, 53, 63–64, 90, 126, 135, 139, 141, 142, 143, 146–147 n. 33, 202, 203, 217, 218, 234 n.32
Kharrazi, Kamal, 224, 226
Khatami, Mohammad, 5, 6, 29–30, 32, 33, 53, 63, 108, 123–124, 222; achievements as president, 11, 41–45, 50–51, 200, 222; and democracy, 38, 42, 45–46, 222; and United States, 200–202, 226–227; campaign strategy and platform, 35–41, 200; challenges facing in future, 51–52; economic policy of, 40, 112, 114–120; educational policy of, 42; foreign policy of, 7, 8, 10, 155, 157, 158, 162, 172 n.34, 178, 189–190, 200–202, 203, 229; formation of political parties under, 43–44, 51; obstacles to reforms, 45–50; on culture, 19–20; on "governance of the jurist," 142–143; on women, 66–67, 77, 87–90, 91, 124; reforms of, 2–3, 30, 51, 143, 206; women's support for, 86–87; worldview of, 223–226
Khobar bombing, 9, 188
Khoeiniha, Hojjatolislam Mohammad, 31, 32
Khoie, Ayatollah, 125, 126, 142
Khomeini, Ayatollah Ruhollah Musavi, 1, 2, 6, 10, 11, 20, 27 n. 21, 31, 32, 36, 37, 46, 48, 62, 77, 97, 123, 124, 125–126, 131–139, 140, 141, 193, 195, 196, 208 n.7, 212, 214–217, 219, 223, 229
Khordad, 43, 90
khums, 129
kidnappings, 1
Kissinger, Henry, 192
Kosovo crisis, 154
Kuwait, 176, 181, 183, 197, 198, 219–220
Kyrgyzstan, 163, 173 n.43

Larijani, Mohammad Javad, 41
law, rule of, 3, 4, 11, 30, 42, 200, 224
Lebanon, 9, 176, 178, 185–186, 188, 195, 198, 202, 216

Majles, 23, 32, 34, 42, 46, 52, 83, 97, 115, 119, 131, 135, 138, 196, 200, 217, 218
marja-i taqlid, 6–7, 27 n. 21, 47, 125–126, 129, 130–131, 138–140, 141, 145 n.15, 217
McFarlane, Robert, 196
Middle East, 11
Ministry of Intelligence, 43
Moderates, 100
modernists, 14, 21–22
modernity, Islam and, 15–16
modernization and development, 11
Mohajerani, Ataollah, 49, 87, 174 n.50
Mohtashemi, Ayatollah, 34, 53
Mojahdin-e Khalq, 201
Montazeri, Ayatollah Hossein Ali, 27 n. 21, 33, 48, 141, 196, 203, 207–208 n.6, 208 n.7, 217
Mossadeq, Mohammad, 42, 177, 180, 203, 227
Mostafavi, Zahra, 77
Motlalefe-ye Islami, 40
Mottahari, Ayatollah, 37
mu 'amalat (human-human relationship), 137
mujtahid, 6, 125, 129–130, 131–133, 134, 139, 140–141, 143, 144 n.7, 145 n.15
al-Mulk, Khajeh Nezam, 213
Murphy, Richard, 197
Mussavi, Mir Hussein, 33, 35, 87
Mykonos killings, 178, 179, 189

Nabavi, Ibrahim, 74 n.15
Nagorno-Karabakh, 7, 153, 161–162, 165, 184
Naini, Ayatollah, 37
Naini, Mirza Mohammad Hossein Gharavi, 30
Nateq-Nuri, Hojjatolislam Ali Akbar, 3, 29, 30, 34, 35, 36, 39–40, 41, 63, 83, 86, 124
nationalism, 7, 18–19, 71, 73 n.6, 214
NATO, 153, 154, 155, 159, 162
Neshat, 43
Netanyahu, Benjamin, 9
Nixon, Richard, 192
North Korea, 153, 186
Nouri, Abdullah, 73 n.12, 90, 209 n.17
Nuri, Sheikh Fazollah, 30

oil markets, 5, 101, 111–112, 171–172 n.30 and 31, 225
Oklahama City bombing, 9, 188
Organization of Iran's Islamic Revolution, 35
Oslo Accords of 1993, 185
Ottoman Empire, 213

Pahlavi, Mohammad Reza Shah, 5, 42, 61, 192, 203, 213
Pahlavi rule, 11, 211
Pakistan, 153, 162, 164–165, 176, 183–184
Palestine, 9, 140, 185
Parsa, Farrokhru, 79
Participation Front of Islamic Iran, 44, 74 n.19
Peres, Shimon, 204
Persian Gulf, 1, 8, 149, 150, 157, 166–167, 179–180, 187, 200, 202, 205, 215, 219, 220
personal liberty, 34
pluralism, 3, 16, 34
political violence, 22
popular sovereignty, 3, 4, 30, 38, 46, 48, 51, 222
"Pragmatic-Islamic interest," 212, 217–222
Pragmatists, 32, 33, 35, 36, 42, 49
Prophet (Muhammad), 127, 129, 135–136, 216

Qassemlu, Abdel-Rahman, 189

Rabin, Yitzhak, 204
Rafsanjani, Ali Akbar Hashemi, 2, 3, 5, 7, 10, 32, 33, 34, 35, 38, 40, 47, 53, 77, 83, 89, 91, 97, 104, 110, 112, 124, 178, 196, 215, 217, 218, 219–220, 222, 228, 234 n.32
Rahnavard, Zahra, 77, 87
Ras al-Khaima dispute, 180, 182
Reagan, Ronald, 194–195, 196
reforms, Iran, 2–3
Reformists, 44–45, 48–49, 70–71, 202
Rejaii, Atefeh Sadighi, 34, 76
Rejaii, Mohammad Ali, 47, 53, 76
religion, role of, 3
"republic of virtue," 20–22
Resalat, 43
Revolutionary Council, 81, 193
Revolutionary Courts, 31, 49
Revolutionary Guards, 69, 90
Reza Shah, 11, 78, 177
rights and freedoms, religion and, 16
Rushdie affair, 177, 178, 216, 226
Russia, Iranian relations with, 7–8, 41, 149–167, 186, 220

Sadeghi, Zohreh, 87, 91
Safavi, Rahim, 69, 74 n.16
Safavid Empire, 211, 213
Saidzadeh, Mohsen, 84
Salam, 49–50, 74 n.16
saltanah (political power), 132
Sassanians, 213
Saudi Arabia, 1, 7, 9, 164–165, 183, 188, 192, 200, 216, 219, 225–226
SAVAK, 36
science and technology, religion and, 16
Second Khordad coalition, 42, 45
secularism, 15
secularization, 21–22
Servants of Construction, 34, 35, 44, 63
shariah, 21, 67, 90, 128, 129, 136, 140
Shariatmadari, Ayatollah Kazim, 140, 145–146 n.23 and 24, 223
Shiis, 6–7; jurisprudence of, 13, 20–22, 31, 37, 48, 123, 214, 223; modernists, 14–15; religious leadership in, 124–143
Shiism, 31, 154, 213, 214, 221

Shojai, Zahra, 87, 91
shura (consultation), 15
social justice, 109–110
Society of the Combatant Clerics of Tehran, 32, 35, 63
Sorush, Abdolkarim, 21, 42
Soviet Union, 149, 150, 151, 160, 165, 175–176, 184, 192, 195, 204, 215, 217, 218, 219, 220–221
Special Family Courts, 83, 89
"Sultanic interest," 212–214, 236 n.71
Supreme Leader, office of, 6
Syria, 175, 185, 187

Tajikistan, 7, 8, 152, 153, 160, 162–163, 165, 173 n.40, 184, 222
Taleqani, Aazam, 76, 83
Taleqani, Ayatollah, 76
Taliban (Afghanistan), 41, 88, 154, 163, 164–165, 170 n.18, 177, 183
taqlid, 128–129, 130, 144 n.9
Tatarstan, 154
Tehran Stock Exchange, 103, 110
Tehran Times, 151
tolerance, institutionalization of, 30, 42, 86
Tous, 74 n.15, 90
Turkey, 159, 164, 165, 218
Turkmenistan, 162, 163, 164, 165
TWA 800, 9, 188
Twelve Imams, 46, 128

United Nations, 180–181, 183, 194, 197–198, 200, 208 n.11, 214, 215, 219, 224, 225
United States, 7, 9; and Afghanistan, 183; freezing of Iranian assets, 10, 94; hostility toward Iran, 8, 9, 199; influence on Iranian foreign policy, 150–151, 152–153, 157–160; policy of containment of "Islamic threat," 8, 155; policy toward Iran, 157–160, 163, 164, 165, 176, 179, 180, 191–207, 216–217, 218; sanctions against Iran, 5, 10, 101, 120
Uzbekistan, 158, 159, 163, 165, 171 n.27, 173 n.40, 222

vali-e faqih, 63, 124, 134, 138, 139, 142
velayat-i faqih, 4, 6–7, 10, 15, 20–22, 30, 37, 39, 40, 42, 46, 48, 51, 61, 123–143, 145–146 n.23 and 24, 214, 222
Velayati, Ali Akbar, 220

weapons of mass destruction, 9, 10
West, Islam and, 16
wilayah, (authority to govern) also *wilayat*, 131, 132, 134, 137, 138, 143 n.1
women, activism of, 5, 74 n.14, 75–6; and NGOs, 83; as culture bearers, 4, 65–68, 85; as elected officials, 45, 76–77, 79, 81; dress, 76, 78, 80, 82, 84–85, 90–91; in personal status law, 78, 80, 84, 88; in public space, 67, 76–77, 80–83, 85, 91; in sports, 85, 91; protests by, 77; rights of, 4–5, 14, 66–67, 74 n.15, 76, 78–84; role of, 59; segregation of, 81, 82, 85, 88–89, 90, 91; status of, 3, 14, 24 n.1, 39, 77–92; voters, 77, 86; "women's question," 75–92
Women's Organization of Iran, 79
working class, 3

Yazdi, Ayatollah Mohammad, 46, 89
Yazdi, Ibrahim, 192–193
Yeltsin, Boris, 41
youth, 3

al-Zahra University, 87
zakat, 129
Zan, 89, 90–91
Zan-e Ruz, 90
Zanan, 86, 87, 88, 90
Zanganeh, Bijan Namdar, 118
Zhazali, Ayatollah, 40

GPSR Compliance

The European Union's (EU) General Product Safety Regulation (GPSR) is a set of rules that requires consumer products to be safe and our obligations to ensure this.

If you have any concerns about our products, you can contact us on

ProductSafety@springernature.com

In case Publisher is established outside the EU, the EU authorized representative is:

Springer Nature Customer Service Center GmbH
Europaplatz 3
69115 Heidelberg, Germany

www.ingramcontent.com/pod-product-compliance
Lightning Source LLC
LaVergne TN
LVHW041626060526

838200LV00040B/1458